D1599199

The Anthropology
of Violence

The Anthropology of Violence

Edited by
DAVID RICHES

Basil Blackwell

© Basil Blackwell Ltd 1986

First published 1986

Basil Blackwell Ltd
108 Cowley Road, Oxford OX4 1JF, UK

Basil Blackwell Inc.
432 Park Avenue South, Suite 1503,
New York, NY 10016, USA

British Library Cataloguing in Publication Data

The Anthropology of violence.
1. Violence
I.   Riches, David
303.6'2   GN493
ISBN 0-631-14788-8

Library of Congress Cataloging in Publication Data

The Anthropology of violence.

Selected papers from a conference on "Violence as a Social Institution" held in St. Andrews, Scotland, in January, 1985.
Includes index.
Contents: The phenomenon of violence / David Riches — Insurrections in Spain / J. R. Corbin — "le Mal Court" / Elisabeth Copet-Rougier — [etc.]
1.   Violence—Cross-cultural studies—Congresses.
I.   Riches, David.
GN495.2.A57   1986   303.6'2   86—11755
ISBN 0-631-14788-8

Typeset by Pioneer, Perthshire
Printed in Great Britain by
The Camelot Press Ltd, Southampton

Contents

Preface

'Violence is understood best when it is examined over a range of cultural settings, and in a full variety of social situations.' Such is the view offered in this book about one of the most intractable phenomena in contemporary human society. The following chapters are presented by nine social anthropologists and four sociologists who first came together at a conference on 'Violence as a Social Institution' in St Andrews, Scotland, in January 1985, and whose main concerns were to consider the social rules that so often seem to enjoin the performance of violent behaviour, and to make sense of the images of violence that frequently stand out in ideology, mythology and aesthetic culture. The distinctive methods of anthropological research are evident in all the chapters. The contributors' findings stem from field studies in which they were immersed in the 'community', or 'small-group' level of society: for all the contributors, to *participate* in the level of society in which social life is *lived*, and in which the social rules and ideologies that influence the conduct of social action are constructed, is a key method of research. The volume as a whole proclaims that a balanced account of violence in any one society — in our 'own' society, in Japan, or among the Australian Aborigines — is enhanced through the knowledge that violence in 'other cultures' can have a variety of purposes and take on a variety of meanings. And *if* there is a single process which engenders the violence which seems to be present or latent in all human social settings, it is more likely to be discovered through the kind of cross-cultural research of which this collection consists.

A large amount of important work on the study of violence has already been achieved by sociologists working in 'Western industrial' society. Now that anthropologists have realized that anthropological techniques may be applied not only in examining non-industrial and Third World societies, but also in investigating community life in the 'Western' milieu, an overlap of interests is bound to arise. Reciprocally, the sociologists' interest in the various 'subcultures' within industrial society is going to be highly consonant with the anthropologists' preoccupations with 'other ways of life'. To be cited in this regard are the several papers dealing with social organization and values among juvenile delinquents, prison inmates, etc. in the recent, predominantly sociological, collection on violence edited by Peter Marsh and Anne Campbell (*Aggression and Violence*, Oxford: Basil Blackwell, 1982), and in some respects the present volume is a complement of Marsh and Campbell's. Certainly, the experience of the St Andrews conference was that the non-anthropologists present addressed their chosen topics through methods and analyses which the anthropologists found perfectly palatable — or, at least, as palatable as they found one another's approaches! The increasing interdependence of the world's communities and the rapid social changes that have resulted and which are described in some of the chapters that follow, means that greater co-operation between the various disciplines of the social sciences is likely in the future.

The contributors to this book deal with violence in its many different forms (from simple threats of violence at one extreme through to homicide at the other) and in a very wide range of social settings (from Amazonian Indians to Northern Ireland). But 'wide coverage' in these respects is not the fundamental aim. The intention is more to grasp what *underlies* the striking capacity of violence as a social and cultural resource: why is violence so readily chosen to satisfy social goals? Why are images of violence so culturally prominent, even in 'peaceful' societies? The subject of violence is therefore more prominently approached here along the dimensions of: practical versus symbolic usages; visible versus invisible manifestations; physical versus cognitive effects; and inner-directedness (stemming from the perpetrator's personal capacities) versus outer-directedness (stemming from the forces of society). The guide in all this is the tradition of mainstream socio-cultural anthropology. The 'anthropology' of this volume is not one where human behaviours are treated like animal behaviour or are thought to be directly subject to the control of genes. Rather it is one in which human social forms are seen as a product of a distinctively human imagination, and as moulded by the constraints of social structure and culture.

As convener of the St Andrews conference, I must express gratitude to the Economic and Social Research Council (Great Britain) which supported the conference with a generous grant, and to the University of St Andrews for providing secretarial assistance. I am indebted to the nineteen participants for their enthusiastic contributions: I have no doubt incorporated quite a few of their ideas in the first chapter without acknowledgement. The papers published here are a selection from the conference extensively revised and rewritten. Those not included (papers by A. Blok, M. Gilsenan, M. Hobart, P. Marsh and P. Worsley) will be published elsewhere, several of them as parts of larger works. My thanks are also due to my colleagues Richard Fardon and Ladislav Holy who acted as discussants, and to Mark Hobart, Peter Marsh, Garry Marvin and David Parkin who made innumerable suggestions whilst the conference was being arranged. I hope that the following chapters will also be accessible to non-specialist readers, and I have therefore appended, at the end of the book, a glossary of the technical terms that appear in the text.

David Riches

1

The Phenomenon of Violence

David Riches

THE MEANING OF VIOLENCE

The call is frequently made to anthropologists and sociologists to cut down on the 'jargon' they employ: 'use the language of ordinary people', they are admonished. But then problems arise. To employ the language of everyday life in sociological[1] analysis risks distorting the social processes due to be uncovered. In the first place, the terms of everyday language are used in particular situations by particular individuals who have particular designs; the sense these terms convey is therefore bound to vary subtly with the context. Second, everyday language is something the analyst takes for granted and uses without reflection; the full implications of its meanings may therefore remain concealed (cf. Riches 1985). Not least because of the emotions it tends to arouse, 'violence' must stand close to the top of the list of words which invite danger from these points of view.

For anthropologists to declare that they are studying 'violence' especially courts such danger. The social actions performed by people in 'other societies' and the collective representations (mythology, aesthetics, etc.) of 'other cultures' may strike the English-speaking lay person as 'violent' — yet some of the essential meanings in the Anglo-Saxon idea may be missing from them altogether. Indeed, it may be that there will not be a word in the language of the 'other culture' which marks off exactly the same range of acts and images that 'violence' denotes in the Anglo-Saxon world. Then again, to the Anglo-Saxon mind, 'violence' strongly connotes behaviour that is in some sense illegitimate or unacceptable — as noted in several chapters in this book. However, for the performer of violence this particular implication may well be played down or even be completely absent. This is a point brought out

---

[1] 'Sociological' refers here to the social sciences in general; it includes social anthropology.

strongly in Edmund Leach's discussion of violence perpetrated by terrorists (1977). Leach draws a remarkable parallel between terrorists in a society and the society's leaders (authorities), noting that in a crucial sense both may be regarded as 'outsiders' competing to impose their will on the populace at large. Locked in a supreme opposition, each side represents the other's acts of physical force as barbarism but considers its own as heroic.

There is a second danger in employing the term 'violence' in sociological study. This is that the analysis could be damagingly influenced by the 'folk' theories about violence which obtain in the analyst's lay culture. Stressing the apparent universality, intractability and unacceptability of the problem of violence, the theories prominent in Anglo-Saxon lay culture focus strongly on the irrationality and bestiality of violence. It is certainly tempting to remark that the approach to violence advocated in the discipline of ethology — in which violence is seen at least partly as having genetic determinants — is rather close to Anglo-Saxon folk ideas, though I am sure that the ethologists themselves would reject the view that their theories have been influenced in this way (cf. Eibl-Eibesfeldt 1979; Riches 1986). But more than this, anthropologists can also stand accused of being influenced by their informants' theories and rationalizations as Graham McFarlane shows in his chapter in this book on violence in rural Northern Ireland. In McFarlane's opinion, the anthropologists' long and intimate association with particular communities, whose members believe it is barely thinkable for one member to carry out violence against another, may well have led to analyses which emphasize the communities' harmony and integration and which can be seriously at odds with reality.

How realistic, then, is an attempt to appreciate violence cross-culturally? The fact that actions which 'we' recognize as violent may be understood rather differently in other cultures, epitomizes the doubts which many have expressed as to whether 'violence' can be a sociologically useful category of action (Heelas 1982). But I would not wish to pre-judge the matter; perhaps some universal 'core' understanding can be uncovered. In any event, the point of departure in this chapter *is* the Anglo-Saxon notion — transparently a meaningful category for most English-speakers! For a cross-cultural analysis to be reasonable it must do justice to people's understandings, so there is some sense in my deploying the everyday categories of my own cultural world — even though the explanations of violence that I eventually offer will have been filtered through the 'language of ordinary people'. In the end, I hope to deduce certain social processes implicated by Anglo-Saxon ideas of violence which possibly can be discerned in other cultural — especially non-Western — settings. But, before beginning, I might mention that in the closing chapter in this book David Parkin offers the complementary procedure, showing that the analysis of certain non-Western ideas provides insights into Anglo-Saxon understandings.

An apparent paradox may be noted as a guide to the following discussion. This is that 'violence' is very much a word of those who witness, or who are victims of certain acts, rather than of those who perform them. Yet what is required is that *performance* should be understood and explained. Indeed the cross-cultural appreciation of the performance of actions deemed violent is the major aim of this chapter. In the face of this paradox I believe the focus must initially be put squarely on the witness and victim, examining 'violence' in its fundamental sense: we consider the *use* of the term 'violence' by the English-speaking lay person. However, because such use is predicated in *the political[2] relations between performer and witness*, it turns out that important insights into the performer's perspective can be generated quite quickly.

THE WITNESS'S PERSPECTIVE (ANGLO-SAXON CULTURE)

A significant background of cultural values and norms is plainly the context for the major meaning of the term 'violence' in Anglo-Saxon culture. The salient point is that when a witness or victim invokes the notion of violence, they make a judgement not just that the action concerned causes physical hurt but also that it is illegitimate. By implication, Anglo-Saxon understandings indicate that 'physical hurt done to others' counts as violence only in certain social contexts. In a negative sense, the salient context in this respect is the state. The physical force employed by the state is, as Radcliffe-Brown told us some years ago, government ('political organization') and not violence (1940: xiv). Also, the fact that such physical force does not normally amount to 'violence' implies some idea of social order, to which the notion of violence is inextricably counterposed. In the affairs of the state, and in world affairs, the concept of peace is typically invoked to describe the ideal condition of such social order. In David Parkin's chapter in this book, the opposition between legitimate and illegitimate uses of physical force is shown to be nicely captured in a London Metropolitan Police poster, which seems to be inviting the public to respond to the activities of the petty criminal with physical force. The poster's effect is clearly intended to derive from the fact that for an arm of the state apparently to be inciting the populace to violence will be seen as highly paradoxical and arresting.

---

[2] I shall be using 'political' in its most general sense, referring to that component of social life in which people seek influence or control over the actions of others. There is a political dimension in all social relationships.

4 *David Riches*

It is evident then that when the term 'violence' is being used, attention should crucially be focused on *who* is labelling a given act as such and most especially their social position. It follows that violence is a concept which can easily be manoeuvred into an ideological ambience, coming particularly to symbolize moral impropriety in a range of actions and policies. Through leaps of imagination people can ensure that acts of violence are inextricably linked with other acts implying social disorder (e.g. strikes, political unrest, etc.). So it has been with the moral panics about football spectator violence that have arisen in Britain during the past century. These have undoubtedly been occasioned through such violence being identified with rather different activities which threaten the social fabric in a considerably more profound way (here I refer to the chapter in this book by Eric Dunning, Patrick Murphy and John Williams). Sometimes the ideological possibilities of violence are explicitly recognized by certain individuals in the community. The pronouncement by an Anglican bishop, at the time of the British miners' strike in 1984—5, that the social and economic neglect of mining communities in certain parts of Britain should be regarded as a 'violence', is an example. What arises from this discussion is that analysts using the term 'violence', even in simple descriptions of certain acts of physical hurt, might well be forthright about the possible ideological stance they themselves are entertaining, especially when they employ such arguably controversial phrases as 'state violence' or 'working-class violence'.[3]

THE PERFORMER'S PERSPECTIVE (ANGLO-SAXON CULTURE)

The analytical focus in the study of violence which requires that the performer's actions command central attention is bound to be compromised slightly, for the performer may well deny that the actions concerned can properly be called 'violent' — especially when violence is allowed its connotation of illegitimacy. But the anthropologist's task is more to explain actions than to label them, so this difficulty should not be troubling. For convenience, the performer's actions can be called violence, corresponding to the commonsensical meaning of the term as 'the intentional rendering of physical hurt on another human being'. But one thing does follow from the shift in interest from witness to performer. The connotation of violence as disorder is lost. As we shall see, the focus in this chapter is on what goals —

[3] My stance in social analysis, empathizing with the performer of action, suggests that the illegitimacy imputed in an act or image that is deemed violent should be regarded with scepticism.

'practical' or 'symbolic' — people achieve by behaving violently, and on why, from among other alternatives, people specifically choose violence to strive for these goals. To the extent that performers conceive of violence as something which can be predictably deployed to meet some end (including changes in the social system), ideas of *order* could reasonably be pertinent to the analysis. However, my preference is to consider the performers' actions through such concepts as *strategy* and *meaning*. It is these notions which lie behind the examination of the performer's perspective in what follows.

For the performer of violence in the 'Anglo-Saxon' society, a particular act will very likely have several explicit purposes, one of which will probably predominate and will therefore give the act its primary sense or meaning. But for the act to fall into the category of 'violence' suggests that some 'core' purpose, common to all acts of violence, is at least implicit in its performance. It is obviously worthwhile to uncover this purpose and illustrate its presence in specific examples of violence.

To discern the 'core purpose', the political relations between performer and (dissenting) witnesses look to offer the most promising context. An essential aspect of such political relations is that the performer will argue for the act's legitimacy, whilst the witnesses (and victims) will deem it illegitimate. In rival attempts to uphold their respective stances both sides will appeal to social rules and values, each entering the claim that justice lies with *their* performance or opinion. I suggest that the core purpose of violence stems from a contradiction in this situation which performers have to face. In the first place, violence is a means of social advancement whose recipients — victims or witnesses — are, by definition, unwilling recipients. But, at the same time, victims and witnesses have to be persuaded of the act's acceptability, for the performer will certainly wish to dampen down the possibility of a like reply. The purpose of violence which best meets this contradiction — through which advancement is achieved *and* a measure of legitimacy claimed — is tactical pre-emption, i.e. securing practical advantage over one's opponents in the short term through forestalling their activities. For performers of violence, then, the notion of tactical pre-emption is vital, in that pressed to give an account of themselves they can offer defence through making the idea explicit — though it is hardly necessary to say that when someone insists that the need to meet this purpose outweighs the suffering caused victims and witnesses may well *not* concur.

But why tactical pre-emption? I deduce this from two facts. First, social acts in general may be most readily justified if they can be presented as unavoidable, and second, that in a violent act the immediate effect is to impair a victim's faculties. The ultimate defence for all violent acts will accordingly be given as the unimpeachable necessity of immediately halting some aspect of the social activities of the person to whom violence is imparted. Tactical pre-emption is what has happened when this necessity is met.

By way of clarification and illustration, let me extract this core purpose from three quite different examples of violence (I continue to refer to Anglo-Saxon societies). Firstly, the violent acts associated with rape may be cited as an extreme — some would say controversial — instance. In this example, the violence by which the woman is restrained would be defended as a means to mitigate or prevent the physical protest she will offer, and which the rapist could find seriously endangering.[4] The second example, at a very different part of the moral spectrum, reveals the core purpose much more plainly. I refer here to the deployment of violent actions as a means of pre-emptive self-defence, particularly the homicidal actions that have come to be known in the United States as 'deadly force'. The sympathy aroused in the American public in 1983 for the subway passenger who shot and seriously wounded four young men whom he claimed were attempting to rob him indeed testifies to the efficacy of making explicit the core purpose in violent acts.[5] The third example refers to acts of vengeance, and specifically homicidal vengeance. Here we hardly need confine ourselves to Anglo-Saxon societies; for example, we could equally be speaking of the inter-group feuds common in tribal and some peasant societies. The background to the practice of homicidal vengeance as tactical pre-emption is, of course, that those destined to receive the violence (they may be specific individuals or groups) have already proved *their* strength by perpetrating homicide on some prior occasion. In terms of the 'core purpose', vengeance's aim reflects the importance of immediately disabling this opposition, undermining their capability for continuing in the same manner.

Of particular interest in the case of vengeance is that the core purpose is largely concealed. As the word 'vengeance' implies, the perpetrator normally speaks in terms of exacting retribution, of retaliation — of paying back. Any

[4] The sexual penetration itself is better thought of in terms of mental harm (cf. Corbin 1977). To consider it as violence would be to detract from the serious physical hurt that usually accompanies sexual intercourse in rape.

[5] The genocide of women and children in warfare, which some writers have considered irrational in relation to warfare's aim, is surely similar to 'deadly force' (cf. Kelman 1973). In terms of 'core purpose' it is designed to forestall women and children giving emotional and economic succour to enemy fighters. Of course, from the perpetrators' point of view, the women and children only pose an indirect threat — but such is the case in other instances where the tactical pre-emption is obvious, for example when soldiers massacre an enemy to forestall their commanding officer executing them for disobeying orders.

practical advantage stemming from the act is effectively disclaimed, and the act is entirely rationalized in terms of what has happened in the past. That the tactical pre-emption in vengeance homicide remains largely hidden in this way is probably because vengeance is typically thought of in relation to conflict among political equals. In this regard to enunciate the act in terms of what has gone past claiming that no present advancement is being sought, mitigates the likelihood of further conflict. To put it another way, lest the act of violence invite still more contention, it is better declared as designed simply to retrieve lost honour than as a means to forestall the other side deploying its capabilities. Yet an act from which there is no practical advantage vis-à-vis some other is impossible (cf. Riches 1985); when this is made explicit among the people involved, the core purpose of vengeance violence will have to be revealed.

If Anglo-Saxon understandings of violence are to enable us to appreciate comparable practices in other cultures, then cross-cultural analysis is bound to dwell on the fact that these practices will be deemed by some as illegitimate. The importance of the 'core purpose' is that, among violence's many possible aims, it is the means by which its legitimacy will ultimately be argued — the core purpose, so to speak, constitutes the *substance* of violence's legitimacy. In probably only a minority of instances is tactical pre-emption the initiating purpose (or 'primary meaning') of violence: many ambitions can stimulate acts of violence, but the core purpose itself is not often evident as one (though instances of 'deadly force' would be an example). The salience of the core purpose is, rather, that it amounts to a necessary condition of violence. The tactical pre-emption in an act of violence may be incidental to the act's primary purpose, but the knowledge that it is nonetheless being produced allows performers to contemplate the violent solution to a particular problem; confident that their actions command a gloss of legitimacy they are able, with some equanimity, to satisfy their ambitions through deploying physical harm.

THE DYNAMICS OF VIOLENCE: TOWARDS THE CROSS-CULTURAL VIEW

Can we discern in other human societies and cultures, social processes and images corresponding with Anglo-Saxon notions of violence (even though such processes may not be exclusively marked off with a particular linguistic term)? If this can be done, can we then grasp — again with all human societies in mind — what it is about violence that makes it so efficacious in action and potent in imagery? The capacity of violence to achieve certain ends may seem obvious to the Western mind, yet it is plainly a risky adventure

8   *David Riches*

(E. Marx 1976).[6] Violence as a course of action is especially difficult to control and, in very many societies particularly liable to censure. Other means are normally available to achieve the desired ends. As several contributors to this book point out, though people may be in conflict this by no means explains why they select violence in order to achieve their aims at their opponents' expense. To consider these questions is effectively to examine the scope of violence, which is evident in the richly varying specific purposes to which it is put, in different settings and in different societies. The scope of violence turns out to be very largely enabled by its 'core purpose'.

But the groundwork laid in previous sections, explicating Anglo-Saxon meanings of violence, is inadequate as it stands. In the first place, it must be recognized immediately that in many non-Western societies much physical hurt is *invisibly* enacted. Thus, witchcraft and sorcery, their reality as unquestioned as is the reality of visible physical hurt, must be included as instances of violence, even though their performance has to be inferred from their eventual result: the misfortune, injury or death of the recipient. But more importantly for the moment, we have to admit the realities of violence in human society will hardly be grasped through a simple institutional analysis, encompassing the performer, victim and witness of violence in so many social roles. A superior model is required, which captures the fundamental tension in this basic triangle of violence. The aim must be to reveal the dynamics present in the triangle. We shall see that these dynamics reflect the *spirit* of the Anglo-Saxon notion as this has been examined so far, yet they exemplify a new perspective. This perspective is secured through putting the focus on the act of violence itself, rather than separately on the roles of performer, etc. Violence now comes to be seen as 'an act of physical hurt deemed legitimate by the performer and illegitimate by (some) witnesses.'[7]

---

[6] In his interesting study of Galilah, an immigrant town in Israel, E. Marx offers useful comments about the riskiness of violence. What emerges here is that immigrants who employ violence against state authorities normally command a certain level of wealth and resources, which they can fall back on if the violent strategy has adverse repercussions. Those who are totally impoverished dare not risk the violent solution, such is their material dependence on the authorities whose decisions to supply state resources can be quite capricious (E. Marx 1976: pp. 37, 46—7).

[7] A limiting case is apparently where the victim gives approval of the actions perpetrated against him. But such action still qualifies as violence, since (masochists apart) approval is invariably voiced only after the event. (Rather similarly to the way in which *performers* of violence may be contrite after the event.) Thus, Yanomamö wives give approval of their husbands beating them, for the latters' power to defend family integrity is thereby demonstrated. But the beatings themselves are always contentious affairs: the husband has to give an account of his wife's particular failing, which she assuredly will deny; excessive beating is certainly condemned (Chagnon 1977: pp. 83, 95).

Once the tension in the relationship between performer, victim and witnesses is drawn out, the vital question of the potency of violence as an act and as an image can be approached.

The tension in the relationship between performer, victim and witnesses consists of two elements: an element of political competition and an element of consensus about the nature of the violent act. I deduce the element of competition from the fact that the act of violence never fails to be one of contested legitimacy. What marks the contestability of violence is that, as acts of physical hurt unfold, performers, witnesses and even victims may be expected to alter their opinions about this legitimacy. Witnesses may come to accept the performer's view of things or may come to detract from this view; performers may come to accept the opinions of detracting witnesses — and cease or modify the acts they are perpetrating. For anthropologists who have studied political action, the mobilization of resources and information which leads people to be persuaded to change their minds in this way is known as 'subversion'; I accept the view of Bailey (1969) that this is a universal feature of political strategy.

Argument and dispute about the sorts of occasion when the use of violence is appropriate, and about the sorts of relationship which may obtain between performer and victim, are indicative of the possibility of such subversion. Societally arranged compromises may be expected on behalf of those who are likely to find themselves 'on opposing sides of the argument'. As is well-known, few societies are without norms stipulating how violence should be organized — specifying, for example, the sorts of weaponry that might be used against particular adversaries. The famous case is that of the Nuer of southern Sudan, for whom fighting between members of the same village is restricted to clubs whilst people from different villages may use spears; likewise, with fighting between different tribes there are restrictions against molesting women and children, destroying huts and byres and taking captives. This sort of ruling is only suspended where the opponents are non-Nuer (Evans-Pritchard 1940: pp. 121, 151). In much the same manner, in the Canadian arctic, where I conducted field research in the early 1970s, the fighting among Eskimos which typically accompanies the consumption of alcohol is never carried on with firearms, though these are always at hand; nor does it involve Eskimos physically harming the European-Canadian administrators present in the village, despite the fact that the latters' policies often give rise to very considerable grievances.

And yet . . . exacerbating the inherent contestability of the violent act and effectively countering societal constraints on its deployment, human control over the practice of violence is strikingly fragile. Whatever the weapons, the discharge of violence is bound to be grossly unpredictable, both in terms of the actual physical harm done, and in terms of how a sequence of violent acts develops.[8] Nowhere is this more plain than in those pre-industrial societies which anthropologists have made famous for their fighting and bellicosity, such as the Tausug of the Philippines and the Yanomamö of Venezuela. The Tausug recognize that such is the nature of violence that it tends to go beyond right and appropriate levels; intellectually they accept that tit-for-tat reprisal killing is self-defeating (Kiefer 1972: pp. 83, 92). In such societies, a hallmark of leadership is to exercise a restraining influence in this regard — though people who become leaders seem to be provided with precious few resources to help them impose authority, apart from their own personalities, determination and ambition. The duty of the Tausug leader is to stress the long-term implications of violent activity (1972: pp. 92—5). Meanwhile, Yanomamö leaders have to be 'even-headed', and work to limit the effects of fights (Chagnon 1977: p. 91).

The second element in the tension in the performer/victim/witness of violence relationship is the degree of consensus among those involved as to what qualifies as violence. Notwithstanding the multifarious purposes of violent actions in various societies, and at different levels in particular societies (e.g. violence within the family, violence between members of a community, and so on), everyone implicated in violence is very likely to recognize it as such. The main ambiguities, and therefore misunderstandings, will certainly come from people's inability always to spot acts of hurt which are primarily meant as playful or ritualized, as opposed to those which are directly serious in intent. Even so, all these various acts are very likely to connote violence in one way or another, for those that are 'playful' or 'ritualized' are commonly designed as 'threats' of serious violence or as dramatic metaphors of the value of being, or being prepared to be, violent in the society concerned. To emphasize the point: the tension amongst those implicated in violence stems from the fact that the people concerned — be they performers, victims or witnesses — are unlikely, deliberately or otherwise, to mistake the activity for what it is. Suppose one's experience of violence has been limited to one level of society, such as the family, the fact that it is being practised at another level (e.g. between members of different communities, or even different ethnic groups) will be immediately noticeable, and one will then be unable to avoid the implications of its central property — its contestability. This recognizability of the violent act is, of course, enhanced by its very visibility. The sight and sound of violence, and the tell-tale marks of physical distress it leaves, are matters upon which elaboration is hardly needed.

[8] But such unpredictability may be somewhat reduced if the actions concerned are ritualized, as is the case in some tribal warfare.

THE POTENCY OF VIOLENCE

The capacity of violence as a social and cultural resource draws on four basic properties, which I believe have cross-cultural validity. The first three of these properties have in fact been introduced already.

1 The performance of violence is inherently liable to be contested on the question of legitimacy.
2 The discrepancy in basic understandings amongst those implicated in the performance of a violent act, or in experiencing a violent image, is likely to be minimal: in its key sense, as the 'contestable giving of physical hurt', violence is unlikely to be mistaken as such.
3 The practice of violence is highly visible to the senses.
4 The performance of violence to a moderate degree of effectiveness requires relatively little by way of specialized equipment or esoteric knowledge. The manipulative and strength resources of the human body, and knowledge that these resources are capable of destroying physical objects, are sufficient to enable a minimally successful act of hurt against another human being.[9]

These properties, each on the extreme end of a continuum, reveal violence to be unique among social acts. Other social acts are likely to be less inherently contestable, more ambiguous as to their meaning, less visible, and to require resources and knowledge of greater degrees of sophistication and complexity.

The potency of violence stems from the way in which its four key properties make it highly appropriate *both* for practical (instrumental) *and* for symbolic (expressive) purposes: as a means of transforming the social environment (instrumental purpose), and dramatizing the importance of key social ideas (expressive purpose), violence can be highly efficaceous. So it is that the desire to achieve a very wide variety of goals and ambitions is a *sufficient condition* for acts of violence to be performed.

To employ the solution of violence to transform the social environment plainly reflects its fourth property. The strategy of advancing one's social

---

[9] Adjuncts to plain physical strength will of course add substantially to violence's effectiveness. Sorcery and witchcraft constitute esoteric knowledge which contributes considerably in this regard. Indeed, so devastating are these techniques that in some societies they may completely substitute for the use of physical violence. But the images that sorcery and witchcraft inevitably conjure reveal their basis in the observation of the essential efficiency of visible physical strength.

position through offering physical hurt to one's opponents could indeed be entered as a 'natural social experience', together with the fact that weaponry and other devices can increase exponentially the results from this strategy. Thus while powerful social constraints, especially those articulated through the rules and values of kinship, may very substantially dampen the incidence of violence amongst a quite large proportion of the population, this natural tendency to employ the violent solution is quickly revealed in relations among people who fall outside the purview of such constraints. In my view, the Piaroa of Venezuela, described by Joanna Overing in this book, offer the perfect example. Because of kinship-type constraints, objective everyday relations among this people are almost totally free from violence. But in relations with outsiders — be they non-Piaroa or beings of the supernatural world — violence is allowed full sway. I should note at this point that theoretically to treat violence as a strategically, consciously employed resource — as I do here — is at odds with the opinions of some scholars, for whom violent tendencies are seen as in some sense biologically innate or as imprinted in the human subconsciousness. I cannot comment here on the contributions of the ethologically-minded anthropologists on the subject (see later), except to say that whilst they see the etiology of violence as comparable with the biological 'drives' towards sex and eating (e.g. Fox 1982), the parallel I prefer is between the practice of violence and the tilling of the soil.

The expressive function of acts or images of violence capitalizes, firstly, on the visibility of violence, and secondly on the probability that all involved — however different their cultural backgrounds — are likely to draw, at the very least, some basic common understanding from the acts and images concerned. These two properties of violence make it an excellent communicative vehicle. Some commentators have remarked that the symbolic usage of violence has been neglected (e.g. E. Marx 1976); but this is not the case in this book.

The relation between violence and what it signifies can clearly be metonymic or metaphoric. It is the former when extraordinary violent acts or images are used to make a statement about the general political capability of, say, a particular social group, where the readiness to deploy violence is an ordinary part of this capability. Public executions are an example, as is the kneecapping of informers favoured by some paramilitary organizations in Northern Ireland. At a simpler yet possibly more profound level, metonymic signification is evident where an individual uses violence tit-for-tat fashion in retaliation against violence perpetrated by others. While such violence, among other purposes, effectively (and instrumentally) pre-empts further violence by the original perpetrators through incapacitating them, it is also a statement about the retaliating individual's general political strength in the long term. In this regard, just as violence may be a natural social experience for the achievement of instrumental aims, it may be the same as regards the realization of expressive goals. Since individuals or groups will always at least contemplate violence as a means to secure a practical political advantage, then, should people wish to announce themselves as worthwhile political associates it makes sense that they consider demonstrating their own persohal capacity for violence. Certainly, to represent themselves as worthwhile associates people cannot always rely on displaying economic resources which they command or social connections that they enjoy, since the availability of such 'assets' tends to be uncertain and not necessarily under their control; in contrast, their physical capacities — especially their physical strength — are much more readily available, constituting as they do a 'resource' of which an individual can boast remarkably comprehensive knowledge. Suggested from this is that the seeming propensity for 'violence to breed violence' stems not from something inherent in the psychological constitution of the human individual, but rather from some basic — and possibly universal — logic in human and social interaction. This 'basic' social structuring is indeed quite transparent in the institutional complexes of a number of societies — among them, most famously, the societies of the northern Mediterranean (Spain, Sicily, Greece, etc.) such as are discussed by John Corbin and Garry Marvin in this book.[10]

Where violent images are used in metaphoric signification, the challenge is to uncover the rationale through which violence has come to represent ideas which are not themselves normally associated with the imparting of physical hurt. This is the theme of Brian Moeran's chapter in this book, dealing with certain Japanese film genres and other artistic media which centrally embody images of violence and sexual pornography. It is surprising that violence is such an obsession in this classically ordered industrial society, but Moeran shows that it is especially linked to the experience, which the Japanese deeply feel, of the transience and impermanence in the passage of time. Images of violence, for which there is plainly a high aesthetic regard, function to represent a protest against this passage of time; in this respect death, in particular, provides a sense of liberation and purification.

Since images of violence are among the few social images which are likely to be well understood across major ethnic divisions, the communication of these images may be expected to frequently take place in an ambience of substantial conflict and opposition. And because the idea that is most basically communicated in such images is the idea of a contestable social act, violence

[10] When such discussions about social advancement refers to the explicitly *public* domain of politics, *men* become the chief actors. Then the control of women, especially their sexuality, becomes a statement of political worth as well as control over one's own physical body — as the Mediterranean examples indicate.

14 *David Riches*

is peculiarly appropriate for directly expressing this opposition. Thus, specific
acts of violence may be arranged in a way that one 'side' will deem them
legitimate, whilst the other side will judge them unacceptable — and in this
respect each side may be fairly confident about the interpretation the 'other' is
giving. From the standpoint of witnesses on one side of a divide (ethnic or
otherwise), the violence perpetrated and displayed by people on the other side
comes to symbolize the existence of an alternative way of life — a way of life
which, though mysterious in detail, plainly has integrity in its own terms and
is therefore profoundly challenging and disquieting.

For such messages of political opposition to be effectively relayed, the
witnesses need not — and perhaps should not — be directly the victims of
violence. Such is the position of the British middle classes, watching passively
from the stands or on their television screens, as football hooligans from the
'rough' working classes fight among themselves in the stadium. The message
they receive is that the middle-class way of life is not sacrosanct and that the
working class may have a supremely viable alternative (cf. Marsh and Campbell
1982; Dunning, Murphy and Williams, in this book).

One presumes that the successful communication of political opposition in
this way will be better achieved through some acts of violence than through
others. The selection of 'appropriate' violence here may require judgements
of some subtlety — which gives the lie to the view that violence is mindless or
irrational. For example, the 'opposing side' will have arrived at its own
internal compromises about what is acceptable and what is unacceptable in
violence, so intending perpetrators will be obliged to estimate exactly where
this line of legitimacy has been drawn; *their* violence can then be all the more
effective for having been pitched precisely on the 'wrong' side of the line. Of
course, in the internal affairs of any group the question of acceptable and
unacceptable violence is likely to be a compelling concern; indeed, a group's
internal compromises may come to be a symbol of its cultural distinctiveness.
One may therefore suppose that, of any aspect of the opponent's culture,
outsiders will know its conclusions on this matter. The Eskimos in my
Canadian arctic community certainly knew where European Canadians 'drew
the line'; whenever they had engaged in a violent drinking bout the latter
would keenly attempt to re-educate them. In fact, the more the Eskimos
departed from Canadian norms, so the stridency of Canadian sermons on the
subject would increase — and so the Eskimos' conclusions about the Canadians'
opinions were confirmed yet again. In the next section, I consider in some
detail the Eskimos' deployment of violence as a strategy of political opposition.

However, whilst the communication of political opposition may be their
aim, perpetrators of violence do not necessarily seek complete political
dissociation from the group they oppose. For example, their intention may

merely be to signal a desire for an improvement in the political balance in their favour, within the context of some overarching political system which embraces both sides. In this case, there will be limits to the level of violence by which opposition may be suitably expressed: the perpetrated violence will have to be considered illegitimate by the other side, but it should not be completely indiscriminate or 'beyond the pale'. Such a state of affairs is brought out clearly in Fogelson's exemplary analysis (1971) of the race riots which occurred in the black ghettos of many United States' cities in the 1960s. What marked these riots was apparently the relative restraint of the blacks' violence set beside the physical potential for death and destruction. The blacks' targets seem to have been selective (white policemen, certain other whites venturing into the ghettos, particular economic exploiters), and their wielding of physical force kept for the most part in check — very few whites were killed in the riots, and even fewer deliberately killed (1971: pp. 73, 92). However, if there was a subtle political message here, not all whites seemed to heed it.

ALCOHOL AND VIOLENCE

The anthropologists' approach to violence is bound to concentrate on the way its practice is mediated by social constraints and values in the society at large. Childhood experiences, personality traits and other factors 'internal to the individual', which possibly predispose particular manners of behaving, will be less prominent in the explanations offered by anthropologists. Behind the anthropologists' perspective is the assumption that social acts are designed to make an impact on the wider social environment, and that a measure of shared understanding between an act's perpetrator and its recipients and witnesses is a precondition of the act's intended effect being produced. Social values importantly underpin this shared understanding. So it is that the predominant focus in this book is on the social ideas which give sense to the acts and images of violence and which provide for the exceptional social reaction that the acts and images command and evoke.

But this is not to say that anthropologists will totally ignore the inner determinants of violence. Thus, implicit in Suzette Heald's chapter in this book (which, with material from an East African people, associates cultural ideas about violence and aggression with aspects of initiation ceremonial) is the hint that a subconscious propensity to act violently may be fostered through certain 'ordeal'-type experiences featuring psychological processes akin to brainwashing — certainly such ordeals seem to prepare people to be courageous *in the face of* violence. But Heald's cautious discussion of the

Gisu circumcision rituals suggests that if such experiences are to have this effect they will have to be fairly drastic, and even then one could only draw tentative conclusions that the effect actually occurs. However, there is one field dealing with inner determinants of violence in which anthropologists have, contrastingly, pronounced with confidence though with resounding disagreement. I refer to the relationship between alcohol consumption and violence (cf. Everett et al. 1976). On this particular topic it is worthwhile to draw out the respective ideas and debates, for clarifications of some of the issues of contention are suggested from the analysis of violence in general, offered in the preceding part of this chapter. The main discussion on the significance of alcohol consumption in human society is about whether or not (or to what extent) alcohol consumption actually produces particular styles of social behaviour. No-one disputes that alcohol induces substantial *physiological* changes in the human body; the question is whether such changes directly translate into distinct patterns of action.

The ferocity of the argument about the role of alcohol in human action is fuelled by the immense variability in the behaviour with which alcohol consumption is empirically associated. Thus, writers who link alcohol with the practice of violence have to confront the many societies where alcohol is connected with peaceable and quiescent behaviour (MacAndrew and Edgerton 1970). Generally the styles of behaviour, be they violent or peaceful, adopted when alcohol is consumed seem to be rather exceptional compared with sober everyday styles. Yet, from society to society, it is very difficult to predict what these exceptional styles will turn out to be. To be sure, the most common pattern associated with alcohol does involve violence, but even here there are puzzles and paradoxes. My data from a Canadian Eskimo community are typical in this regard. In this community, alcohol — either 'home-brewed' wine or imported beer and spirits — is consumed only in connection with particular social events, most especially at parties held to celebrate the return to the community of people who have been away for some time, on hunting expeditions, at development conferences or in hospital. When violence occurs at these parties it tends to develop only after an event has been under way for some time, usually replacing boisterous but essentially friendly interaction; the physical assaults that take place are typically connected with particular grievances which the Eskimos involved hold against one another. What is noteworthy is that even though the physical assaults are quite frequent and not in the least unexpected, after the event, many people — often including the perpetrators — voice the opinion that such behaviour is a thoroughly bad thing. And here is the puzzle: in spite of this, retaliative action is barely ever attempted even against the most persistent offenders (Riches 1976). Instead, in the familiar manner, the perpetrator's violence is excused — on the grounds that they were drunk. This fact may be kept in mind as I now turn to two prominent theoretical approaches to 'alcohol violence' in human society.

With the first theoretical approach, I introduce the well-known hypothesis that alcohol violence may at least partly be attributed to the fact of alcohol consumption itself. I believe a mark of this approach is that it either baldly treats alcohol violence as deviant behaviour, or else implies that those who practise it are virtually on an emotional scrapheap; and I am therefore sceptical. However the analysts who favour this approach normally present alcohol violence in rather more positive wrappings, pointing to certain beneficial effects — to the individual or to the society — which it seems to engender. It is claimed, for example, that in those social settings where norms of everyday behaviour suppress such emotions as anger and ill-will, violent alcohol events function as a culturally-approved vehicle for the release of the tensions which invariably result. In a variant of this view, typically enunciated about aboriginal peoples who are confronted with abrupt social change forced on them from the outside world, alcohol violence is explained as a simulation of feelings of power — in an ambience where real power has been lost to the outside. Klausner and Foulks's study of Eskimo social change and oil-related developments in North Alaska includes this latter opinion (1982). On the face of it these sorts of proposals make sense of my Eskimo material as well.

But for all these arguments, this general approach plainly treats alcohol violence as deviant behaviour in that it includes the view that alcohol consumption works physiologically to lower people's inhibitions, and so is instrumental in fostering actions which run against everyday social controls. It sees the agents of action as virtually on an emotional scrapheap in its assumption that, like the alcoholic in Western society, the perpetrators of alcohol violence are victims of forces they can barely control and against which they strike out blindly. In my view, these are not especially helpful points of departure for understanding behaviour whose potential for damage is so enormous. It is immediately noticeable that their conclusions seem to concord very closely with the opinions my Eskimo informants express about such behaviour after the event (see above); analysts who favour this approach appear to be tackling the problem of alcohol violence from the standpoint of the perceptions of those who witness violence. Yet any explanation should properly address the situation of the performer of violence at the moment of performance. Being disposed to this latter perspective I shall have to find an alternative explanation for my Eskimo data — one in which the Eskimo is seen to practise violence as a rational and entirely considered means of social advancement.

A 'performer's perspective' may be introduced through MacAndrew and Edgerton's stimulating contribution (1970), to which I alluded above. Theirs, indeed, is the second theoretical approach to alcohol violence that I shall be considering. These writers argue convincingly about the relationship between alcohol consumption and social behaviour, claiming that, whatever its style, 'alcohol' behaviour is specified culturally and is not directed by the fact of alcohol consumption itself. They remind us that people can learn that, from the way a social situation is defined, a particular style of behaviour is expected. Thus once a situation has been designated as, say, a 'party', or 'fiesta', the appropriate behaviour will tend to be forthcoming at the appropriate time — indeed, with a party it will tend to be forthcoming whether or not or however much alcohol has actually been consumed. What is proposed then is, that among those social events for which alcohol happens to be an intrinsic part, violent behaviour (supposing it occurs) is learned behaviour. And this certainly fits with two vital observations: first, very often in human social settings where violence is performed, alcohol is not being consumed; second, alcohol consumption can be connected with entirely peaceable behaviour. For present purposes, the first observation is crucial: if violence can be perpetrated without alcohol accompaniment, then violence associated with alcohol does not have to be caused by that alcohol.

I find this approach helpful and ask two questions from it. First, why is violence *deemed appropriate* in certain social situations (events) where alcohol is also consumed? And second, why is alcohol considered the *proper accompaniment* to these situations? Limitations of space mean that I can only sketch in the directions for the answers. But a condition of them being satisfactory is that they will also explain the consumption of alcohol in situations where peaceable and quiescent behaviour is expected.

One promising interpretation of alcohol violence treats this behaviour as symbolic behaviour, the investigator's aim being to work out what message the behaviour is expressing. Support for this view comes from considering the violence that seems to be especially prominent in drinking situations among native peoples in North America (cf. MacAndrew and Edgerton 1970). Two points are important. First, although Indian and Eskimo violence is normally directed in a straightforward way against people with whom there is a grievance, the victims of attack almost invariably fall in the same basic social category as the perpetrator: they are inevitably fellow Indians or Eskimos. To put it another way, it is notable that Europeans[11] are only rarely the victims of, for example, Eskimo drunken violence — even though their policies and activities quite often give cause for very substantial resentments. The second

[11] From now on, I shall use 'European' as an abbreviation for the cumbersome 'European-Canadian' or 'European-American'.

point is that Indian and Eskimo violence seems peculiarly ineffective when judged in purely instrumental terms. Thus, as much as providing an *outlet* for the expression of grievance, its very practice *produces* further antagonisms and thereby heralds the likelihood of yet more violence later on.

If the Eskimo or Indian alcohol violence is to be interpreted as primarily symbolic behaviour, then to grasp its message the ambience of European-native relations offers the most promising context. The salient fact about these relations is that authority and resources lie overwhelmingly on the Europeans' side. Admirably capturing the expressive implications of Eskimo and Indian violence, a number of writers (e.g. Brody 1977; Lithman 1979) have in fact already proposed that the function of this violence is to make a statement of opposition, or rejection, towards the social values of the American or Canadian authorities. Accepting this, the question which then follows is, what makes alcohol situations special that they should be particularly appropriate for the communication of such opposition? The fact that in both European and contemporary native cultures, alcohol situations (especially 'party' situations) are important and given value, suggests the answer. The significance of alcohol situations is that they provide an ambience of common understanding between the two sides, in the absence of which it would be impossible to communicate a message at all. And as to why it is specifically through drinking violence that the opposition to 'European' values is expressed, this may be because (with tedious repetition) Europeans in authority continually stress the necessity of restrained conduct at drinking events — though this is not how they invariably behave themselves. Frequently on the receiving end of the Europeans' sermons, the native people, by behaving in a manner that reverses European proprieties, make the point that European values are ideas with which they find little sympathy.

Through the exceptional behaviour typically occurring in drinking events, we therefore conclude that the communication of a particular social message is the most likely purpose of these events. Yet we still have to ask why certain forms of symbolic behaviour are accompanied by alcohol consumption, and others not. The answer may well be found in the nature of the message being communicated, rather than in the fact that out-of-the-ordinary behaviour is being performed. For, in most societies, behaviour out of character with everyday life quite frequently occurs in the absence of alcohol — one thinks of crowd behaviour, or behaviour associated with ecstatic religious ceremony.

I suggest that there is something contradictory about the social events (we could call them rituals) where alcohol is typically consumed. In these events, the message that is being symbolically communicated seems to be seriously at odds with the reality of the social relations which prevail in (non-ritual) everyday situations. And alcohol consumption's importance may relate to the

20 David Riches

fact that, lest they be confronted with the fact of this contradiction, people need a means for recanting or denying the worth of the symbolic message. The physiological changes — especially the lessened motor control — connected with imbibing alcohol offers this means. Citing such lessened control, people can disclaim responsibility for what the ritual has 'said'.

I believe such contradictions are particularly evident in two broad types of situation. The first, exemplified by Eskimo party drinking, is where rituals of political opposition express confrontation or rejection vis-à-vis some other group, whilst those who perform the rituals are in fact dependent on this other group in rather fundamental ways. Thus European—native economic relations in northern North America are markedly asymmetrical. The constraining influence this has had on Eskimo and Indian action is well documented (e.g. Paine 1971), and illustrated in the Canadian arctic in the continual threat by Europeans to withhold resources (e.g. jobs) should Eskimos not be forthcoming with certain required behaviour — usually behaviour in the 'European style'. Alcohol rituals enable Indians and Eskimos to accommodate such effective subordination with expressions of insubordination. So it is that, when promised with the loss of social welfare payments because they have been brawling, the Eskimos protest to the European administrator that 'it was the drinking that was responsible.' In this way, insubordination is masked and the Eskimos' economic fortunes preserved.

Second, contradictions between 'ritual messages' and 'everyday reality' arise when the ritual is meant to express social solidarity, whilst everyday social relations are plainly not at all 'solid'. Events of alcohol consumption where 'peaceful' behaviour is the norm are appropriate to this sort of contradiction — and drinking events among the *Europeans* in the Canadian arctic provide an example. In frequent parties, the Europeans vigorously proclaim their sense of social intimacy — yet these people are essentially strangers, thrown together in an alien setting and not infrequently engaged in bitter disputes (Riches 1977). In a similar vein, Brody (1971) remarks on the bar-room conviviality of Indian migrants to a Canadian city (the bar-room *is* the Indians' society), yet these Indians come from widely different regions and are of disparate ethnic origin. Again, Szwed (1966) links the increase in social drinking in a remote Newfoundland parish to the increased social isolation among its component families stemming from social changes brought about by greater contacts with industrialized society. Such social isolation is also typically characteristic of many peasant societies where fiesta-type drinking is prominent. In all these cases, the unproblematic solidarity asserted in the drinking rituals stand, in the everyday, to be exposed as highly problematic. To be able to cite the lessened control that alcohol engenders means that, if need be, the actors are provided with the capacity to dismiss the ritual message, presenting it as an aberration.

END REMARKS

The study of violence in the contemporary social and behavioural sciences seems to be dominated at the one extreme by the view that such behaviour has a strongly innate component, or some other form of genetic basis — and, at the other extreme, by theoretical approaches which appear to insist that virtually all social acts be metaphorically, or even literally, treated as 'violent'. Before the main arguments of this chapter are summarized, these two themes merit brief discussion.

Studies offering the view that violence has a genetic basis normally discuss it under the rubric of a broader notion — aggression. Comparisons between human and animal behaviour feature strongly in such research. Very many definitions of aggression have been offered in the past, but one that is widely purveyed is the view that it is behaviour leading to the spacing of a (human or animal) population by means of repulsion (e.g. Eibl-Eibesfeldt 1979). Where animals are concerned a considerable range of behaviour evidently qualifies as aggression, from fighting to postures implying fighting, and indeed to any communications behaviour, such as birdsong, which is territory-maintaining.

Directed as it is by insights into animal behaviour, this 'biological' approach is distinctive in its lack of interest in human understandings, and in its being disposed to give explanations in terms of function — i.e. in terms of what the social behaviour brings about, rather than in terms of what prompted it in the first place. This is not to the taste of many social anthropologists. But to draw parallels or analogies between human social forms and animal behaviour is, in any case, contentious in its own right (Fortes 1983). Certainly, comparisons between aspects of human violence and aspects of animal aggression often seem to be drawn very superficially. Whilst a biological component to violence need not be ruled out, I believe that much in human violence is perfectly amenable to explanation in terms of the human being's unique mental capacities. As an illustration of this point we might consider the question of 'threats of violence' — be these actual mild acts of physical hurt, gestures, or verbal utterances.

Threats of violence have been given considerable attention by sociologists and anthropologists (e.g. Marsh, Rosser and Harré 1978) and are sometimes spoken of, appropriately, as rhetorics of violence. All of course agree that the function of threats of violence is to demonstrate a capacity to use real, or more serious, violence in order to prevail over an opponent. However, what is at issue is the relationship between a so-called threat and the real violence that might ensue. Those for whom parallels between animal and human behaviour are decisive suppose that threats of violence obtain unconsciously (perhaps from natural selection), so that real violence never, in fact, happens. Through threats of violence adversaries are repelled, yet since one side withdraws the species is not endangered through someone, or some group, suffering serious physical impairment or even death (cf. Fox 1977). The alternative approach to such behaviour — which sees threats of violence as a product of a distinctively human imagination — considers it as reflecting something which is actually known and experienced about serious violence. As I have indicated, this second approach is the one I would prefer. I simply suggest that threats of violence should be seen as an appropriate (and far from arbitrary) *symbol* of 'real' violence, based in the fact that people know that real violence can develop inexorably from quite mild acts of physical hurt. In short, knowledge about the uncontrollability of violence underpins the connection between the 'threatened' and the 'real', and not natural selection and the drive for species preservation.[12]

The second 'recent theme' about violence concerns the way in which in certain branches of sociological understanding a very wide range of social acts have come to be denoted by the term 'violence'. Thus, acts which result in mental anguish can be spoken of as 'violent', and Bourdieu (to take just one example) introduces the idea of 'symbolic violence' — meaning the capacity to secure a lasting hold over someone through economic means or through the manipulation of affective obligations (1977: p. 191). For many commentators, to employ 'violence' in this way is intuitively unreasonable. Yet respectable justifications can be put forward. In the first place, 'broad usages' of 'violence' result from profound cogitation on the analyst's part on such matters as the nature of human society, or the relationship between the human individual and the wider social forces which encompass him. Supposing the analyst decides that it is in the nature of interpersonal relations that they are intrinsically alienating with respect to one party in an interaction, then the notion of violence could reasonably be employed as a means to conceptualize the essence of social relationships. In the second place, broader usages of 'violence' may be justified as reflecting something in the reality of very many non-Anglo-Saxon cultures, where a concept or label referring specifically to the 'giving of physical hurt', is entirely lacking. Such, for example, is the case with the Tausug, the notoriously violent people of the Philippines, for whom the only relevant term is *maisug*, which simply connotes a supreme masculinity and bravery (Kiefer 1972).

---

[12] But species preservation may *incidentally* be favoured through such symbolic manipulation of 'threats of violence': no one would dispute that an element of repulsion is at least an unintended consequence of 'threatening' behaviour. I might mention that elsewhere I have considered the question of the 'dehumanization' of the victim in violence in similar terms to the examination of threats of violence given here (Riches 1986).

Yet, there are counter-arguments to broad uses of the term 'violence'. Firstly, the theoretical approaches which inspire such uses are by no means going to be universally accepted. And alternative theories simply may not invite the 'broad use'. Such would be the case with those theories (which I confess I favour) which see reciprocity and bargaining as key elements in human social interaction (Riches 1985). Similarly, to take the example of mental anguish (mentioned above), I would prefer to see this in terms of a loss of social prestige than as an assault on the human psyche, and would therefore be less likely to favour it with the label 'violence'. However, I must emphasize that this chapter should not be taken as representative of the theoretical standpoints implicit in the chapters which follow. The chapters in this book do take a very broadly similar line but they are not identical in this respect, as is evident from the following chapters by John Corbin and Elisabeth Copet-Rougier. 'Violence' is evidently not privileged among social acts in being uniquely able to command a theoretical agreement among those who analyse it.

On the other issue — the fact that, in many cultures, categories of action corresponding with Anglo-Saxon notions of violence may be missing — it may be a mistake to allow discussions about violence to be dictated by the presence or absence of particular terms in particular cultures. (Though it is true that the terminology of Anglo-Saxon culture is bound to influence the preliminary avenue of enquiry where English-speaking analysts are concerned.) Social processes and meanings that are distinctive in human societies may in fact not be graced by exclusive terms — as students of kinship behaviours in society have discovered.[13] So it is that the aim of this chapter has been to discern specific social processes and meanings present in Anglo-Saxon culture corresponding to the English word 'violence', and to indicate that, marked by an exclusive term or not, these specific processes and meanings may well obtain cross-culturally.

But among the anthropologists in the orthodox traditions there is one agreement that can lead us into our concluding summary. This is that social and cultural factors, together with ecological setting, are the chief factors influencing the type and frequency of violence in any social situation. A large number of studies have been conducted on this theme and most of the present chapters contribute to it.

Thus, cultural factors specifying the main ambitions people should hope to realize can crucially affect the performance of violence if the ambitions

[13] It would of course be interesting to establish cross-culturally the social and cultural variables that influence the presence or absence of a linguistic term corresponding exactly to the English 'violence', and of other terms with related meanings.

concerned are ones which violence can possibly achieve. In this way, among the Eskimo and among the Yanomamö, the abduction of women from other groups is a vital trigger of violence (cf. Riches 1986). The social structure, identifying domains of altruistic relationships and domains of strangership and enmity is also influential. The study by Elisabeth Copet-Rougier in this book, which reveals the peaceability which prevails within a corporate community and the warlike behaviour that occurs between such communities, is an excellent example of this theme. Among different social structures, some allow the individual person a high level of autonomy. Here, unsupported by a definite wider group, someone ambitious for public political success has to rely very much on his or her own resources, especially physical resources, for advancement. If enemies are close by, such people may be instrumental in organizing frequent raiding, as occurs among the Tauade of New Guinea (Hallpike 1977). Alternatively, the ambitious person, by the judicious use of violence in dramatic gestures, can come to dominate a political following — this happens among the mafiosi of Sicily (Blok 1974). Then again, there may be specialized institutions fostering the planning and organization of violence, for example the men's houses in some New Guinea societies (Hallpike 1977: p. 230). Where there is conflict between people within a community, the level which it attains may partly be a product of members being in a position to pressurize one another for resources and support, as David McKnight shows at some length in his chapter on violence in an Australian Aborigine community (cf. Hallpike 1977: p. 116). Finally, factors external to the society as a whole may vitally affect the levels and types of violence which prevail within the society. For example, Hallpike presents the counter-intuitive opinion that in some tribal settings a permissive *ecology* may foster warfare[14] and violence, allowing the disputing parties the crucial mobility to enable them to reorganize their social groupings after a defeat, find refuge out of range of the enemy, etc. (1977: p. 206).[15] And the state structure's relations with the local society will be equally vital. Where state authorities are pervasive in the administration and direction of a local society, violence is likely to be confined to trivial incidents (albeit possibly frequent ones), as E. Marx demonstrates in his discussion of an immigrant town in Israel (1976). Providing a contrast, the theme of Blok's book (1974) on the fluctuating fortunes of the Sicilian mafia is that extreme mafia violence

---

[14] I am not making an issue of warfare in this chapter, simply treating it as violence which is subject to a certain level of organization.
[15] For discussion of the rival view, which links warfare to *pressure* on resources, see Ferguson (1984).

comes to dominate the affairs of Sicilian communities during periods when the Italian state's 'effectiveness' in the area is in decline.

And so we could continue. Obviously all these socio-cultural variables are relevant to some degree in all societies, and separately should be seen either as aggravating or as detracting from the likelihood of violence in any particular social setting. But in every instance, the relationship between social structure and violence is one of *influence* and *opportunity*; there is no suggestion that social structure *compels* violence — there are always alternative courses of action. The aim of this chapter has been to examine why people nonetheless seem so inclined to opt for the violent solution. With genetic factors ruled out, the answer must reveal something fundamental — possibly universal — in human social experience.

I suggest three main factors underpin the capacity of violence as a social and cultural resource. First, *with equal efficacy*, violent acts fulfil both instrumental and expressive functions. It is true that the instrumental function may be the more fundamental, for the 'core purpose' of violence, tactical pre-emption, implies instrumentality — if an act of violence has no instrumental aim, it would not be performed. Even so, a particular act of violence will, at the same time, transform the social environment in a practical sense *and* strikingly dramatize important social ideas. Indeed, the same act or image of violence will certainly achieve more than one expressive purpose. For example, the British football hooligan engaged in fighting against a rival group of fans offers to his group a statement about his own worth as an associate, to the rival group a statement about his own group's political and social capabilities, and to the watching middle classes a 'sceptical' view of working-class opinions about middle-class values.

Second, violence may be manipulated most prominently in the context of political conflict and contention, including between distant and separated groups. Particular attention can be drawn here to a peculiar combination of properties. On the one hand, the same basic meaning to violent acts and images is likely to be imputed by people who in other respects subscribe to very different cultural ideas. On the other hand, the notion of violence connotes the idea of an act whose legitimacy is highly contestable. Accordingly, acts and images of violence offer a highly appropriate medium for the expression of broad political opposition, not least in the context of major ethnic cleavages.

Third and finally, for all these properties and capacities the performer of violence requires remarkably little by way of specific resources and knowledge. The physical strength of the human body, together with the knowledge that such strength effectively transforms the physical environment, is minimally sufficient to indicate that, appropriately directed, such strength can affect the social environment. Whether this affect is directly practical or whether it is symbolic (functioning to communicate the individual's worth as a social associate), violence may be said to amount to a strategy which is basic to the experience of social interaction.

REFERENCES

Bailey, F. 1969: *Stratagems and Spoils*. Oxford: Basil Blackwell.
Blok, A. 1974: *The Mafia of a Sicilian Village*. Oxford: Basil Blackwell.
Bourdieu, P. 1977: *Outline of a Theory of Practice*. Cambridge: Cambridge University Press.
Brody, H. 1971: *Indians on Skid Row*. Ottawa: Northern Science Research Group.
———1977: Alcohol, change and the industrial frontier. *Inuit Studies*, 1, 31—46.
Chagnon, N. 1977: *The Yanomamö: the Fierce People*. 2nd edn. New York: Holt, Rinehart and Winston.
Corbin, J. 1977: An anthropological perspective on violence. *International Journal of Environmental Studies*, 10, 107—11.
Eibl-Eibesfeldt, I. 1979: *The Biology of Peace and War*. London: Thames and Hudson.
Evans-Pritchard, E. 1940: *The Nuer*. Oxford: Oxford University Press.
Everett, M. Waddell, J. and Heath, D. (eds) 1976: *Cross-Cultural Approaches to the Study of Alcohol*. The Hague: Mouton.
Ferguson, R. B. (ed.) 1984: *Warfare, Culture and Environment*. London: Academic Press.
Fogelson, R. 1971: *Violence as Protest: a study of riots and ghettos*. Garden City, New York: Anchor Books.
Fortes, M. 1983: *Rules and the Emergence of Society*. London: Royal Anthropological Institute.
Fox, R. 1977: The inherent rules of violence. In P. Collett (ed.), *Social Rules and Social Behaviour*, Oxford: Basil Blackwell.
——— 1982: The violent imagination. In P. Marsh and A. Campbell (eds), *Aggression and Violence*, Oxford: Basil Blackwell.
Hallpike, C. R. 1977: *Bloodshed and Vengeance in the Papuan Mountains*. Oxford: Clarendon Press.
Heelas, P. 1982: Anthropology, violence and catharsis. In P. Marsh and A. Campbell (eds), *Aggression and Violence*, Oxford: Basil Blackwell.
Kelman, H. 1973: Violence without moral restraint. *Journal of Social Issues*, 29, 25—61.
Kiefer, T. 1972: *The Tausug: violence and law in a Philippine Moslem society*. New York: Holt, Rinehart and Winston.
Klausner, S. and Foulks, E. 1982: *Eskimo Capitalists: oil, politics and alcohol*. Totowa, New Jersey: Allenheld, Osmun.
Leach, E. 1977: *Custom, Law and Terrorist Violence*. Edinburgh: University Press.
Lithman, Y. 1979: Feeling good and getting smashed: on the symbolism of alcohol and drunkenness among Canadian Indians. *Ethnos*, 44, 119—31.

MacAndrew, C. and Edgerton, R. 1970: *Drunken Comportment: a social explanation.* London: T. Nelson and Sons.

Marsh, P. and Campbell, A. (eds) 1982: *Aggression and Violence.* Oxford: Basil Blackwell.

Marsh, P. Rosser, E. and Harré, R. 1978: *The Rules of Disorder.* London: Routledge and Kegan Paul.

Marx, E. 1976: *The Social Context of Violent Behaviour.* London: Routledge and Kegan Paul.

Paine, R. (ed.) 1971: *Patrons and Brokers in the East Arctic.* St John's, Newfoundland: ISER Press.

Radcliffe-Brown, A. 1940: Preface, in M. Fortes and E. Evans-Pritchard (eds), *African Political Systems.* London: Oxford University Press.

Riches, D. 1976: Alcohol abuse and the problem of social control in a modern Eskimo settlement. In L. Holy (ed.), *Knowledge and Behaviour* (Queen's University Papers in Social Anthropology, vol. 1). Belfast: Queen's University.

_____ 1977: Neighbours in the 'bush': White cliques in an arctic settlement. In R. Paine (ed.), *The White Arctic: anthropological essays on tutelage and ethnicity.* St John's, Newfoundland: ISER Press.

_____ 1985: Power as a representational model. In R. Fardon (ed.), *Power and Knowledge: sociological and anthropological approaches.* Edinburgh: Scottish Academic Press.

_____ 1986: Violence, peace and war in 'early' human society: the case of the Eskimo. In M. Shaw and C. Creighton (eds), *Peace and War: sociological approaches.* London: Macmillan.

Szwed, J. 1966: Gossip, drinking and social control: consensus and communication in a Newfoundland parish. *Ethnology*, 6, 434—41.

2

Insurrections in Spain:
Casas Viejas 1933 and Madrid 1981

John Corbin

In the major cities of Spain, on 8 January 1933, the Spanish anarchist syndicate, the *Confederación Nacional de Trabajo* (CNT), rose to abolish the state and establish libertarian communism. The revolution was suppressed quickly with little violence. Two days later the anarchist agricultural workers of the Andalusian village of Casas Viejas, armed only with shotguns and agricultural implements, rose alone in support of the failed revolution. Three policemen were killed and many more wounded; in retaliation, twenty-one villagers were killed and others wounded and beaten. Few of those killed were insurgents; two were women and two were old men.

In Madrid, on 23 February 1981, Lieutenant Colonel Antonio Tejero Molina of the Civil Guard arrived at the *Cortes* (the Spanish parliament) with two hundred armed traffic police in six school buses to occupy the building, take the assembled deputies prisoner and hold them hostage. In support, a few other right-wing officers mobilized soldiers and tanks and took over national radio and television headquarters. The rebellion failed: the rebels surrendered without fighting. Despite all the soldiers, tanks, guns and shots fired, no-one was hurt.

Separated by nearly fifty years, these two insurrections pivot on a third. In 1936 General Francisco Franco led a right-wing military rebellion which provoked a left-wing social revolution. The combination of rebellion and revolution reproduced violence on the scale of Casas Viejas throughout Spain. Franco won the ensuing civil war and established a military dictatorship which lasted until his death in 1975. The transition to democracy which followed was opposed by right-wing officers. The insurrection of 1981 by some of these officers was modelled, however ineptly, on the Franco rising, and aroused fears of a repetition of the events of 1936.

Historians and political scientists have analysed the conflicts of which these insurrections are part, but the analyses throw little light on the quixotic behaviour they sometimes entailed[1] and ignore violence as such, by default understanding it as conflict. However, violence seems to vary independently of conflict. The insurrection in Casas Viejas was far more violent than the risings in other parts of Spain at the time, yet the rising in the village threatened the government far less than the risings in the larger cities. In contrast, the Tejero rising was far less violent than the Franco rebellion, but like its predecessor it threatened immediate overthrow of government and constitution.

This chapter offers an anthropological discussion of these insurrections, drawing on theory and ethnography to focus on quixotic behaviour and violence, arguing that understanding the former is a means to understanding the latter. The 'symbolist' theories of anthropologists such as Leach (1976), Douglas (1966), Turner (1969), and Lienhardt (1961) can provide a basis for understanding the meaning of violence (Corbin 1977). These theories imply a dialectic between mental maps and the physical world — between the ideal and the real. The structure of the physical world is continuous, but that of mental maps is discontinuous. Reality flows; the ideal is fixed. Maps falsify reality; reality challenges maps. The resulting dialectic leads to maps being changed to fit the world and the world being changed to fit the map. Concern for coherence is a basic engine for human action.

A symbolist perspective insists that violence is mental as well as physical. Physically it involves the application of force to distort, damage or destroy objects; mentally it involves violation of identities. Violation occurs whenever a term in the map is threatened, the intensity of violation depending both on the strength of the threat and the importance of the term in the map. Destructive physical force applied to the material object to which the term corresponds can pose such a threat. The term may be in the mind of a person using force, of a person on whom force is used, of a person witnessing force being used, or of a person combining any or all of these experiences. In this regard, the boxer, who both gives and receives blows, is both violator and

---

[1] Hobsbawm (1959) follows Diaz del Moral (1929) and Brenan (1960) in treating Andalusian anarchism as a millenarian movement. He has been criticized by other historians such as Kaplan (1977), Lida (1972), Calero (1976), and the anthropologist Mintz (1982) writing as a historian, all of whom insist on the rationality of anarchist action. My own view, that Andalusian anarchism was both millenarian and rational, is being prepared for publication by Gower Publishing under the title *The Anarchist Passion: Class Conflict in Southern Spain, 1810—1965*. The Tejero rising is too recent to have generated much academic debate in print, but Preston (1984) refers to 'comic opera' aspects.

violated. People witnessing the bout, while not experiencing the physical force, may experience the violation of the boxers; indeed such an experience is the point of witnessing the bout.

Violence, then, is destructive physical force associated with experiences of violation, but the relation between physical force and violation is complex, and much slippage between one and the other is possible. First, physical force is not a necessary condition of mental violation. We speak sometimes of 'mental' or 'psychological' violence, which in terms of the present argument is violation without violence. Second, physical force is not a self-evident, universally recognized category. Force is detected by its effect and may lack a visible agent. 'Wind' and 'gravity' are examples from our own culture, and 'witchcraft' and 'sorcery' from others. Once the existence of such forces is accepted, the possibility arises of invisible forces behind visible agents. The man knifing another may have been driven to it by the devious manipulations of others, by the retributive hand of God, by witchcraft or by moonshine. Third, the degree to which force is experienced as violating varies. Violation may be means instead of end; force may be intended to 'destructure' in order to restructure. Instead of wishing only to harm, users of force may want to purify, correct, restrain, reconstruct, or restore order. Our own culture condemns violence as end but may condone or legitimate violence as means. Thus a fist fight between boxers is less violating than a fist fight between two people who are quarrelling; the former inflict damage on one another to win the match and earn a living; the latter 'just want to hurt' one another. A knife wielded by a surgeon is less violating than a knife wielded by a murderer; force used by the police is less violating than force used by the mob. Generally speaking, 'legitimate' violence is more circumscribed, more formally organized and regulated, than 'illegitimate' violence. The problem with such considerations is, of course, that people may disagree about means and ends, about legitimacy and about whether the force used by those entitled to use it is of the right degree and kind.

Given the scope for disagreement and the large range of meanings, motivations and justifications which can be attributed to any use of force, any definition of violence should depend minimally on particular renderings. The concept of physical force cannot be avoided, but defining violence as physical force that is illegitimate or intended only or primarily to harm can and should be avoided. To be sure, 'destructive physical force to which experiences of violation are attributed' will not be recognized as a separate or distinct category in every culture, but it will occur. As much as possible the meaning of violence should be a variable to be investigated ethnographically and not a constant to be built into the definition.

Of particular interest here is the suggestion that taking violent action is often, perhaps usually, an attempt to restructure; its aim being to alter both the real world and the ideal world with which it corresponds. Often the restructuring consists in restoring parity by returning violation for violation, or harm for harm. This implies a conceptual structure in which equivalence of identities and violations can be calculated. It also implies some impetus (perhaps the need and wish to maintain the conceptual structure itself) for keeping these violations balanced.

Sequences of reciprocal violence can start accidentally or tangentially, for people can feel violated even if they have not been subject to damaging force, and can blame their experience of violation on others even though the others intended no violation. Once started, the degree and type of violence may stabilize or change. Change often shows signs of positive feedback, increase or decrease becoming progressively greater with each instance. Each reciprocation may acquire a peculiar autonomy, each being thought of as a justified response to the immediately preceding injury, however much the preceding injury itself may have been justified reciprocation. In such sequences grievances never end and balance is never restored, for each reciprocation establishes balance for one and imbalance for the other. Further development of this argument would need to consider the factors which make the violence increase, decrease, stabilize or end.

Violence differs from conflict in that violence is about structures of integrity while conflict is about structures of control. The two are related in that violence may be a tactic in conflict, and in that control itself may violate the integrity of those controlled. Though the two may occur separately they are often found together. The Spanish insurrections in question are by definition conflict, for they are armed attacks on the agents of state control. To focus on them as violence is to focus not just on the armed attack but also on the experiences of conceptual violation the attack responds to and produces. In these insurrections the key conceptual structure is personal integrity, specifically honour, about which there is a wealth of ethnographic evidence.

Honour is a commonplace of Mediterranean anthropology; it is said to be a key value of Mediterranean societies (Peristiany 1965). The honour at issue here is that of Spaniards, most of whom are Andalusians, for Casas Viejas is in Andalusia (Spain's southernmost region), and all the informants who talked to me about the Tejero rising are Andalusians. Like most Spaniards, Andalusians are intensely concerned with their personal integrity, with their reputations and their conduct and what it signifies (Pitt-Rivers 1971, 1977; Corbin and Corbin 1984), and they express this concern in a few culturally important terms.[2] Andalusian culture is centrally concerned with qualities of *vida* (life), with variations in *vida*, and with the place of humans in this scheme of variation (Corbin and Corbin 1986). The distinguishing characteristic of *vida* is the ability to transcend the limitations of inert material, and in particular to become self-determining. Thus plants have more *vida* than things, animals more than plants, humans more than animals and God more than humans. From the human perspective, then, the world divides into superior and inferior orders, with humans occupying an order of their own between the two. Subordinate to human beings are things, plants and animals, and the space to which these belong — the *campo* (country); superordinate is God in the *cielo* (heaven); between are humans and their corresponding urban space, the *ciudad* (city), and *pueblo* (village).

Human existence is a struggle to transcend bodily limitations, to achieve enhanced *vida* and to become self-determining. In this world, success is necessarily temporary and contingent. The young have yet to develop it; the old are losing it; illness and impairment can threaten it at any time. These qualifications are coped with by confining them as far as possible to the highly bounded, private *casa* (house) — reserving *calle* (street), the space between *casas* in the human urban domain, for the more successful manifestations of enhanced *vida* in this-worldly existence. Precisely because self-determination is so necessarily qualified, individual autonomy is merged in a higher domestic autonomy. Domestic structures are the primary processors of individual identities, dealing not only with overlapping identities of kinship and affinity but also with extensions of individual identities into the material world, that is, with private property. Since this is an agrarian society, private property includes farms, livestock and crops in the *campo*. Each domestic unit should be self-sufficient; it should be able to sustain all its members with its own labour on its own property. Employment outside the *casa* violates domestic autonomy. With etymological aptness, the economy should be domestic.

Politics consists of extra-domestic encounters in the *calle*, and is open to all adult men with *casas* on that *calle*. These encounters may involve competition in which honour, predicated on domestic identity and underwritten by domestic resources, is at stake. Each man engaged in such politics defends his own honour, questions the integrity of his opponents and discusses that of others in the *calle*. The substance of such politics is the exercise of influence; the man who is successful is the man who is respected and whose views and

---

[2] This analysis is based on fieldwork in Andalusia, but some of the actors to be discussed are not Andalusian. I cannot say with authority that their actions can be analysed in terms of Andalusian culture, though my informants did not hesitate to do so. As Andalusian culture is a variant of Spanish culture, the analysis is probably valid.

opinions on matters of public interest are noted and given weight; he is the man who can shape and guide public opinion. Competition in the politics of honour makes sense as a means of producing contingent and temporary inequalities between those of similar means; it is pointless if the means are so unequal that competition starts from absolute and permanent inequalities. The culture is more suited to a society of independent domestic enterprises — farms, shops or workshops — than to Andalusian society, which consists mainly of many poor employees and a few wealthy employers. To be employed is to yield autonomy; it is to accept authority, to abandon contestation of the *calle* and to move in the direction of *casa* and *campo*. To be employed demeans; it symbolically emasculates, infanticizes, impairs, and animalizes.

Andalusian culture, then, values domestic autonomy and treats that autonomy as an index of success in achieving a higher order of life — an order which is culture rather than nature, human rather than animal, civilized rather than savage. This culture renders politics as civic affairs and 'politicking' as the exercise of personal influence. But Andalusians are subject to the Spanish state, which is founded on authority, equates politics with government and renders 'politicking' as the exercise of office in the maintenance of legal order.

The two insurrections to be considered were both attacks on the government, the Tejero rising an attempt to gain control of the state and the Casas Viejas (anarchist) rising an attempt to destroy the state. In both, the politics of honour clashed with the politics of office as violation led men to take restructuring action. I shall consider the Casas Viejas rising first.

Anarchism in Andalusia attacked the existing distribution of land and other means of production which denied the vast majority of the population the means to subsist autonomously, and it sought to destroy the state as a system of authority. It insisted on spontaneous action, and on occasions was able to mobilize masses of people with minimum organization. As a movement it was marked by sporadic bursts of activity and enthusiasm, alternating with long periods of quiescence.

One outburst occurred in 1933.[3] In the preceding years a division had developed between older moderates and younger radicals, and by 1932 the latter had gained control of the CNT. A railroad strike threatened, and to coincide with it the radicals planned an armed uprising, so that during the

---

[3] This account is based on J. R. Mintz (1982). Mintz collected oral histories from many of the participants in the events of 1933 during fieldwork in Casa Viejas. From these and documentary sources he constructs a narrative of the rising, its antecedents and consequences. His main concern is to correct the historical record. He cites neither anthropological theory nor ethnography.

strike the Government would be unable to move troops. The major battles were expected in large cities such as Barcelona, but the CNT called for local sections throughout Spain to rise so that troops would be dispersed. Among the local sections which responded was that of the Andalusian village (population 1800) of Casas Viejas. The village was a satellite of the town of Medina Sidonia; municipal authority in the village was represented by a deputy mayor and state authority by four civil guards.

The rising in Barcelona was set for 8 January 1933. Local sections in Andalusia were advised not to rise until they had heard on the radio that the battle had been won in Barcelona. Unfortunately, the smaller towns lacked electricity, so a plan for visual signs was made to cover the area which included Casas Viejas. First, the workers in Jerez, the largest town, would cut the electricity supply at night. Then the workers of Medina Sidonia, on seeing the lights go out, would themselves rise. They would also light a fire to signal Casas Viejas that the rising had begun.

In the event, the national rising failed. Some violence did break out in Andalusia on the 10th, but the workers of Jerez did not succeed in cutting the power supply. But a written message from the syndicate in Jerez had reached Medina Sidonia and been passed on to Casas Viejas. The message read: 'At ten o'clock at night, no matter what the consequences'. That night, the workers of Medina Sidonia, waiting for the visual signal from Jerez, dispersed when a contingent of civil guards arrived. That same evening the workers of Casas Viejas met at syndicate headquarters to discuss the contradictory reports they had received. The elected leaders, who were older and more moderate, urged caution, but the younger radicals prevailed. Three of the leaders signed a note stating that they resigned their office and could not be held responsible for any action taken in the name of the syndicate. One threatened to inform the Civil Guard of the plans; he later carried out the threat. Another actually did continue as leader during the rising. A fourth man, the president-elect, slipped out of town and went into hiding.

That night the insurgents sealed off the village — cutting telephone lines, digging a ditch across the main road and posting men to guard all entrances and exits to the town. Armed guards were posted behind walls where they could cover the doors and windows of the Civil Guard barracks. The deputy mayor was visited separately by an older and a younger leader of the workers. The older told him to instruct the civil guards to stay in their barracks, claiming that nothing would happen if they did. The younger leader demanded that the mayor instruct the guards to surrender. The messages were delivered but ignored. The sergeant in command of the unit led two of his men out and around the barracks to reconnoitre. They were fired on, but the workers had loaded with birdshot and the pellets did not penetrate the heavy capes worn by the guards, who quickly retreated to their barracks. The guards went upstairs. The sergeant presented himself at the front window with his rifle; a guard peered over his shoulder. Again they were fired on, but this time they were hit with buckshot, and both men were to die from the wounds they received. The remaining two guards returned the fire but hit no-one.

Apart from guarding the entrances to the village and trying to keep the civil guards in their barracks, the main activities of the insurgents the next morning were to mount an enthusiastic parade with banners through the streets and to ransack a records office, burning the papers in the streets.

Later that morning a telephone repair man accompanied by three civil guards arrived, discovered the cut line and reported to Medina Sidonia that something was wrong. A squad of nine civil guards arrived at two o'clock in the afternoon and entered the town, running and firing their rifles into the air. The insurrection collapsed with the workers fleeing, most of them to the country, a few to their homes. The police patrolled the streets, firing at anything that moved. At least one villager was killed and another wounded. At five o'clock, a further force of four civil guards and twelve riot police arrived under the command of a lieutenant. They found the streets quiet, and the lieutenant ordered the villagers to open their doors and resume normal activities. A house search for insurgents was started. One of the men besieging the barracks had been recognized. He was captured in his home and beaten. When his pregnant wife protested she was struck with clubs. His brother-in-law was also beaten, and one or both revealed the names of the others who had fired on the barracks. Among those implicated were two brothers, and the guards went to their house. In the house were the two men, a third militant worker, and six other people related to them, including a man of seventy, a boy of thirteen and three women. The guards forced the door; one was shot and killed trying to enter, and another was wounded in the exchange that followed. From the surrounding darkness other villagers fired on the guards. The lieutenant called for reinforcements. Another twenty-two men, one officer, hand-grenades and a machine-gun had arrived by ten o'clock, but the machine-gun would not fire, the grenades would not explode, and the lieutenant did not dare to move his men.

At two o'clock in the morning another forty men, under the command of Captain Rojas, arrived with orders to take swift and uncompromising action. These men had been sent from Madrid two days earlier and had not rested for forty-eight hours. By this time the machine-gun was working, and the villagers providing supporting fire from the darkness were forced to retreat. Rojas called on the occupants of the besieged house to surrender; when they refused he ordered it to be set on fire. One woman and the thirteen-year-old boy managed to escape. The other seven people in the house were killed.

The next morning the house search for insurgents was resumed. Rojas ordered his men to shoot anyone who resisted. A man of seventy-five tried to shut the door on them, protesting that he was not an anarchist. He was shot and killed through the door. Twelve men were arrested. One of them had been among those firing on the guards the night before. The police who arrested him did not know this, and none of the others arrested had taken part in the insurrection. The prisoners were taken to the burnt-out house. Rojas told them to go in and see what they had done and had them shot, firing on them himself with his pistol.

Most of those who fled into the countryside drifted back some days later. Some were arrested in the streets, many turned themselves in. Interrogations, beatings, trials and convictions followed. No-one was executed.

Three years after the Casas Viejas rising, the Franco rebellion split the country. The issue was finely balanced, and three years of civil war were required to resolve it in Franco's favour. During Franco's regime the main threat to the state came not from class conflict but from regional, and in particular Basque, separatism. The Basques had supported the Republic in the Civil War, and after the war the Franco dictatorship suppressed Basque nationalism. An underground opposition developed and Basque terrorists attacked policemen, soldiers and other officials. Killings usually took place in public — in streets or bars.

In the last years of his regime Franco sought to ensure an orderly and conservative succession by installing Juan Carlos, grandson of the last king of Spain, as king, but after Franco died in 1975 the king appointed Adolfo Suárez to oversee the transition to democracy. Suárez assembled a political alliance called *Unión del Centro Democrático* (UCD), which fought and won the elections of 1977 and 1979. His government tried to counter the influence of the Francoist old guard among the military by assigning the liberal Lieutenant-General Manuel Gutiérrez Mellado to 'democratize' the armed forces. The government also tried to defuse separatism by a policy of regional autonomy, but the more militant Basques were not satisfied and the terrorist campaign continued. Suárez refused to launch a full-scale military campaign against the terrorists, thus further antagonizing right-wing officers already suspicious of democracy and opposed to regional autonomy.

Tejero was one of these officers, a lieutenant-colonel in the para-military Civil Guard.[4] He had been implicated in the Galaxia plot, which was named

---

[4] Sources for this account include *Todos al Suelo* (a narrative written by seven Spanish journalists immediately after the event), the academic discussions of P. Preston (1984) and P. Vilanova (1983), and my own observations. The deliberations of the *Cortes* were being

after the Madrid cafeteria in which the plotters gathered to discuss their plans. The plot, if such it was, was uncovered and defused before any action was taken. Tejero is also reported to have rebelled on one occasion in Malaga. On hearing that two civil guards had been shot by terrorists, he trapped his commanding officer in a lift between floors in the headquarters building, took over the garrison and ordered the guards into the streets. The rebellion was short-lived and hushed-up. Tejero was reprimanded and transferred.

In January 1981 Adolfo Suárez resigned as head of government. The business of the *Cortes* on 23 February was to elect a new head; nearly all members of the government and deputies were expected to attend. During the meeting Tejero, accompanied by guards with submachine guns, entered the chamber waving his pistol. He shouted '*todos al suelo*', ordering everyone to get down on the floor. When they did not obey he ordered his men to fire over their heads, showering them with plaster. Most of the deputies, including Felipe González, leader of the socialist party, and Manuel Fraga, ex-minister under Franco and leader of the conservative *Alianza Popular*, dived into the space between the row of seats in which they were sitting and the back of the seats in front. Three politicians did not obey the order to get down. One was Adolfo Suárez, who remained upright in his seat off to one side. Another was the seventy-year-old Gutiérrez Mellado, who came unsteadily forward to remonstrate with Tejero. Eventually Suárez came down and managed to lead the general away. The third was Santiago Carrillo, leader of the communist party, who remained seated upright. Tejero repeatedly ordered him down, and when he refused salvos were fired over his head. After several such sequences Carrillo inclined his body to one side, and this gesture was accepted as submission. Later, the guards removed Carrillo, González, Alfonso Guerra (deputy leader of the socialist party), Gutiérrez Mellado, and Rodríguez Sahagun (Minister of Defence), from the main chamber, placing them in another room under close supervision. Those who remained behind feared that they were being taken away to be shot.

Tejero claimed to be acting in the name of the king and under the orders of Lieutenant-General Jaime Miláns del Bosch, commander of the military region of Valencia. Miláns del Bosch declared martial law pending instructions from the king and put troops and tanks into the streets of the city. Captain Martínez Merlo of the Brunete armoured division occupied the offices of

---

recorded for television when Tejero arrived, and I saw the opening sequence of the occupation on British television news. Any anthropologist doing fieldwork in Spain shortly afterwards, as I was, would have heard informants discussing the event. Among my informants was a deputy to the *Cortes*, who was taken hostage by Tejero.

national radio and television near Madrid with eighty men. Major Ricardo Pardo Zancada, also of the Brunete division, joined Tejero in the *Cortes* with a unit of military police. The king opposed the rising and used all his influence to prevent further defections. No other troops joined the insurrection. By the early hours of the morning Martínez Merlo and Miláns del Bosch were persuaded to withdraw their troops. The king appeared on television to announce that the insurrection had failed. Tejero continued to hold the *Cortes*.

As the occupation wore on, some of the junior civil guards told their captives that they had never planned to join an insurrection, and that they had been told that the *Cortes* had been attacked by Basque terrorists and that they were on their way to rescue the deputies. Several slipped away and surrendered. Alfonso Armada, a high-ranking staff general with personal ties to the king, offered to negotiate with Tejero. Eighteen hours after invading the *Cortes*, Tejero and his remaining companions surrendered. Generals Miláns del Bosch and Armada, along with several other officers, were accused of conspiracy and arrested. Most were eventually tried and convicted, the leaders receiving heavy prison sentences.

These two insurrections are part of a well-understood conflict over the legitimacy of the state and the form it should take. In Spain, as in the rest of continental Europe, the Napoleonic aftermath of the French revolution effectively undermined king and court, shifting power and authority to parliament. Military pressures, rather than elections, were the principal means of changing governments, and insurrections played a major role in this system of 'praetorian parliamentarianism' (Carr 1966). These insurrections were not *coup d'etats*; military force was seldom used to depose the government and take control directly. Instead, the insurrection usually took the form of a *pronunciamiento*, a declaration by a rebelling officer or garrison that the existing government was unable to exercise its functions and that in the interests of the nation a new ruler should be named, often the leader of the rebellion. Others were then invited to pronounce against the government and in favour of the new ruler. As news of the rebellion spread through the country, other garrisons, town councils, and similar authorities would decide whether to join the *pronunciamiento*. If support was sufficiently strong the *pronunciamiento* would succeed; if support was slight or non-existent the existing government would stay in power. In either case the losers would retire from active politics, go into exile, or perhaps suffer a brief period of imprisonment. In effect, the system was a kind of extra-official, irregular election — in this case, of a supreme authority by lesser authorities. In some instances, however, support for and opposition to the *pronunciamiento* was more even. When this occurred the resolution of political uncertainty was usually by battle, sometimes developing into full-scale civil war.

After 1875 this system was supplanted by one in which political agreements between parties to alternate in office were legitimated by elections. The military were still inclined to intervene when they thought the government incapable of maintaining order, with *pronunciamientos* in 1923 and 1936 leading to military dictatorships. Franco's rebellion in 1936 was a *coup d'etat* as well as a *pronunciamiento*.

The Tejero insurrection has some of the features of a *coup d'etat*. In Spain it is known as the *golpillo*, 'little coup', and academics have referred to it as a coup (Preston 1984).[5] There may have been three plots. First, Alfonso Armada, who thought he could use his position and connections to depose the government temporarily, aimed to take power himself to mount an offensive against Basque terrorists, returning government to civilians once the operations were completed. Second, Miláns del Bosch and other right-wing generals, who, on being told by Armada that he could secure support from the king, plotted to do away with democracy and return to Francoism. They planned to rebel in May. Third, Tejero, who shared the aims of the generals but was too impatient to wait. His premature action in February caught the generals unprepared.[6]

Tejero acted more like someone engaged in a *pronunciamiento* than in a *coup d'etat*. He issued a proclamation declaring that the occupying force was opposed to separatist regional autonomies, that it rejected impunity of terrorists, the decline in the prestige of Spain, and civil disorder, and that it accepted and respected the king whom it wanted to see at the head of the country backed by its armed forces (Cid et al. 1981: p. 201). Overtaken by events, this proclamation was never published. Taking the *Cortes* could never have produced the change Tejero wanted; he clearly expected that action to

---

[5] Preston's explanation of the rising includes the assertion that the Spanish military are a clannish, in-marrying group with their own schools, stores and residences, and that this accounts for politics at odds with the rest of society. I have not made a specialist study of the military, but most of the wealthy families in the town in which I worked included men in the military; the views that the military expressed were not noticeably different from the other members of their families, and, in the social circles to which the families belonged, military and non-military mixed easily. My material suggests that the conservative politics of the officer corps is less an exotic product of a military hot-house than an extension of the politics of the class from which it is drawn.

[6] This interpretation was offered by a well-connected and informed source. Cid et al. (1981) speculate that there was only one plot, that Armada was its leader, and that he deliberately launched the fanatic Tejero at the *Cortes* to scare the opposition into accepting him when he came forward to offer himself as a 'moderate' military solution.

spark off a more general military rebellion. However, the political circumstances were not propitious. In the past, *pronunciamientos* had been successful when the government was clearly unable to govern, to maintain public order and to protect private property. Basque terrorism was a threat mainly to police and military, not to the public.[7] The resignation of Adolfo Suárez had left a minor power vacuum, but the successor to Suárez was certain to be a member of his party, and in the end a viable government of the centre was formed which ruled until the next elections in the autumn of 1982.

The Tejero rising illustrates the divisions within the Right in Spain. All conservatives are committed to authority but are less agreed on the ultimate basis of legitimacy and social order. The main competing principles are monarchical — personified by the king, military — represented by Tejero and the Francoist plotters, and democratic — represented by Manuel Fraga and his *Alianza Popular*. On this occasion monarchy allied itself to democracy and militarism was defeated.

Popular insurrections have an even longer history in Spain than *pronunciamientos*. Most were limited attacks on government authority, local risings of the populace in protest against a local grievance causing little more than a temporary disturbance. The development of working-class movements after 1870 — anarchism, socialism, communism — led to explicitly revolutionary popular insurrections. Interpretations of the effectiveness, sense and rationality of the actions taken by insurgents differ in many respects, but agree that economic inequality is the basic cause of these actions. However, analysis of insurrections as struggles for control of property or the state leaves to one side the terms in which the struggles were cast for insurgents and their opponents. Analysis of these terms permits a better understanding of apparently mistaken, irrational, utopian or quixotic behaviour. Men who value honour and engage in conflict may defend or enhance their honour even if they lose the conflict and may lose their honour even if they win the conflict. Action in pursuit of risky or hopeless causes is not irrational if it permits something highly valued to be attained.

The clash between anarchist workers and police in Casas Viejas pivoted on

---

[7] Some civilians had been killed; indeed, shortly before the rising the head of a nuclear-fission plant in the Basque country had been kidnapped and, when the government refused to shut down the plant, executed. The Right also claimed the country was suffering a general moral decay, that crime and drug-taking were on the increase, that the streets were no longer safe, and that the police were too fettered by liberal safeguards to cope. Few people were personally affected by either problem.

concerns for honour. In general, Andalusian workers resent any treatment which denies them fully human status. They resent refusal by the upper class to socialize in the *calle*, which the latter usually express by disdaining to speak. Speech is, of course, the main feature distinguishing human from animal, infant from adult; talking is the main *calle* activity. People who quarrel are said 'not to be speaking'. If conversation is refused without the justification of a personal quarrel, the refusal implies that the refuser regards the other as unable to speak. Andalusian workers also resent levels of pay which do not give them 'means to live' (*medios para vivir*) and conditions of work in which they are treated as labour rather than as persons, for in their terms this equates them with animals (Gilmore 1980; Corbin and Corbin 1984). All these themes appear in comments of the anarchists of Casas Viejas. One reflected: 'We knew it would be difficult, but if one didn't protest, one would be an animal — some species other than man' (Mintz 1982: p.185). Another noted: 'There's a new generation now to continue the struggle. Man was born not to be a beast but a man' (Mintz: p. 315).

The police, also, were concerned with honour. Mintz thinks that the deputy mayor, on conveying the anarchist demands to the Civil Guard on the night of the rising, may have conflated the instruction from the older moderate that they stay indoors with the demand from the younger radical that they surrender. Mintz says 'the anarchosyndicalists quickly realised that the sergeant was not about to abandon his honour' and quotes the sergeant's reply to the mayor: 'We not go out? I've gone out in Cadiz, am I not going to go out here?' (p. 202). Mintz's narrative further suggests foolhardiness on the part of the sergeant and one of his subordinates when they exposed themselves at an open window to armed men who had just shot at them.

The Tejero rising, too, was conditioned by concerns for honour. Many of the officers killed by Basque terrorists were known to have refused bodyguards and other security measures in public, even though they were well aware of danger. The term 'honour' was used often by right-wing officers. One of those who quarrelled with Gutiérrez Mellado coined the slogan 'honour before discipline'. The day after the rising, the king told political leaders that eighty per cent of officers believed the conspirators to be 'patriots and men of honour'.

Tejero is reported to have rallied his men for the attack on the *Cortes* with the cry that they had to save the honour of Spain. His posture during the occupation was one of an officer willing to accept death and defeat but not dishonour. When General Aramburu, the commander of the Civil Guard, came in person to order him to surrender, he replied: 'If you take one step more I will shoot you and then shoot myself.' The commander responded to the challenge by trying to draw his pistol, but his adjutant physically prevented him from doing so and is credited with saving the commander's life.[8] As it became clear that the *pronunciamiento* had failed, Tejero refused to surrender to either overwhelming force or bribery. Threatened with attack, he replied that the deputies would be his trench. Offered safe-conduct to an aircraft so that he might leave the country, he refused. Finally, Tejero negotiated the terms of his surrender with the chiefs of staff, insisting that none of the other ranks who took part in the rising should be prosecuted. In effect he took charge of his own surrender, shaking hands with his men before leaving in a military car.[9]

The three politicians who refused to prostrate themselves to Tejero risked being shot. The rest were more prudent or more panicked, and some at least were slightly ashamed. As one deputy, a member of Suárez's centrist party, commented, 'I too threw myself down. The only thing which saved my honour a little is that when I looked around I saw that everyone else was doing the same. I felt a lot better when I saw the difficulty Fraga was having forcing his large arse down between the seats.' The conservative Fraga presumably had less to fear from military insurgents than other major leaders. Later comments on all three men expressed admiration for their courage. However, one ex-military conservative assessed Gutiérrez Mellado rather less flatteringly: 'He wasn't really valiant. You know how officers are accustomed to dressing down their subordinates. He just thought "I'll brace this one for what he's done". That is all.'

As negotiations for the release of the hostages proceeded, a guard reported to the deputies that Tejero had said he would make them strip to their underpants before sending them out into the street. One deputy reacted ambivalently:

When I heard what Tejero planned I said to myself 'That's enough. I am not going to walk out there in my underpants.'
Then I thought 'This is silly. Do I really want to leave my wife a widow and my children orphans?'
And then I thought 'But I won't do it.'
And then again 'But my family . . .'
And so I went on.

---

[8] Another version of this encounter had the commander waiting for Tejero with his pistol drawn, and when Tejero entered the room he, too, had his pistol in his hand. The adjutant pretended to knock the pistol accidentally out of the commander's hand, retrieved it, and handed it back with apologies for his clumsiness. The commander then was able to holster his pistol without loss of face, and Tejero followed suit.

[9] Cid et al., unequivocally opposed to Tejero, observe that though he entered the *Cortes* like a *pistolero* (gunman), he left it like a *caballero* (gentleman) (1981: p. 139).

The connotations are worth underlining. Underpants are associated with the privacy of home, intimate relations, biological functions. In city streets little boys, never grown men, wear shorts. Adult men only wear shorts on the beach or for hiking in the country. Moreover, to 'drop trousers' to another man implies subjection to him, becoming female to his male. (Brandes 1980: p. 95) To force the deputies to appear in the *calle* in their underpants symbolically depoliticizes by domesticating, animalizing, infantilizing, effeminizing.

Public judgement of honour was based on individual comportment and was little influenced by party sympathies. Of course, left and right reversed their judgements of heroes and villains, but few regarded Tejero, Suárez, Carrillo, or the king as men who lost integrity by their actions, or Felipe González and Manuel Fraga as leaders who rose above the rest in their response to danger. Considerations of success or failure had equally little effect on honour. Thus the right-wing rebels failed, the 'impartial' monarch succeeded; both emerged with honour enhanced. But such judgements did not noticeably affect later legal or political process. The rebels were jailed. Adolfo Suárez left the UCD to form his own party; he retained his seat at the next election but his party failed miserably. Santiago Carrillo was also returned at the next election, but his party did not improve its share of the votes. The socialist party headed by Felipe González won the election outright, and the conservative party headed by Manuel Fraga substantially increased its vote to become the chief opposition party.

In both insurrections, then, men used or threatened violence to retaliate for violations of their honour, and in doing so provoked violence or the threat of violence in return. Both insurrections were episodes in reciprocities of violence. Couched in Andalusian cultural terms, the sequence in Casas Viejas begins with poor workers generally feeling that their circumstances prevent them from being full men in the *calle*. On previous occasions they had taken action, with little success, to improve the domestic means which are a precondition of such public status. On this occasion they decide to take control of the *calle* directly and immediately. They do this by attempting to keep their opponents off it and parading through it themselves. In thus asserting their honour, they threaten that of the Civil Guard. Unlike the other villagers who do not sympathize with the rising, who stay indoors and are not molested, the Civil Guard contest the *calle*, but are forced to retreat. Up to this point the affair remains entirely *calle*. However, firing on policemen is a transgression for an ordinary man, and two of these policemen are now standing at a window looking into the *calle* with rifles in their hands. The pendulum of violence for the first time then crosses from *calle* to *casa*; the policemen are shot through the window. The building in which they are shot is, however, partly *casa* and partly *calle*, for the *casa-cuartel* of the Civil Guard is both private residence and public office. The guards retaliate when reinforced by retaking the *calle*, in the process tangentially killing at least one villager and wounding another. Reinforced even more, they return the pendulum unambiguously across the *casa* boundary by invading the houses of the villagers, beating at least two men and one pregnant woman. A policeman is killed trying to enter another house. More reinforcements arrive, the house and its occupants are destroyed. The police continue their search of houses, killing one and arresting twelve. The twelve are taken to the destroyed house where one policeman and seven villagers had been killed, and are shot. In summary, the sequence of killings is preceded by shots fired at police in the *calle*, begins with two police mortally wounded by shots fired from the *calle* into their ambiguous *casa*, continues with the police killing a villager in the *calle*, a policeman being killed trying to enter a *casa*, that *casa* being destroyed with seven of its occupants, another villager being killed resisting police entry to his *casa*, and climaxes with twelve villagers executed by the police at the destroyed *casa* where eight people had already died.

Some of the factors affecting this sequence are circumstantial. The arrival of mounting numbers of police who did not know the locals contributed to the scale of violence against the villagers. Normal relations between police and villagers were neither friendly nor harmonious, and beatings of suspects seemed to have been common; but normal policing involved some degree of integration in the local society, some knowledge of likely and unlikely suspects and some possibility of giving orders without having to enforce them at gunpoint. Normally, when the police wanted to interview or arrest someone, they would do it in the *calle* and not force entry to the home of the person they wished to see. This practice, in suspension during the rising, was restored afterwards. One of the workers who fled to the country after the rising returned three days later.

I went to the barracks and asked if Salvo, one of the guards, was there. They said no, he was in the street; but as I was going up to my house, I met him, and I said, 'Salvo, I'm here.'

He said, 'You ran away.'

I said, 'Not ran away. Like everyone else, I left.'

He said, 'All right. You come down to the barracks tomorrow at 12:00.' (Mintz 1982: p. 255)

The worker was arrested, beaten by Salvo among others, tried, convicted and jailed.

The violence during the rising could have been worse. The two surviving local civil guards intervened to prevent several people being arrested or shot during the house search. The brother of one of the men killed did not take part in the rising but knew that he had been seen carrying a shotgun in the street.

When they killed my brother, I thought they had killed him because of me. I went straight away to find the civil guard. I wouldn't have cared if they killed me.
Then I said to Salvo, the guard who had survived, 'Come out.'
Then he came to me and gave me his condolences. He greeted me. They had killed my brother. They had killed him, but he wasn't at fault.
I said, 'Look, this is what I think. You know what my brother was like. He was the sort of man who never bothered anyone or anything. If they wanted to kill those in politics, all right. But my brother was a man who never got involved in anything like that, nor me either. But I came down to see what happened.'
And he said to me, 'What happened with your brother is that I could not get in there in time. I couldn't be everywhere.' (Mintz 1982: pp. 244−5)

Another circumstance which may have added positive feedback to the sequence of violence was the arrival of Rojas and his force of forty police who had not slept for two days. He became ranking officer and his force outnumbered the other police in town. The death toll before his arrival was three policemen and one villager. After his arrival nineteen villagers were killed. The inhumanity of Rojas and the tiredness of his men may have contributed to the final nineteen deaths.

In essence, however, the deaths occurred because at several key points men either refused to retreat to the home and so retreat from politics, or refused to accept that a retreat from the *calle* was a retreat from politics. Charged with authority to maintain public order, the police chose to defend a challenge to that authority at all costs, regardless of the consequences for public order. Had the civil guards stayed in their barracks on the morning of the rising, there probably would have been no killings. Had the workers accepted that the police, on retreating to their barracks, were no longer contesting the *calle*, they would not have shot the two policemen 'foolhardily' looking out of their window. Had the police then accepted that insurgents who had fled to their homes were no longer a threat and simply settled back to wait for them to drift out, the suspects could have been arrested in the normal manner without loss of life.

The initial violation leading to the Tejero rising is well outside the range of this paper, as presumably it relates to the sense of outrage of some Basques at the subjection of their country to the Spanish state. As I know little about Basque culture or the process by which a sense of violated nationality can lead individuals to terrorism, I cannot comment. The killings with which the terrorists reciprocated provoked a desire to retaliate by the military which was not allowed by the government. Consequently, some rebelled against the government. The insurrection itself was remarkably low in violence. On several occasions it threatened to escalate but did not. In the *Cortes* this happened with the threat to Carrillo when he refused to get down, and again later when five prominent opponents of the insurgents were separated from the others. It also threatened during the confrontation between Tejero and his commanding officer. Sending the deputies into the streets in their underpants might have caused violence had some of the deputies resisted and would certainly have escalated violation.

Conflict, violation and violence are complexly related in these insurrections. Both start with 'structural' violation, that is, unintended violation which results from legitimate social process. The economic inequality which denied the poor of Andalusia the means to full honour was not intended by people with such means; it resulted from historical processes of accumulation and inheritance. Similarly, the incorporation of the Basque country into the Spanish state was not intended as violation; it resulted from processes of state formation little different from those which incorporated other regions without producing feelings of violated nationality. In both cases this structural violation created conflict in which the violated sought to alter the structure and by doing so threatened violation to others. In both conflicts violence became a tactic; it violated the honour of members of the armed forces and other members of these forces were provoked to illegal violence by the violation. But the violence was significantly different. In Casas Viejas many people were beaten and wounded and twenty-four were killed; Tejero held people against their will but did not wound and kill.

Some of the factors in these events were accidental, such as the muddle over signals and instructions to rise in Casas Viejas; others were circumstantial, such as the arrival of large numbers of police who did not know the locals; others were idiosyncratic, such as the cruelty of Rojas or the impetuosity of Tejero. Some are well-known from studies of conflict, such as the generally lower incidence of damage done in conflicts which quickly produce clear winners and losers, an example being the contrast between the military rebellions of 1981 and 1936. Equally familiar is the observation that the voluntary or involuntary placement of a third party between opponents may limit conflict. The confrontation between Tejero and his commanding officer, resolved by the intervention of the adjutant, is a good example. The placement of the government between the military and the terrorists is another case in point, for in rebelling against the government Tejero was not attacking those who had committed violence against the military.

Violence in these events was also conditioned by the symbolic meaning of actions — meaning which is implicit to the actors and not always apparent to observers. The violations of integrity on which these insurrections pivot produced more violence when they invaded the *casa* than when they occurred on the *calle*. The extreme violence of the Casas Viejas rising was marked by movement of the confrontation from contestation of the *calle* to fighting on the *calle/casa* boundary, where most of the deaths clustered. It increased rapidly and progressively by reciprocal transgressions of this boundary, reached extraordinary extremes and then collapsed. In contrast, the Tejero rising remained a *calle* affair and avoided bloodshed.

In this culture, competitions in which honour is at stake are integral parts of the life of the *calle*, and violations of individual honour in the *calle* are more legitimate and less provoking than violations of the integrity of the *casa*. Even so, competition in the *calle* should stop short of killing. Deliberate killing exercises God-like control or reduces the person killed to the subhuman. Proper politics cannot be conducted if opponents are destroyed rather than defeated. Personal honour in the *calle* cannot be maintained if individuals cannot appear in the *calle* without armed guards.[10]

Consideration of what did not happen in the Tejero rising is illuminating. It could have been more violent as a *calle* affair; shots could have been exchanged in the attack on the *Cortes* and someone wounded or killed; Tejero and his commander could have shot one another; Carrillo, González and the others removed from the chamber of deputies could have been executed. Such violence would have violated those killed by taking their lives, but it would not have violated them by taking their honour.

Violations of the *casa* seem more damaging to honour. The Tejero rising did not provoke a revolution; left and right did not, as in 1936, invade the homes of their opponents, remove them, often to the *campo*, and shoot them. Even so, many Spaniards who thought they had something to fear from the rebels were afraid to sleep at home on the night of the rising. The closest the Tejero insurrection came to crossing the boundary dividing *casa* from *calle*

---

[10] Discussions of honour in Mediterranean society often emphasize qualities of physical strength, aggression and willingness to do violence. Blok (1981) argues that state-formation, and the civilizing movement, have made the terminology of honour using the idiom of the physical person obsolete — the term 'civility' being more appropriate to denote honourable behaviour. I agree that a violent pastoral code of honour has been superseded by a much less violent urban code of honour but not that this results from the development of the modern European state. Andalusian ethnography suggests that civility is not a product of the large-scale nation state, that its structural base is the much older Mediterranean city, and that the politics of civility are often at odds with the politics of the modern state.

was with the symbolic implications of expelling men into the streets in their underpants. At least one deputy was willing to balance the violation of honour that this would have entailed against the violation of being shot.

The *casa* produces and processes human identities before they are subject to competition in the *calle*, and in doing so must deal with and rise above the unavoidable animal aspects of man. The resulting balance of humanity and animality is delicate, and to protect it the *casa* is apolitical and reserved for the problems of coping with nature. To invade the *casa* with the problems of politics (of the exercise of will by man over man) is to violate a fundamental order. Normally the streets are the place for willed *vida*, and the house for natural *vida*. When natural death comes it can be coped with by the *casa* and acknowledged by the *calle*. When willed deaths invade the *calle*, savagery threatens civility; when they invade the *casa*, animality threatens humanity.[11] Thus the pursuit of honour can destroy the public competition which normally frames it and go on to destroy the domestic structures from which it springs. If the irony of the Tejero rising was that most of those who gained honour lost authority while some of those who lost honour gained authority, the irony and tragedy of Casas Viejas was that in the pursuit of honour men destroyed the civility and humanity which gives honour meaning. No-one emerged from Casas Viejas with honour intact.

This analysis is specific to Spain. Many cultures distinguish private from public, associating the former with women and the latter with men. There is no reason to assume that these distinctions will have the same place in every culture and that their violation will have the same consequences. Each culture constructs and lives its own meanings, each experiences its own violence, and each must be investigated in its own terms.

REFERENCES

Blok, A. 1981: Rams and billy-goats: a key to the Mediterranean code of honour. *Man*, 16, 426—40.
Brandes, S. 1980: *Metaphors of Masculinity: sex and status in Andalusian folklore.* Pennsylvania: Pennsylvania University Press.
Brenan, G. 1960: *The Spanish Labyrinth: an account of the social and political background of the Spanish Civil War.* Cambridge: Cambridge University Press.
Calero, A. M. 1976: *Movimientos Sociales in Andalucia (1820—1936).* Madrid: Siglo Veintiuno de España.

[11] Corbin, 1982, is a film, entitled 'Symbolic Deaths', made for the BBC Open University course *Inquiry* which applies these arguments to Picasso's *Guernica*. See also Garry Marvin's discussion of the bullfight in this book.

Carr, R. 1966: *Spain: 1808—1939*. Oxford: Clarendon Press.

Cid, R., de la Cuadra, B., Esteban, J., Jaúregui, F., López, R., Martínez, J., and Van den Eynde, J. 1981: *Todos al Suelo: La conspiración y el golpe*. Madrid: Punto Critico.

Corbin, J. R. 1977: An anthropological perspective on violence. *Intern. J. Environmental Studies*, 10, 107—11.

_____ 1982: *Symbolic Deaths*. Milton Keynes: Open University Educational Enterprises.

Corbin, J. R. and Corbin, M. P. 1984: *Compromising Relations: kith, kin and class in Andalusia*. Aldershot: Gower Publishing Company.

_____ 1986: *Urbane Thought: culture and class in an Andalusian city*. Aldershot: Gower Publishing Company.

Diaz del Moral, J. 1969. (Original publication 1929): *Historia de las Agitaciones Campesinas Andaluzas*. Madrid: Alianza Editorial.

Douglas, M. 1966: *Purity and Danger; an analysis of concepts of pollution and taboo*. London: Routledge and Kegan Paul.

Gilmore, D. 1980: *The People of the Plains: class and community in Andalusia*. New York: Columbia University Press.

Hobsbawm, E. J. 1959: *Primitive Rebels: studies in archaic forms of social movement in the nineteenth and twentieth centuries*. Manchester: Manchester University Press.

Kaplan, T. 1977: *Anarchists of Andalusia, 1868—1903*. Princeton: Princeton University Press.

Leach, E. R. 1976: *Culture and Communication: the logic by which symbols are connected*. Cambridge: Cambridge University Press.

Lida, C. 1972: *Anarquismo y Revolucion en la España de XIX*. Madrid: Siglo de Veintiuno.

Lienhardt, G. 1961: *Divinity and Experience: the religion of the Dinka*. Oxford: Clarendon Press.

Mintz, J. R. 1982: *The Anarchists of Casas Viejas*. Chicago: Chicago University Press.

Peristiany, J. (ed.) 1965: *Honour and Shame: the values of Mediterranean society*. London: Weidenfeld and Nicolson.

Pitt-Rivers, J. 1971. (Original publication 1954): *People of the Sierra*. Chicago: Chicago University Press.

_____ 1977: *The Fate of Schechem or the Politics of Sex*. Cambridge: Cambridge University Press.

Preston, P. 1984: Fear of freedom: the Spanish army after Franco. In C. Abel and W. Torrents (eds), *Spain: Conditional Democracy*, London: Croom Helm.

Turner, V. W. 1969: *The Ritual Process: structure and anti-structure*. London: Routledge and Kegan Paul.

Vilanova, P. 1983: Spain: the army and the transition. In D. S. Bell (ed.), *Democratic Politics in Spain: Spanish politics after Franco*. London: Frances Pinter (Publishers).

3

'Le Mal Court': Visible and Invisible Violence in an Acephalous Society — Mkako of Cameroon

Elisabeth Copet-Rougier

Alarica	Avant tout, ce qu'il faut c'est que coure le mal. Le mal court. Vous le voyez? Comme il court bien! Furet! C'est un plaisir. Le crime . . .
Célestincic	Quel crime? Quoi encore?
Alarica	Le crime serait de prétendre l'arrêter.
Célestincic	D'arrêter qui?
Alarica	Le mal. D'arrêter le mal, quand il court. Je ne commettrai pas ce crime, sûr que non.

Jacques Audiberti, *Le Mal Court*

INTRODUCTION

When we compare the word 'violence' in English and French, we immediately see that it is conceptually ambiguous and relative. The primary English sense is of physical aggression — of physically inflicted wrong which is in some way illegal. In French there are two basic meanings. One relates to the English, and the other has the idea of 'exerting pressure on someone in order to make them comply'. In the latter meaning we are speaking of indirect, moral violence. The duality in the different perspectives is reproduced on two levels: legal/illegal, physical/indirect.

The significance of expressing the two levels as dichotomies is that each of the terms in a given pair intrinsically implies the other. In an edition of *Etudes Rurales* devoted to the problem of violence (1984), the legal/illegal dichotomy encompasses the opposition of Weberian and Durkheimian positions, which treat violence as an instrument, respectively, of social order and disorder. While one pole in the dichotomy (legal violence) *is* to do with the way a social order may be set up and maintained, it at the same time implies the other pole (illegal violence), which refers to breaches of social law and is concerned with the 'nature of events, accidents, and "noise"' (1984: p. 11).[1] Here, through the one extreme we may see societies being founded on violence, while through the other we may perceive the development of an aesthetic.

Before I clarify my own interests relating to this dichotomy, let me say immediately that I find it difficult to accept R. Girard's view (1972) that the *possibility* of social order is based on some *original* act of violence, which thereafter must constantly be expelled through ritual. M. Augé rightly criticizes this genetic view (1979: p. 76). It is moreover a romantic one. For why should social order be heralded in this way? Are we to suppose a prior state without violence? Such a view assumes a Rousseau-like blindness to the banality of violence and of the fact that it is expressed and used differently in different societies. My approach is close to that of J. Bazin and E. Terray (1982), who distinguish *polemos* (war against others) and *statis* (dispute, civil war, self-violence, disruptive violence). These writers further counterpose violence in the context of state society, and violence in the context of segmentary societies, of which an example is the 'acephalous' society (so named because its constituent clans and lineages lack co-ordination through some permanent institutionalized authority). Within state society, the only internal violence allowed is that of repression; the only other legally acceptable forms of violence which its members can perpetrate must be carried out beyond state boundaries. In the stateless societies, by contrast, this separation is not so clear. Some such societies allow the feud to develop after homicide between members of different clans, while others have precise rules of compensation after such a killing; sometimes, both arrangements co-exist, as among the Nuer or the Maasai. However, homicide among members of the *same* clan is so serious that it may result neither in revenge nor compensation, but in contamination that has to be purified. This is a crucial fact for subsequent discussion in this chapter. Speaking of societies in general, I believe that the intimate social units in which members are identified one with another by both insiders and outsiders (*l'entre-soi*), and within which violence is forbidden in this way, may range from the nuclear family to the clan (or a cluster of clans), and even in some cases to the level of the state. Yet, I would note that even within the narrow confines of the nuclear family

[1] All citations are my own translation.

there is still a certain play between notions of inside and outside, and legal and illegal acts. (I could find no easy English translation for '*entre-soi*', so I shall retain it in what follows.)

In human societies, acts of violence within the *entre-soi* are usually regarded as the most unacceptable instances of violence. For example, in my society, there can be nothing more horrible than such murders as the parricide committed by Pierre Rivière and discussed by M. Foucault (1973). Indeed, in many stateless societies *entre-soi* violence cannot be repressed by force emanating from sources external to the unit, for it concerns much more than the law. Typically, only purification can absolve it. Such violence is in fact defined as the ultimate in anti-social acts, in that it involves a confusion of categories whereby the 'same' is taken for the 'other': in this sort of violence, one's fellow is treated as an outsider.

So far, I have taken the idea of violence in the classical Anglo-Saxon sense, of causing physical hurt to someone (see Riches's chapter in this book). If we now examine the second of the French senses, we touch on the idea of constraint, or *indirect violence*. This idea has produced the broadest of interpretations of the notion of violence. Bourdieu thus distinguishes two types of indirect violence, on the one hand 'open' violence (implied by economic obligations), and on the other hand 'symbolic' violence (implied by moral and affectively-based obligations); typifying primitive society, this last violence is censured and 'euphemistic', and 'has to be made incomprehensible in order to be recognized' (1980: p. 217). According to this analysis, indirect violence, though mild and veiled, plays a part in perpetuating the social order and therefore fits the Weberian perspective (see above). Apparently, there is nothing 'illegal' about it — rather, the contrary. Indeed, can there be such a thing as illegal 'symbolic' violence? We shall see shortly.

In this chapter, which focuses on the Mkako, a West African society of eastern Cameroon, I shall concentrate on the contrast between notions of physical (visible) violence and 'invisible' violence (see below), which, it will be shown, apply respectively outside and inside the local community. I shall demonstrate that this contrast is linked to the opposition between legality and illegality to which I have just alluded.

The Mkako are an acephalous society for whom the notion of *entre-soi* comprises a cluster of localized clans. These make up a territorial group, or more precisely a 'tribe'. Accordingly, this group is defined politically as a conglomerate within which war is forbidden and where all physical violence is banished — even violence of a repressive kind, in contrast to what prevails in state systems. For the Mkako, the expulsion of physical violence from the *entre-soi* stems from the view that shared social identity is based on consanguinity. As I shall explain, this image of consanguinity and identity draws upon the key concept of blood, around which cluster such notions as pollution, purification, murder, interiority and externality, and time and space.

A salient fact about this society is that disruptive and repressive violence is to be found, located beyond social law, in an *invisible* world containing transgressions and their repression, and killers and their victims; in this world witchcraft, sorcery and magical medicines hold sway. This invisible violence is no mere reflection of social relations. Indeed, far from being a passive metaphor or an inverse image of social life, invisible violence *is* action and is as immediately tangible as physical violence. A typical 'Western' view of invisible violence — that it, in fact, represents something else — is not shared by the Mkako. We must therefore separate out the concrete and specific actions making up invisible violence, from the representational efficacy of such violence which, as an integral part of ideology, prevents transgressions and stifles individual wills through the threats it embodies. So far as violence in general is concerned, two levels evidently have to be distinguished: first, there is external physical violence and internal invisible violence; second, there is the threat of the use of either, reflecting the efficacy of ideology.

Within this invisible violence, thought of as an act rather than a metaphor, we may possibly find the illegal 'symbolic' violence that we were seeking earlier. We are then confronted with the question of the basis on which actual instances of violence are allocated to these various categories. Who or what, says one instance is illegal, and another, if not legal, is at least part of the social order? The answer is: none other than that through which they are defined, namely power.

We can only understand these different aspects of violence in terms of their relationship to power. Nevertheless we have to guard against any temptation to reify power. The Mkako example usefully presents us with different powers operating against a background of contradictory tendencies. Thus, while social order among the Mkako requires that the powers be scattered, individuals seek to concentrate them. But accumulating powers in this way leads to their re-scattering through the actions of rival individuals (and not through any social consensus). This results in Mkako society undergoing irregular oscillations of concentrated and scattered powers. More generally, we here come up against the perverse structure of power. Violence by itself says nothing, for it is not a pure concept. In order to understand it, we have to conceive of the opposition, noted at the beginning of this chapter, between violence supporting the social order and violence transgressing and reacting against it. It is precisely this intrinsic relationship of opposition that provides our anthropological topic. From this standpoint, J. Jamin rightly says 'that the same term . . . denotes a class of phenomena and its opposite, the exercise of law and its violation' (*Etudes Rurales* 1984: p. 17). In another way, E. Claverie asserts that, '. . . to commit violence is to give an intrinsic, destructive quality to a social relationship' (*Etudes Rurales* 1984: p. 16). But we must recognize the consequences of this position: the violence that perpetuates the social order contains within itself barbarous forces of destruction. The power, *all* the power, that it reproduces has this wild and destructive element. For this reason power does not exist by itself, and in *its* capacity to reproduce also carries the capacity to destroy. As M. Foucault suggested, 'Murder is the point at which history and crime meet. . . . Killing sets up an ambiguity in the relationship between legitimation and illegality' (Foucault 1973: p. 271).

This irreconcilable nature of power and violence seems especially evident in acephalous societies, as I shall now try to show.

FORMS OF VIOLENCE

I begin by presenting some examples of both regulated and disruptive violence among the Mkako. I shall refer to them as my argument unfolds.

Example 1 In the 1890s, Lieutenant Lizon crossed the Gbaya and Mkako country and found only 'ruins, burning villages, destroyed gardens'. He wrote, 'We have evidence that war between these pagans is not a game. The beginning of the "main street" of Boné is closed off by a line of grizzly heads, half-dried by the sun; everywhere, there are corpses, scattered limbs and the scraps of cannibal meals' (Mizon 1895: p. 336).

Example 2 Old Mkako men recount the story of the separation of two main clans who previously lived together in the east of the country, the Bolesse and the Mbessembo: two leaders were competing, and one of those, called Mbwa, took the initiative when the other leader, Ndelele, left the village to go hunting with all his men. Thus, Mbwa attacked and raided the village. 'They killed old Mkako men who remained in the village; they cooked the corpses with banana plantain in their cooking pots, covering them with banana leaves, and ate them.'

Example 3 On another occasion, the leader Ndelele tried to attack the main Mkako group in Batouri, called the Mkako Nbwako; the adversaries stood on either side of a little river; one of Ndelele's young warriors could not resist engaging in a fight and let fly an arrow at the enemy; in response the Nbwako killed two of Ndelele's men with their arrows. It was a bad sign, an omen, and as it was about to rain the fight stopped; everybody went home.

Example 4 Sometimes these war stories relate that as soon as the first or second man was killed, his heart would be taken out and medicine made from it and put inside a special drum, which was then played. They say that the sound was so unusual and terrifying that everybody knew of the fight, and war would then stop.

Of course, these acts of violence are viewed as legitimate by those who carry them out, and as illegitimate by victims, who call the perpetrators barbarians. One notes that there are no examples of such violence within the local community. But we do have a second group of stories, which describe fighting and murder taking place in the invisible world:

Example 5 Two men who were witches were competing for the same woman. They started to fight during the night in the invisible world. One was wounded by a sword; the other was wounded with the butt of a gun. In order to keep secret the fact that they were witches, they decided to 'change the terms of the sickness.' The more seriously injured man said he was sick in the stomach and accused a third person of wanting to kill him; he died the day after.

Example 6 Another story concerned two agnates — non-siblings — who were not witches. The younger agnate was envious of the big coffee plantation of his elder and decided to kill him through sorcery. He stole some items of clothing, some nail cuttings and hair from his elder agnate. Then, he caught a chameleon and hung it up with a medicine made from the stolen things. The animal took a long time to die and even longer (a year or two) to drop, dry and shrivelled, to the ground. The elder meanwhile grew thinner and thinner, and ended up as a skeleton with dried skin. Several weeks after he died, the junior agnate bragged that he had killed him, and provided details of the death. He did so when drunk, for drinking parties are an occasion for violent talk, self-vaunting and boastful confessions.

Example 7 The last story is about a girl cured by a witch-doctor. One of her female kin, an agnate living in the same house, was a witch and out of jealousy ate the young girl's blood and part of her heart. In an invisible fight against the witch during the night, the witch-doctor restored the stolen heart and put it back in place.

It might be argued that the second group of stories (5—7) are of a different order from the first (1—4). While the first group deals with violence which is physical and visible and has political aims, the second appears to be based on an imaginary and invisible violence, caused by jealousy and merely reflecting the inevitable tensions of social relations within the community. I shall try to argue, however, that the two types of violence share a common nature, supported by the same cultural category, and that they both often arise from an obligation to take revenge or in some way respond to war and dangerous social confrontations. They also function similarly, in maintaining or destroying both internal and external political boundaries — even though in other respects they are sharply distinguished, as respectively outer- and inner-directed. They are complementary aspects of a process by which social antagonisms are set up and different kinds of power distinguished. Just as the old political order of Mkako tribes was defined and maintained through external violence, so invisible and internal violence defines what kind of competition and domination are socially acceptable within the community.

PHYSICAL VIOLENCE AND SOCIAL ORDER

Violence, in the Kako language, is most commonly termed *sosur*. It refers to ideas of breath (*msosu*) and dryness (*soso*) and denotes a kind of inexplicable force that occurs without reason, like a breath or gust of wind. But it also contains an idea of excess (perhaps leading to disruption) — in the way that dryness comes from an excess of heat. The notion of heat (*woso*) itself connotes the dangers of aggression, and also the kind of controlled violence which can emerge on occasions such as the funeral of a great man. Heat is thus opposed to *weinate*, which means both peace and coolness. But another word, *mguru*, is also used to term violence, connoting an idea of legitimacy by reference to hunting and war. There are a further number of words linked to the idea of violence, depending on the context.

Among the Mkako, physical violence is allowed (it is, indeed, enjoined) only outside the community; it cannot occur within, except in special rituals[2] or between husband and wife (provided the man is stronger). Fights between equals, that is, between adult males, are totally forbidden inside the community.

In contemporary times, Mkako communities have each comprised several villages; but traditionally they formed just one village with an average of between 500 to 1000 persons localized in the middle of its respective territory.[3] Thus, formerly, such a community would complexly consist of several patrilineal clans of unequal size: one of these, because it was large, was the dominant clan, and other small clans or parts of clans were grouped near it. The social solidarity of this community was weak, and even localized clans

---

[2] Such as when the corpse has not been 'paid for' at a funeral; however even here the fight is ritualized.

[3] Formerly, the Mkako were mostly hunter-gatherers with some limited cultivation of yams and bananas, but nowadays they grow maize and cassava.

hardly constituted corporate groups. However, this community derived some political solidarity and definition from a common recognition of the limits of war and physical violence. Authority was continuously evident only in relations between elders and juniors, men and women, and old and young people. No instituted chiefs or centralized political institutions existed. The elders — particularly elders of big families — especially tried to emphasize their prestige and powers. They would use supernatural sanctions relating to illness and ill-fortune (but not physical sanctions) in order to control and punish those who broke the law of the ancestors.

The Mkako still have patriclans and a patrilocal rule of residence, but no real lineages. In their descent lines, true consanguineal links are hardly recognized beyond the level of grandfather. The rule of patrilocality effectively requires the families of full and half-brothers, and their descendants, to gather together in a homestead called a 'fire'. Each family grows its own crops, but families eat together, this being the basis of the 'fire's' unity — so much so that any refusal to engage in commensality inevitably causes the 'fire' to split. In this society, antagonism, competition and segmentation form the basic framework for social relations. Segmentation makes use of polygyny and the principle of seniority in order both to keep the priority of the nucleus of the line and to scatter genealogically junior lines. These latter become autonomous a few generations later, and each one can then choose either to integrate with another dominant line in the same clan, or stay under the domination of the senior line, or try to set itself up politically through exploiting affinal links. All these strategies capitalize on ties of co-residence within a chosen 'fire'. Thus an elder might gather around him the support of kin in order that his prestige and power be increased; this was the basis of the competition between important elders.

In the traditional Mkako society, then, social relations drew their dynamism from the fluidity of social units, limited genealogical memory, an absence of centralized authority, competition for prestige, and the accumulation of people in the context of segmentation. The general social trend was territorial dispersion; this was inhibited by two factors: the threat of other communities, and endogamic alliances. As regards the first factor, nobody could go further than one day's walk without being captured or killed. Permanent hostility was the rule between different groups, although some of them were linked for a while by blood treaty resulting from the exchange of sisters between their leaders' families. But these treaties never lasted long and allies could become enemies on any pretext. On the second point, most marriages took place within the local community. However, since an Omaha system of kinship and marriage prevailed, these marriages would, significantly, tend to be scattered, thereby effectively establishing internal alliances within the community. This is because marriages had to be contracted among people unrelated by (i) bi-lateral kinship, (ii) any one of several clanship links, and (iii) certain pre-existing alliance ties. Meanwhile, the Omaha system also provided for the specification of the larger zone of kinship relationships which each marriage initiated. This system apart, a limited number of marriages did take place outside the local community. These could be said to parallel the 'dispersed alliance' effect which the Omaha system engendered within the community: they were viewed as a political means of setting up some necessary areas of peace outside the community. Indeed, since the clan system precluded exchanges between groups (there was an absence of clan dispersion, and a localization of clans within a political group), affinal and matrilateral links were critical for enabling persons to circulate from community to community.

For Mkako local groups, physical violence in former times was restricted to war, and therefore amounted to external violence. War (*ndjambi*)[4] was not an exceptional occurrence, but was part of the social and political order. Homicidal feuds between clans of the same community led inevitably to the split of the two parties and to the departure of one of them. (Such feuds were the result of previous political and competitive antagonism between two lines or clans.) A murder had to be avenged, but it would result in fission because physical violence could not occur inside a community.

Warlike capacities were certainly emphasized during the initiation of young men. *Djeinate*, the generic term for initiation in the Kako language derives from *dje*, to press or constrain by physical strength, and implies a kind of violence. Derivations of the word *dje* are *djeso*, to obey, and *djesi*, to respect. What is significant here is that order and power find their roots in the discourse about violence, as a threatening response. From contemporary observations, initiation procedure straightforwardly employs violence and involves little esoteric learning, and it is the only example of controlled violence within the community. It is very harsh and it is not uncommon for some young men to die during the performance (thereafter being buried in the bush as criminals).[5] The only teaching included concerns hunting and war. These two activities belong to the same symbolic and semantic fields, in that just as a hunter has to perform a ritual of purification after killing certain kinds of game in order to protect his blood from sickness (*simbo*), so must the warrior who has killed men in battle. Special songs and dances are about both

---

[4] *Ndjambi* is also the word for a hunting beat (the closely-related term, *ngambi*, means aggression); there is indeed a continuity of meaning from hunting to war.
[5] This is a theme that Suzette Heald develops in her chapter on the Gisu of Uganda.

war and hunting. A key point is that the only possible physical violence inside the community derives from a breach of initiation rules, such as when an initiated man is insulted by a non-initiated one. The former must return the insult by fighting, and even killing, for failure to do so will result in his death. The power of words is so dangerous that it jeopardizes the strength of the initiated man's blood: the weakness of a non-initiated man's blood could contaminate it.

This emphasis on warlike capacities certainly fits with the ancient practice of permanent hostility. By means of such hostility, war leaders (*bende*) could emerge. When war was threatening, people (mainly the elders) chose a man to organize war expeditions. If he was prestigious, strong, had charisma and retained the elders' support, he could try, after a successful war, to transform his military leadership into political capacities by becoming the chief of the community. Although this position could not be inherited, he could try at a later date to hand it on to a member of his family. War made chiefship more or less permanent, providing, in this acephalous society, a measure of centralized authority for external affairs. At the same time, war provided the leader with the opportunity to reinforce his prestige and power within the community, thus increasing its political strength and unity. Such inherent competition inevitably led to conflicts with another 'great man' inside or outside the group, and possibly to fission or further war. The relative strength of rivals rested on their use of magical power, on the support they could get from the spirits, and on their possession of a specific power (*duma*) which derives from the strength of a man's blood. A leader's defeat proved the weakness of his blood and of his medicine, leaving him unsupported and leading to the collapse of political unity; clans or clan segments would then join other communities through kin or alliance relationships, or if they were large enough, settle in a new place. Thus, war was an indirect means of maintaining and reproducing a specific order. It did not lead to the evolution of new social forms: rather, *as external violence, it was fundamentally an external means of reproducing an internal order*. Were this not the case, every clan would have split into small hamlets, as happened among the closest neighbours of the Mkako, the Gbaya (Burnham 1980), who share a similar social organization but have fewer warriors. Reminiscent of the Mkako, the Maka, another similarly-organized neighbouring society, are referred to as 'aggressively egalitarian' by Geshiere (1982), because the levelling forces at work in that society come up constantly against a contrary tendency for powerful men to emerge.

War was subject to strict rules, especially according to the relationship with the enemy. Any kind of disruptive violence, including anthropophagy, was

permitted against the most foreign and remote enemy (example 1, above).[6]
Neighbouring peoples, whether they belonged to the same ethnic group or to
another, could be treated differently. Depending on whether the conflict arose
from migration, raids, revenge, challenge or competition for power, violence
could be disruptive (with anthropophagy — as in example 2), or could be
curtailed as soon as the first man was killed (examples 3 and 4). A specific
rule was that people standing in the relationship of mother's brother to sister's
son (real or classificatory) could not in any way fight against each other: wars
would be stopped when such people found themselves on opposed sides.
Above all, kinship defined the field of possibilities for war and anthropophagy
— one could neither kill kin nor eat them (in 'reality' or symbolically). Thus,
one might fight against a remote kinsman who was not of the same local
group, but one could never eat him even if he were killed by a member of
one's own group who was not his kinsman. On the other hand, fighting was
disallowed among both kin and non-kin belonging to the same community.
Non-kin living in the same local group were viewed ideologically as sharing a
putative consanguinity, in spite of the absence of explicitly recognized social
links of blood. In this respect, both criteria — ties of blood and ties of territory
— fixed the boundaries and possibilities of physical violence.

KINSHIP, BLOOD AND VIOLENCE

The Mkako kinship system specifies a large set of kin and, as I have noted, is
defined in terms of an Omaha system of terminology and marriage
prohibitions. Although the Omaha kinship system is patrilineal, bilateral
links up to the third cousin are recognized. Such kin, as well as people
belonging to any of the four patriclans defined by one's great-grandfathers, are
forbidden as marriage partners.

The concept of blood is cited in Mkako explanations of the taboos connected
with kinship, alliance and violence. Procreation originates from a mixture of
the blood from the man's sperm and from the woman's uterus at the end of
the menses. Until the fourth month the foetus is composed solely of separate
'blocks' of blood. These are then transformed into 'blocks of child'. Two
months later the spirits unite them, giving a soul. The sex of children (as well
as witchcraft) is unilineally determined in terms of the sex of the parent. If the
mother's blood is stronger than the father's, then the child will be a girl, and

[6] Such 'total' strangers as white men, from whom the distance was too great, were
excluded.

vice versa (Copet-Rougier 1985). Sometimes the sex of the child is inadequate because the blood of the sexually opposed parent is too strong and continues to fight. If such inadequacy is not remedied, the child will die.

But procreation is possible only if totally *different* bloods are mixed; mixing the same blood produces death. And it is because death results from even a partial sharing of the same blood, that all kin recognized as such by the kinship system (even remote kin) are forbidden to marry. There is no special word for incest, only *mmi* (dirt, pollution). However, Mkako themselves identify incest with the eating of one's own blood, and regard both actions as the same. In both cases, a deadly sickness, *simbo*, is produced, characterized by swelling in the belly and legs (effectively, bad death). In short, 'same' linked with 'same' leads to death, life stemming only from the coupling of differences. Eating kin is self-anthropophagy, and *self-anthropophagy is incest.*[7] Similarly, physical violence inside the community is forbidden because spilling the blood of one's kin, whether real or putative, is equivalent to shedding one's own blood and leads to *simbo* and to death. Certain rituals of purification (which the word, *simbo*, also connotes) can be performed at this juncture, since their purpose is to curtail both systematic revenge and excessive shedding of blood — the ritual brings together different categories linked to the notions of blood and transgression. But where incest and self-anthropophagy are concerned, the deleterious effects of these faults sometimes outlast the repairing effect of the ritual.

Hostility and conflict in the daily life of the Mkako community are quite common. But since physical violence is not allowed, they take forms which we might regard as 'phantasmal' — but which are quite concrete for the people concerned.

INVISIBLE VIOLENCE

Competition between elders of different clans, mostly based on the pursuit of prestige, is the main factor in the dynamics of Mkako social relations. It is most intense between agnates; by employing invisible violence, elders from different descent lines within a clan or even from within the same line (or 'fire') attempt to improve their position through obtaining the death of the head man or even the deaths of the descendants who make up his following.

[7] Thus the reason why the Mkako bury the placenta is that, should it be thrown, say, into a river and eaten by a fish which is subsequently eaten by a relative of the child, that person has eaten his own blood and will die (as is the case if someone eats his own kinsman).

The background for this is particularly the jealousy and envy which characterizes the daily life of the members of the 'fire', which cannot be made explicit, and so is left within the 'unsaid' at the heart of the '*entre-soi*'. Mkako statements that witchcraft is most likely to occur between agnates (especially agnates within the same compound), and the statistical fact that witchcraft accusations are indeed mostly between agnates of the same 'fire', is not surprising. Of course, the 'fire' splits when the conflict becomes publicly revealed; at some stage, one of the protagonists will, as a reprisal, refuse to eat the common food or share produce. Prior to the division of the 'fire', this offence must be purified and the threat it implies removed.

Witchcraft, then, operates especially among agnates (example 7). Attacks by uterine witches are unknown, for it is a duty for mother's brother and sister's son to offer one another protection against a witch's malevolence, which includes fighting the other's agnates. The most likely way to be eaten by a witch is indeed to stay in the 'fire' with one's own agnates. But living away from the 'fire' does not guarantee safety, for a witch-agnate can ask a local witch to act on his behalf and hand over his intended victim. The whole notion of witchcraft among the Mkako is highly complex, and cannot be discussed in any detail here. One notes that witchcraft is clearly distinguished from both sorcery and magic, but as we shall see later, the definitional boundaries are, in practice, vague, and this allows these powers to be manipulated in relation to one another.

In Kako, witchcraft is called *lembo*, and takes the form of a spider or a crab localized in the belly. It is neither a real animal nor a metaphor for something. *Lembo* certainly falls outside the well-known categories of animals in Mkako culture, yet it has its own existence. For present purposes, a key point is that, of the various types of witchcraft, the 'purest' *lembo* implies ravenousness and blood sucking — in a word, anthropophagic witchcraft. As to whether a person impregnated with witchcraft is aware of the fact, Mkako ideas are contradictory. A person revealed as a witch will disclaim all knowledge of his tendencies and activities; he will present himself as a victim, *lembo* having invaded his body. But those who accuse him will speak differently. The person will be charged with consciously seeking more and more powers through the death and blood of his victims; his *lembo* will be considered to have emanated from within his body.[8] Moreover, it will be said that the witch

---

[8] The relation between victim and murderer continues to the full in the invisible world, the malevolent actions retaining their efficacy. Until the murderer dies, the victim's soul cannot join the place of the dead. The victim wanders endlessly through forests and among trees, and through rocks and springs. To avoid the same fate, the witch-murderer, under pressure from the souls of his victims, has to identify them all before dying, neutralizing their revenge and any debts owed to other witches.

has a conscious choice when asked by his *lembo* to eat someone. The idea here is that a refusal to comply with the request will leave the ravenous *lembo* unsatisfied, so that it will eat the witch as an act of self-violence; thus, the witch's choice is limited but clear: eat or be eaten. The contradictions are hard to miss: depending on what the Mkako say (in fact, depending on their own situation as they speak), the witch has or has not the choice to exert his constraining violence on others or on himself.

Some of the main Mkako ideas about witchcraft may be drawn out if I give an example of a witch confession which I attended. The accused old man had been a victim of leprosy for some time, having lost both his feet. Several times charged with witchcraft by his own agnates (half-siblings living in the same 'fire'), and of 'destroying the family' through having eaten its members, his last response was as follows: he claimed that when he was young he always wanted to fight people and, to be successful, had asked a sorcerer for special medicine. But as part of the bargain, he had acceded to the sorcerer's request to later give one of his agnates, whom the sorcerer would 'eat'. Accepting that his decision to meet the request had been a conscious one, the old man explained that, after a while, he had refused his part of the deal but that, in reprisal, the sorcerer had eaten his feet. The old man evidently felt that to confess such a thing should be enough to confirm his innocence of witchcraft (though it was clear he had been involved in sorcery). But the result was the opposite, as the agnates told me in 'secret'. For them, witches, and not sorcerers, eat people. His confession was seen as simply a means to hide witchcraft and to avoid the duty to reveal it publicly. He would then be able to continue to eat the rest of his family. The problem was solved by the old man's death one year later, which his agnates considered as evidence of his witchcraft, believing he had been killed in an invisible fight by a stronger witch.

As regards relationships of both space and time, it is evident that witchcraft is symmetrically opposed to external violence: the closer people are in space ('fire') and in time (i.e. in agnatic relationship), the greater is the potential for the invisible violence of witchcraft. But how do witches avoid dying after sucking the blood of their kin, as would be the case with visible anthropophagy? The answer is that they also acknowledge certain prohibitions, which protects them. Thus they may not eat blood relatives without sharing them with witches from other clans; once chosen, the victim is immediately given to other witches with whom a vampiric meal is enjoyed. In this way, the ideas of reciprocity in the alliance system are reproduced, in terms of an obligation to exchange. Now indebted, the other witches should in turn offer the blood of their kin. A witch who eats a relative's blood alone will die, because it is his own blood which he is eating — just as in the Mkako theory of incest, the mixture of identical bloods leads to death. Let me elaborate on this.

Vampire witchcraft is the most destructive type of witchcraft because it mixes within a single asocial act the space of the *entre-soi* and agnatic time. This confusion of the categories of space and time, provoked by confronting inside with outside and similarity with similarity, is ultimately unthinkable: it refers to the wild and non-human — to a condition which cannot exist in the socialized world. It is not therefore confusion itself that arouses horror but the unthinkable inhumanity it evokes. Thus, eating one's own relative amounts to a barbarism which can only lead to death. There is only one way for people to think this unthinkable. This is by the idea of difference being reintroduced into this confusion of identities. So it is that there is the obligation that unrelated witches who are not co-resident exchange their victims with one another; in this way, the fundamentals of social law are re-established within the most asocial act.

Pouillon has summed up this idea perfectly by showing that cannibalistic societies set up their own rules for eating people, so that one cannot eat just anyone anyhow. Any deviation from these rules — which will certainly be assumed to be happening in neighbouring societies or among foreigners — will be thought to push people in the direction of the wild and inhuman. (Yet, one is always someone else's barbarian — more so than one imagines.) Accordingly, 'real' cannibalism does not preclude 'imaginary cannibalism, for it is by being opposed to it that it becomes defined' (Pouillon 1975: p. 131). (Even the invisible world of Mkako cannibalism has its own imaginary [i.e. wild] cannibalism, which involves eating one's relative alone.) Thus the 'metaphysical design' behind the prohibition on, say, eating relatives is fear, precisely because this act can be imagined. Every society indeed defines itself through its opposition to nature (which is itself imagined, for no society exists in a state of 'nature'), by rules which are thought to be universal: through these rules 'every society becomes conscious of itself, by becoming opposed in an imaginary way to that which it dreads or dreams, in any event to that which it is not' (Pouillon 1975: pp. 138—9).

THE ESCALATION OF VIOLENCE

In social practice, witchcraft victims are not chosen randomly but are usually people with whom the supposed witch is competing, directly or indirectly. In the latter case, weak people such as women and children belonging to the competitor are typically chosen, thus reproducing the hierarchy of the society. But if the competitors are both witches, and the conflict reaches an extreme, there is sure to be a major confrontation. As witches in the invisible world they let fly arrows, or worse, fight — which inevitably leads to one of them dying. Fights between witches are not imaginary: they are the tangible —

albeit invisible — violence of people competing (example 5). Just as war leaders were rivals, witches are rivals, and are obliged to compete to save themselves from being killed. One of the constraints of witchcraft is the duty of reacting to any aggression. Failure in this duty results in death.

Only certain categories of people are normally accused of having such invisible battles. They are typically elders in the descent line, or supporters of elders, or else persons in receipt of benefits from the modern economy — school teachers, hospital attendants, heads of agricultural posts, owners of large coffee or cocoa plantations, and so on. In Mkako society, as in a number of African societies, anyone who is successful in his career or in some social activity is threatened by the jealousy or envy of witches — to an extent that until the 1980s, nobody dared build a roof in sheet-metal because to do so was a mark of great success, and was too dangerous. Just as, in the past, war leaders had to improve their strength against competitors, so also must successful people today — yet they are sometimes deterred from returning to their villages through fear or witchcraft or, for that matter, sorcery. The Mkako say that those who are not witches can buy magical medicine (*mbati*) from a witch-doctor (*ngan*) to prevent attacks from witches, but that they sometimes use it for their own malevolent aims. All deaths caused by witchcraft and sorcery need to be avenged by some other invisible yet 'legal' violence (*simbo* — see earlier). Death resulting from vengeance is either immediate and brutal, or else marked by a swollen belly and water-filled legs. Death resulting from witchcraft and sorcery (illegal violence) is contrastingly characterized by bodily wasting and loss of blood.

The powers of witchcraft and sorcery, although distinct in the Mkako mind, are commonly mixed in practice. In contrast to witchcraft, the aggressive malevolence in sorcery is held uncontrovertibly to be deliberate, and is moreover premised on the idea that a good reason is needed to exercise the killing (without a good reason the sorcerer will die). But the Mkako also argue that only envy and jealousy — ideas associated with witchcraft — cause sorcery. This contradiction is transcended in the assertion that the jealous man finds an excuse to kill: he asks his kinsman for something which he knows cannot be given, and is then in a position to justify the murder. Witchcraft, then, is closely linked to magic and sorcery, a point which can be reiterated in the fact that magic and sorcery medicines are more efficacious when used by a witch (indeed, some medicines may only be used by witches). Sometimes the difference between witchcraft and sorcery disappears altogether; when a death occurs, people simply accuse someone of having murdered, whether by *lembo* (witchcraft) or other means. As I have noted, one of these other means is to buy magic from a witch-doctor. But this witch-doctor will have previously been a witch who ate many kin but who had since agreed to 'make go out' (i.e. reveal) his witchcraft — which is a way of eliminating its danger for others. So if one kills somebody, even indirectly through the witch-doctor, one cannot avoid having to contend with witchcraft. In the invisible world of the Mkako, violence seems to escalate without end. All malevolent actions need increasingly stronger responses, leading finally to the death of the competitors through the combination of the powers of witchcraft, sorcery and magic.

POWERS AND VIOLENCE

The zones of violence in Mkako society are somewhat indefinite, and because of this have a peculiar capacity to replenish power. It is the big chiefs or war leaders of the past, or the 'great men' of today, who are viewed as having 'powers'. Important among these powers is *duma*, which refers to talent or mystical capacity based on blood and which can be transmitted at death depending on the will of the dying person. Without *duma*, one cannot achieve great things in life; one is a poor sort of person. With *duma* one can obtain all kinds of magic (including war magic), and help from a variety of spirits and jinns. But at the same time, one risks danger because people of the same kind are in competition and if the stakes are important every means may be used, including witchcraft. A powerful war-leader, or a 'great man', is supposed to have substantial capabilities and to be able (probably) to resist the attacks of witches, a quality which may cast him as a witch in turn. As to the relation between *duma* and *lembo* (witchcraft), Mkako say that *duma* and *lembo* cannot go together; yet they also assert that *lembo* and magic and sorcery are associated, for the reason that *duma* is supported by all kinds of magic and sorcery.

In Mkako society, then, powers are not annexed by institutions, chieftaincies, kingdoms, or corporate groups. They are, moreover, theoretically separate and indeed are so in practice for most of the time. Attempts to concentrate powers rests on the social strategy of elders, leaders and any other competitors. This process is a spiralling one, for the better one's position, the more one is in danger, and the more one has to concentrate powers in order to protect oneself. There is danger in this concentration of powers; the egalitarian ideal in this culture is reason for Mkako insisting that the different kinds of powers should be separated. Thus, in contemporary times, people strongly reject the idea of someone accumulating several modern positions and jobs. In this respect, when Geshiere speaks of the 'levelling forces' in the similarly-organized Maka society, this is appropriate. With the Mkako, in like manner, the concentration of traditional powers can or (in the past) could lead to a person's own destruction, because their combined strength could go beyond their owner and kill him.

However, in former times, it is plain that the war leader who wished to maintain the position he had secured by means of physical violence in external affairs had to concentrate in his hands invisible powers of violence available in internal affairs. Operating within a feedback system, *he had to become a warrior of the invisible world in order to remain a warrior in the visible and external world of physical violence.* That is to say, he also needed the forces of illegal violence in order to maintain a position based on legal violence. The lack of definitional boundaries, in practice, between the various kinds of violence facilitated this; it enabled these violences to be concentrated in one person (in contemporary times, a 'great man') who could terrify others with his immense overall power.

The history of Mkako society is one of irregular oscillations of concentrated and scattered powers. Since general power is located in the person (through a concentration of the various powers of violence), we may stress that this oscillation concerns individual relationships and not a social consensus. Thus one Mkako community may, because of prior circumstances, be totally acephalous, lacking any centralized power, its people scattered; whereas another will apparently be based on a strongly centralized power represented by a chief. Should such a chief die without transmitting his *duma* (his power having effectively been vanquished by levelling forces), the community will return to an acephalous condition. The condition of the late nineteenth-century chieftaincy of Bertoua may be cited as an extreme example of this last process. This chieftaincy was composed of both Gbaya and Mkako people, and was engaged in a Muslim Fulani jihad. Its political structure rested on the use of physical violence in war and the slave trade. Comprising a number of acephalous societies, its strength depended above all on its leader, Mbartoua, a person spoken of with fear and as having all possible mystical power. This man's concentration of powers actually made physical violence in the community the means of maintaining the new political order (both physical punishment and taxation were employed, depending on the nature of the fault [Copet-Rougier, in press]). But when he was eventually killed (by German soldiers), the community split and the various kinds and levels of power and authority completely dispersed, except at the level of the 'fire' or family.

CONCLUSION

Although we can speak of the 'non-individualistic aspect of power' (Augé 1977: p. 118) (as in the case of certain collective rituals), we can also conceive of the individualization of power, vested in the person of the leader in an acephalous society. Such individualization emerges when, mutually interacting, all the potentialities of violence — visible and invisible, external and internal — are concentrated in one person. This sort of power is not permanent and disappears when the person dies — very often the victim of a rival or of his own concentration of powers. Thus the political order in an acephalous society incorporates violence which, approaching the boundary of illegality, can be diverted to the benefit of one person. But permanent order cannot be established because there is no possibility that the powers can be embodied in an institution. This does not mean that they disappear totally: they just go back into anonymity or are captured by another person who, to protect himself, will have to fight by means of invisible violence to make them still greater. As in Audiberti's play '*Le Mal Court*' (*The evil continues*), invisible powers — and thus invisible violence — continue by being passed from 'hand to hand', the individuals who assume them holding them for a greater or lesser time. In this way, perhaps, they are prevented from being captured by legal institutions and from being converted into the repressive violence of law.

I should like to close by speaking generally and emphasizing once again that violence is not a concept in itself but rather a *means available* for institutional as much as for destructive use. Accordingly, it can only be understood in terms of its own oppositional relationship, created by rules which each society fashions in its own way. Mkako society provides an example of the insoluble problem of power and violence, evident in the intimate relationship between violence which perpetuates social order (i.e. external, physical violence, and the internal invisible violence of repression) and wrongful, destructive violence (struggles and anthropophagy in the invisible world). In order to overcome the logical restriction on the accumulation of individually scattered capacities, power must here resort to that which it otherwise rejects, namely transgressive and barbarous violence, so carrying within itself the seeds of its own destruction. As Foucault noted: 'Crime lurks within the confines of law, now this side of the law, now beyond it, above and below it; crime turns about power, at one time against it, at another time on its side' (Foucault 1973: p. 271). We may also add that in the context of this vague boundary, power seems sometimes to use violence 'on its side' while, without knowing it, violence is already against it. It is this impossibility of, so to say, deciding which side violence is on that prevents its employment as a useful concept. The ambiguity explains why, for some people, it can indeed lead through the strangeness of the event to the idea of beauty (the aesthetics) of violence.

REFERENCES

Audiberti, J. 1948: *Le Mal Court*. Paris: NRF, Gallimard.
Augé, M. 1977: *Pouvoirs de Vie, Pouvoirs de Mort*. Paris: Flammarion.
_____ 1979: *Symbole, Fonction, Histoire: les interrogations de l'anthropològie*. Paris: Hachette.
Bazin, J. et Terray, E. (eds) 1982: *Guerres de Lignages et Guerres d'Etats en Afrique*. Paris: Editions des Archives Contemporaines.
Bourdieu, P. 1980: *Le Sens Pratique*. Paris: Editions de Minuit.
Burnham, P. 1980: *Opportunity and Constraint in a Savanna Society*. London: Academic Press.
Copet-Rougier, E. 1985: Contrôle masculin, exclusivité féminine dans une société patrilinéaire. In *Femmes du Cameroun, Mères Pacifiques, Femmes Rebelles*, Paris: Karthala.
_____ in press: Du clan à la chefferie. In *Herrschaft und Herrkunft* (Actes du Colloque Franco-Allemand, 'Perspectives anthropologiques sur l'histoire Africaine'), Frankfurt/Main.
Etudes Rurales 1984: *La Violence* (Juillet-Décembre, 95—6.) Paris: EHESS.
Evans-Pritchard, E. E. 1937: *Witchcraft, Oracles and Magic among the Azande*. Oxford: Oxford University Press.
Foucault, M. 1973: *Moi, Pierre Rivière, avant égorgé ma mère, ma soeur et mon frère*. Paris: Achives, Gallimard.
Geschiere, P. 1982: *Village Communities and the State*. London: Kegan Paul International.
Girard, R. 1972: *La Violence et le Sacré*. Paris: Editions Bernard Grasset.
Mizon (Lt) 1895: Résultats scientifiques des voyages de Mr Mizon. *Bull. Sté de Géographie*, XVI.
Pouillon, J. 1975: *Fétiches sans Fétichisme*. Paris: Maspéro.

4

The Ritual Use of Violence: Circumcision among the Gisu of Uganda

Suzette Heald

There has been considerable recent interest in the subjective effects of ordeals and initiations, with writers concerned not only to elaborate upon the ideas mediated through the ritual process but also to speculate upon the effects of the experience on the individual. This chapter looks at a ritual which may be said to use violence to achieve violence — the circumcision ritual among the Gisu of Uganda. My initial concerns are with the kind of sense that may be given to the Gisu view that a capacity for being violent is engendered — indeed created — through the circumcision experience. How should we begin to understand the psychological processes involved?

The Gisu, numbering some 500,000, are Bantu-speaking agriculturalists living on the slopes of Mount Elgon on the Ugandan side of the border with Kenya. Boys are circumcised when they are between eighteen and twenty-five years old, and the practice effectively denotes their sense of ethnic identity and distinctiveness (La Fontaine 1969; Twaddle 1969; Heald 1982). It is the only major ritual observance shared by all. Circumcision is also a classic-type ordeal, an explicit test of bravery, publicly witnessed. The boy stands in the compound of his father or senior relative and must remain absolutely still while his foreskin is cut and then stripped from around the glans penis. He is required to display total fortitude under the knife, betraying no signs of fear; even what might be regarded as involuntary twitches and tremblings, such as the blinking of the eyes, are evaluated negatively. Success, however, is triumphantly celebrated; the watching men roar in unison while the women rush forward ululating as they dance. The boy is then allowed to sit and the onlookers come forward one by one to call him a man and to thank him by presenting him with gifts.

Undergoing the ordeal makes a boy (*umusinde*) a 'man', and the honorific term *umusani* is always used in this context. This is an acknowledgement of the achievement of manhood, for the term is usually reserved for men who have proved themselves through having adult children, especially circumcised sons. In the success of the ordeal, it is used to address both the son and his father. In other respects, too, circumcision gives the son a formal identity with his father since it gives him full adult status, carrying with it the all-important rights to marry, to inherit land and to enjoy such other privileges of adult life as drinking beer.

In a previous paper (Heald 1982), I argued that the ritual can be understood to do far more than formally bequeath a status. Undergoing the ordeal is regarded by the Gisu as having a basic effect on the personality and powers of the individual. The ritual thus has a definite ontological purpose; it is seen to create in the boy the capacity to experience *lirima*, and it is this capacity which critically marks the divide between boys and men.

Lirima is pre-eminently a manly quality. There is no easy equivalent in English. One might start with the idea that it refers to violent emotion, and many of the ways in which the Gisu talk about it suggest that such emotion is also experienced as overwhelming and even out-of-control. Thus *lirima* is spoken of as 'catching' a man and as 'bubbling-up' in him — though 'boiling over' might be more appropriate as the usual simile is with the boiling of milk. While a man is in this state of possession, *lirima* is seen to dictate his attitudes and actions; it gives force to his motivations and impels him to action. Further, *lirima* is linked to the negative emotions, especially to anger, but also to jealousy, hatred, resentment, and shame (the Gisu have an extensive vocabulary for such emotions), which are also seen as capable of inspiring such violent affect.

One could add, though tentatively and bearing in mind the difficulties of directly linking emotions to physiological stimuli (Schacter and Singer 1962), that it is tempting to associate *lirima* with a state of sympathetic arousal of the nervous system, considering the situations in which it is adduced and its breadth of reference. This equation is made more plausible by the fact that the Gisu associate *lirima*, and indeed sometimes define it, with the sensation of having a lump in the throat. Such a symptom could well be produced by the release of adrenalin and the subsequent contraction of the muscles of the throat. While this possibly points to a certain parallelism between the Gisu concept and our own model (or one of them) for understanding intense or extreme emotions, one must be wary of any easy equivalence at this point. At issue is not just the indeterminacy of the (or indeed, any) physiological input in relation to the experience of emotion, but the cognitive associations which set the Western and Gisu models at variance.[1] For example, in Western conceptions, such extreme affect tends to suggest the overriding of reason by passion — a lack of self-control. In contrast, for the Gisu, who do not think of reason and emotion as opposed modalities embattled within the personality, *lirima* can not only be volitional but also an aspect of the control a man should assert over himself and the world — a quality or capacity to be mustered by the individual to achieve and serve his purposes. If a man can be in the grip of *lirima* he can use it to steel himself too. Then *lirima* also has forceful and positive connotations; the force lies behind that strength of character which makes men courageous and determined. That *lirima* bestows such affirmative powers, and is the capacity of men and only men, gives overall poignancy to its more usual associations. In normal everyday life *lirima* is seen to have generally negative effects. It makes men dangerous and is associated with violence, aggression and the disorders which assail the community.

It can be noted here, since it forms part of the problem to be addressed, that the Gisu have long had a reputation for violence in East Africa. In Uganda they are widely feared for their personal aggressiveness. In the 1950s, Richards indicates the attitude of the Ganda towards those Gisu who had taken up settlement in their homeland: 'Ganda just steal but Gisu come with knives and kill you' (Richards 1956: p. 116). In Kenya their reputation is more lurid since they are proverbially regarded as cannibals — cannibalism indeed often being defined with reference to the Gisu. Even within Bugisu this reputation clings to certain clans. That the attribution of violence is not solely a matter of negative 'outsider' definitions is indicated by crime statistics which do indicate relatively high rates of interpersonal violence. Again the pattern is consistent. In the 1940s and 1950s, the Gisu had a homicide rate of 8.2

---

[1] It should not be taken that I subscribe to the James-Lange theory of the emotions, based on the views of William James (1884), where physiological arousal is seen as an essential component of emotion states and which then implies a universal basis to the emotions. I find it more useful to follow the view expressed by Solomon, who defines an emotion as 'a system of concepts, beliefs, attitudes and desires, virtually all of which are context-bound, historically developed, and culture specific' (1984: p. 249). While this does not rule out a physiological element, it throws the emphasis onto the cultural interpretation, so that the type of overlap that then exists between such concepts cross-culturally becomes a matter for ethnographic enquiry. However, of interest for the Gisu concepts is Solomon's speculation that 'a culture that emphasizes what David Hume called "the violent passions" will be ripe for the Jamesian theory, but a culture that rather stresses the "calm" emotions (an appreciation of beauty, lifelong friendship, a sense of beneficence and justice) will find the Jamesian theory and the hydraulic model that underlies it patently absurd' (1984: p. 242).

deaths per 100,000, higher than any of the other Bantu-speaking peoples of Uganda (Southall 1960: p. 228). In the 1960s, the differential was even more striking, with the Ugandan Police figures indicating a rate of 28.4 per 100,000 for Bugisu in 1963, over twice that of any other Bantu-speaking group.[2] It must be emphasized that this killing is almost entirely of an interpersonal kind: there is no raiding, feuding or warfare pattern. Further, it is overwhelmingly male/male, with women only forming 16.7 per cent of the victims and entering the statistics as killers even less frequently — in only 3.6 per cent of cases. The Gisu are cogniscent of this situation and it is not one of which they feel proud. One feature is an almost fatalistic acceptance of violence in the community. After a murder a commonly voiced sentiment was not just that the killer was a bad man but that the Gisu were just bad people and what could one do? This capacity for violence is attributed to *lirima*.

What must be stressed is that, for the Gisu, the ambivalence of *lirima* is a basic fact of life and regarded as inherent in the nature of men. It is central to the transformational purpose of circumcision, for this is the first time in which the boy is expected to display the emotion. Thereafter it is as much a part of his manhood as the circumcision cuts themselves. Moreover, in the context of circumcision *lirima* is accorded a positive and essential role. It is for the Gisu the key to the complete identification of the boy with the ordeal he faces. As the ordeal gets closer it is *lirima* which is seen to drive him on and to dominate his thoughts and feelings. It is *lirima* which allows him to overcome his fear. The induction of *lirima* thus appears both as a technique of the ritual, developed in the boy to allow him to stand the ordeal, and also its aim, to turn him into a man with the capacity thereafter to feel *lirima*.

In a previous paper (Heald 1982) I was concerned to explore the degree to which the ritual leading up to the operation itself — its form and symbolism — could be interpreted from the point of view of its overt aim, to induce *lirima*. Thus I argued that the symbolic forms were best explicated *not* in the latent terms of the standard sociological version as making largely hidden statements about social relationships, but in terms of their manifest purpose — the making of men out of boys in the specifically Gisu way. Thus the rites have an overt transformational aim, a psychological purpose, and this could be

---

[2] The rate quoted here is calculated from Police figures and is the average for the 10-year period, 1945—54. It is thus comparable to the rate quoted for 1963, again calculated from Police figures by R. E. Turner and cited in Belshaw et al. (1966). My own figures, calculated from the Death Enquiry Reports filed by the Police in the District Court, give a slightly higher average annual homicide rate of 32 deaths per 100,000 for the years between 1960 and 1966. The percentage figures given are calculated from the Court Case records for this period (see Heald 1974).

described in terms of what I called Gisu vernacular psychology. Further, I felt
that the rites and the psychological processes built into them clearly 'worked'
— worked in the sense that they provided the means which enabled often
extremely apprehensive boys to overcome their fear and stand the ordeal.
Success here is never assured but I would estimate that the majority, say
seven to eight out of ten, succeeded in displaying the required fortitude.

The ritual, then, can be seen to have pragmatic aims and pragmatic effects.
This leads me to my next set of problems and a much more tricky set, given —
as Audrey Richards (1967) once noted — that British social anthropology is
littered with self-denying ordinances, especially on questions which might
have anything to do with the individual experience or individual psychology.
In brief, my problems revolve around the following query. If the rites can be
seen to be informed by Gisu vernacular psychology and be seen to 'work' in
these terms, can they also be seen to *work* in our psychological terms? Do
concepts such as *lirima*, and the techniques used to induce it, answer solely to
the culturally specific Gisu construction of experience, or can they also be
seen to answer to a universal experiential base?

Clearly this cannot be easily answered given that neither anthropology nor
psychology has given us any way of establishing universal processes and
constraints. The only way of proceeding, I would argue, is in terms of a
process of *translation* — of a seeking of concordances between the models
given by vernacular and Western psychologies. Elucidation can then proceed
by a to-ing and fro-ing between what Geertz (1974) refers to as 'experience-
near' and 'experience-distant' concepts, by which different forms of local
knowledge may be rendered mutually intelligible. One implication of this
approach is that 'our' concepts, except in so far as they are the way 'we'
explicate the world, may initially be accorded no specially privileged status. If
we seek to translate, it is because we desire to perceive the analogies — not
because of an assumption that our discourse, whether scientific or not,
necessarily leads to a better way of construing the original.

The role of violence in ritual revolves around the emotional effects of ritual
more generally. As an anthropologist, one has to admit, with Gluckman
(1964), that one is here quickly 'beyond one's sphere of competence'. Yet
this cannot legislate against curiosity, especially when emotional arousal is
the cornerstone of the Durkheimian theory of ritual, alone accounting for the
power attributed to ritual symbols and their ability to reinforce social values.
Yet, when Leach (1958) commented that the 'puzzle continues to intrigue', it
was at that time little explored, and there was little reference in the British
anthropological literature to actual or imputed psychological processes. In
the Durkheimian tradition, ritual was, in the main, accepted as an intense

socializing experience and left at that. Yet it was not totally uncharted territory. From the literature that has developed since then (I exclude psychoanalysis as beyond my present purposes), it is evident that the commentary can be seen largely as elaborations on the theories advanced by Malinowski (1945) and Radcliffe-Brown (1952) on the relationship between anxiety and ritual.

In simplest terms ritual, for Malinowski, serves as a means of allaying the anxieties evoked by the uncertainty of life, whilst for Radcliffe-Brown it acts to induce anxiety as a means of reinforcing social values (cf. Homans 1941). For Malinowski, the function of ritual was seen from the point of view of the individual for whom it created necessary confidence; for Radcliffe-Brown, its function was seen from the point of view of society, and interpreted as providing an intense socializing experience. The Malinowskian version, in the form of a cathartic model of the ritual process, has been the more widely used. Indeed Scheff (1977) defines ritual in just such terms, and it is central to the work of Turner (1967) and Girard (1977) also. Mentioned by Aristotle, and given further dimensions in the work of Freud, the theory of catharsis has many variants. Without going into the complexities, the common strands, as applied to ritual, are firstly, a prior situation of tension or conflict and secondly, the enactment or representation of this in the ritual with a consequent purging of emotional affect for the participants. This model was used by Gluckman (1963) to give force to his 'rituals of rebellion' thesis, and it appears in several different guises in the work of Turner (1967). But clearly, not all ritual, or violence in ritual, involves catharsis — a position I intend to illustrate by comparing a situation where it does, with Gisu circumcision, where I argue it does not.

From the point of view of a comparison with the Gisu, an interesting example is provided by the studies of Michelle and Renato Rosaldo of the Ilongot headhunters of the Philippines. The Ilongot structure their perceptions of the capacities of manhood in terms of *liget* (energy/anger/passion) — a concept which, on the face of it, has evident similarities with the Gisu *lirima*. Among the Ilongot, however, *liget* is counterpoised to *beya*, 'knowledge', which ideally should inform and govern the raw vitality of *liget*. *Liget* is characteristic of youth and it is the passion behind, and also realized and transcended in, the 'tossing of heads' — the triumphant end of a successful headhunting raid. Then the individual simultaneously proves himself to be the equal of other men in the power of his 'anger', and 'casts' this anger off, lightening his 'heavy heart'. M. Rosaldo writes, 'the gay victors . . . purged of violence . . . will seek out flowery reeds to wear like feathers signifying lightness' (1980: p. 55). R. Rosaldo elaborates: 'To take a head is, in Ilongot terms, not to capture a trophy, but to "throw away" a body part, which by a principle of sympathetic magic represents the cathartic throwing away of certain burdens of life — the grudge an insult has created, or the grief over a death in the family, or the increasing "weight" of remaining a novice when one's peers have left that status' (1980: p. 140). To summarize, headhunting is presented as primarily a cathartic act, celebrated in songs as the source of individual and communal strength and joy.

Gisu circumcision lacks these kinds of connotations. Among the Ilongot the young, by definition, have *liget*, and it is *liget* which is seen to inspire the desire to headhunt. But among the Gisu *lirima* is induced in the course of the ritual, and any catharsis appears as an unstressed by-product. Thus there is obvious relief after the operation; the boy is described as pure and clean, and in a state of passivity his *lirima* is dissipated and inert. For the relatives and spectators, also whipped into a state of intense excitement, the aftermath of the operation is a time for quiet sociability (of drinking beer together in the compound) — though there is also the further drama of the arrival of the father's age mates to demand their customary dues of gifts, as well as continuing anxiety over the boy's health. Relief, however, is not catharsis, and to look at the Gisu ritual in terms of cathartic release would be distorting. The emphasis in Gisu circumcision is not on the release or transcendence of *lirima*, but upon its creation. The power is proved, not purged or transformed into something else.

We turn now to the alternative model, where ritual is seen to achieve its effects through the creation of anxiety. A good example is Spencer's use of 'anxiety intensification' ideas to account for the psychological effects of initiation among the Kenyan Samburu. He suggests

that at a time when social relationships are undergoing change, the uncertainties of the occasion which Malinowski saw as a cause for anxiety, and the beliefs and ritual prescriptions which Radcliffe-Brown saw as an additional cause for anxiety, may serve to induce a mental state in the participants which implements these changes . . . They increase the suggestibility of the participants so that they come to accept the changes (Spencer 1965; quoted 1970: pp. 144—6).

Spencer draws on Sargant's *Battle for the Mind* (1957) to give an additional psycho-physiological account of the process. Sargant's explication is by reference to Pavlov's experiments on the conditioning of dogs, where it was found that when animals are subjected to extreme stress habitual behaviour patterns are disrupted, and in such 'transmarginal' states new behaviour patterns can be induced and remain stable after recovery. From this, Sargant argues that the induction of extreme anxiety, fatigue and forms of physical debilitation are major techniques for political and religious conversion.

A similar 'brainwashing' effect, Spencer maintains, can be adduced in

Samburu circumcision, with the rites impressing upon initiates the ideas of honour and the authority of elders. The rites can be seen to prepare the initiates for a prolonged period — ten or more years — of glamorous but deprived *moranhood* (warriorhood), effectively expelled from the society with wealth and wives being concentrated in the hands of the elders.

There are obvious elements of trauma in Gisu circumcision, and it might well be plausible to adduce this in order to explain the great emotional reaction that adult Gisu men display throughout their lives to the event, as well as (possibly) why the only formal 'teaching' of the boy that occurs takes place so soon after the operation — the circumcisor returning during the night, or, at the latest, early on the morning after circumcision. This last episode is brief but important. The boy is first ritually washed and then handed, one by one, the main accoutrements of adult life. Nevertheless, the values associated with Gisu circumcision, and the atmosphere surrounding it, are sufficiently different from that of the Samburu to make it necessary to look elsewhere for a model of its psychic effectiveness.

Let me expand this difference. One matter of interest is that while Spencer records little information on the preparation of Samburu boys for the ordeal, he notes, 'During the twenty-four hours before the first circumcisions they were generally subdued, a number of them shivered, at least one of them developed a facial twitch and another a fixed frown' (1965: p. 254). And, if the initiates were anxious, a situation of near panic seems to have been characteristic of the onlookers as doubts grew as to whether the boys would stand courageously. Spencer writes that some of the existing *moran* broke down and shook insensibly, while there was the active threat of an affray after one *moran* attempted to strike an initiate who had the temerity to sing of his courage (1965: p. 105).[3] And throughout, he emphasizes the relatively passive role of the initiates: the ceremony 'in every detail and at every stage . . . was under the control of the elders . . . The initiates had to do at each stage what they were told. From beginning to end they seemed thoroughly bewildered' (1965: p. 255). The contrasting themes of Gisu circumcision are:

---

[3] Some caution needs to be exercised with this interpretation since much of it rests on Spencer's understanding of the trembling and shaking of the *moran* as nervous behaviour evidencing anxiety and even 'transmarginal breakdown'. This raises the whole question of our ability to recognize and identify emotions from behavioural symptoms alone, a relevant query when Spencer later tells us that the *moran* link shaking with 'anger'. Given the association in Kenya of shaking with warriorhood — as generally signalling a readiness to fight — it is a pity that further consideration of Samburu concepts was omitted from the discussion. This is not of course to deny the relevance of some form of operant conditioning for an understanding of the psychological processes involved in Samburu rituals.

firstly, that the boy is going to be made formally equal to his seniors; secondly, that throughout the ceremony it is he, and not the elders, who is presented as being in control of the situation; lastly, and most importantly for this discussion, that the boy ought to have overcome his anxiety by the time he enters the circumcision enclosure. To this end, the greatest emphasis is on various preparatory rituals, which normally go on for several weeks prior to the operation. The expectation that the boy should betray no sign of fear involves considerably more than simply not flinching at the end. Ideally, he should be completely relaxed. 'Go, as if it were a mere song', I have heard it said. The conscious psychological frame, as well as the structural situation, is thus different. This suggests that if we are looking for parallels in the area of behaviourist psychology then we should look not at ideas relating to 'brainwashing', but to the possibly more straightforward idea of 'battle-proofing'.

Battleproofing consists of enacting situations of danger, so allowing the person to become accustomed to, and inured against, fear. Peter Watson (1980) writes that military training is most effective when it gives experience of situations of stress of a kind that allow the men to develop confidence in their ability to face danger. Battleproofing, the process of desensitizing the person to danger, is a concept used by military psychologists and it appears to be equally a part of the pragmatic psychology used by the army. An example, in this case reported in a local paper, is the brief account of abseiling exercises by sixteen-year-old army recruits. The major in charge explained that the exercises were very good for building up a young soldier's character, 'They've got to overcome their fear and it's very important for a soldier to know that he can conquer his fear.' These exercises started with one-hundred foot drops and ended with the 'death slide', a drop over a precipice into a river, hitting it at a speed of thirty miles per hour. This, I suggest, is the kind of commonsense vision which the Gisu would immediately comprehend.

The Gisu ritual can be seen to have the same clear-cut aims and techniques; these are particularly apparent in the preparatory rituals, and can be briefly summarized. Firstly, the emphasis is put on the boy being 'strong' enough (*kamani*). This 'strength' implies both physical strength and what we would call strength of purpose. It is evidenced in the vigour with which the boy dances and in the jumps which effectively rehearse the final jump he will make to face the circumcisors. Secondly, the boy is subjected to repeated exhortations by elders and bystanders. They tell him of the ordeal he faces, and how he must stand it. There is never at any stage anything secret about the ordeal; no mystery. Further, he is continually asked if he is sure he can go through with it and urged to withdraw if he has any doubt. He may withdraw, without shame, at any time up to actually entering the circumcision enclosure for the operation. On the ritual level, his determination is tested by a series of smearing rites which are explicitly interpreted as mortifications — as unpleasant and abhorrent — and done to 'anger' him, to incite his *lirima* and spur him on. Additionally, he is encouraged to prepare himself in other ways, for example by pinching his foreskin to give himself some idea of the pain, and so on.

Let me move towards a conclusion. In the previous section I indicated very briefly three different ways in which violence has been seen to have psychological effects in rituals involving ordeals. The examples used have been selective and were chosen to illustrate these processes and provide easy points of comparison with the Gisu material. I have also been concerned to simplify, and it is not suggested that these rituals necessarily utilize only one such mode or that those outlined exhaust the possibilities. Clearly, at one level, it is a matter of emphasis; complex rituals may elicit a wide range of responses in the participants, just as concentration on different phases of the ritual may yield very different interpretations. Nevertheless, such rituals are plainly not all the same type of event, and three main psychological processes can, I suggest, be usefully distinguished:

1 catharsis: in which negative emotions are turned into positive ones;
2 trauma: where the ordeal is seen to have a chastening or even a destabilizing effect on the individual, and is an aspect of repressive socialization;
3 battleproofing (or disinhibition, as the psychologists term it): which involves the use of violence to harden and prepare the individual for violence.

It may be noted that with both catharsis and trauma, violence could be a technique used in ritual, a means of creating or maintaining values which in themselves have little or no intrinsic connection with violence in the non-ritual context — values such as lightening 'heavy hearts', honour, the authority of elders, and so on. However, this is not to deny that the ritual would tend to generate an association and, among both the Ilongot and Samburu where there are clear continuities between the violence in ritual and in secular life, it is difficult to establish any sharp distinction. Nevertheless, I would argue that battleproofing is somewhat different, since here the means are more directly adapted to the ends. Violence is used to breed violence in a more obvious way. It is also, perhaps because of this obviousness, the least interesting as a psychological process. However, what we appear to have in Gisu circumcision is a particularly clear example of it.

Yet if Gisu circumcision as an ordeal seems simple at this level, then the question of both the effects and stability of such experiences on the personality structure looms large. What exactly is the effect of the experience on the boys? In this respect, I suppose one would like to know whether ordeals of this kind do have a long-lasting effect, not only in inuring the individual against pain, fear and violence, but possibly predisposing the individual, or susceptible individuals, to violence thereafter. If the Gisu ritual operates in an analogous way to military training, encouraging men to react in specific ways to certain forms of stress, does it create, in turn, a greater readiness to use violence and to react aggressively at a later time? Is there some form of trigger effect?

As I indicated earlier, there are reasons for this being an interesting line of enquiry in the Gisu case, even if it is outside the compass of this paper. I assume that, in most cultural situations, the psychological or psycho-physiological arousal induced is difficult to separate from more general value orientations; that is, the cognitive frame would be compatible with and validate violent responses towards certain stimuli.[4] Military training in Western countries is a case in point. But this is not so unproblematic for the Gisu for, as I have said, although *lirima* has positive value and is regarded as essential for standing the ordeal bravely it is also seen to create 'dangerous' men. Indeed, the Gisu see their life as plagued by men of violence whose *lirima* may bubble up at the slightest provocation and where it is a constant facet of the personality. Further, this kind of aggressive response is *not* culturally condoned (far from it), and may indeed lead to the offenders being killed.

If one follows this line of thinking then one is faced with a kind of paradox. Circumcision is of central cultural significance: it is tradition in its most valued sense, not only signifying but ensuring the continuity of the people and their distinctive ancestry and heritage. That Gisu boys still desire circumcision is a sign that the ancestors are still a force active in Gisu life and, by the same token, the Gisu believe that if they forswore the custom then they would all die out. Given the strength of such sentiments, it seems unthinkable to suppose that it could disappear. But, from another point of view, it is an anachronism. It seems to be fairly widely accepted that ordeals of this kind are linked to warfare. They are a form of training for the bravery and stoicism of the warrior. Elsewhere in East Africa this association holds, and the evidence is well-summarized by Ocaya-Lakidi (1979). The ideal tribal virtue of manly excellence, he writes, was strongly connected to warfare and 'led the Eastern

---

[4] Where this is not the case, and values are apparently at variance, then the psychological effects are often difficult to establish, as the controversy over television violence illustrates, with both cathartic and disinhibitory effects receiving support from experimental studies (Geen et al. 1975; Kaplan and Singer 1976; Konecni and Ebbersen 1976).

African societies to place undue emphasis on masculinity and manliness, the one to be tested sexually and the other in hot combat' (1979: p. 152). Ultimately, however, the two tests were one, and taking the Kikuyu as an example he elaborates, 'the lengthy initiation rites gave ample opportunity for gauging a man's masculinity, while the supreme pain of circumcision tested his manliness and suitability for warriorhood. That is why becoming a man meant access to physical sex and to warriorhood at the same time' (1979: p. 152).

In a large number of East African societies, male gender identity linked to circumcision has therefore a strong military accent, yet for the majority of these societies the warfare and raiding patterns in which this developed are no longer relevant. Some seventy years after pacification this is certainly the case for the Gisu, just as it is for the Kikuyu and for the Samburu discussed earlier. In the Gisu case all that remains of the association is the idea that the fortitude required of the circumcision candidate is akin to the courage of the warrior. An analogy is drawn: a boy must have faith in his powers and strength in the same way that the warrior has faith in his. But I never heard it suggested that the ritual either would or should make him a good fighter. Indeed, such is definitely *not* the aim. Significantly, of the objects of adult life handed to him in the cleansing rite after the operation, a spear is not included. It is perhaps notable by its absence: the boy receives food, fire, a panga, a hoe, a drinking tube; he is told to use these objects properly, in a socially productive way and not for violence and disruption. Thus the circumcisor, as he hands the boy a piece of smouldering firewood, says,

Kindle this piece of firewood and as you kindle it I say, 'Do not go and burn down the houses of your neighbours. I have made you kindle it so that your wife can cook for you and you can heat water and make tea for yourself' . . . I give you this panga and say, 'Build a house, do not just roam around. I have given you this panga so that you can fell trees and build a house, cut down bananas and banana stems to plant so that you will have your own food. Let me give you this knife so that you can do this work, let me not give it so that you go and attack your neighbours. Nor have I given it to you so you can go and steal the cows of your neighbours and then slaughter them . . .' I give you this drinking tube to hold and say, 'Drink beer and brew it. Do not get drunk and quarrelsome so that you are always fighting with your friends . . .'

I include these long extracts from one such speech which I recorded in order to demonstrate the extent to which the dangers of misuse are dramatically reiterated. That the individual is admonished in this way by moral injunctions highlights the fact that there are seen to be few other checks on violence. Its use is seen to be a matter of personal disposition: the good man controls his anger, the bad man does not (see Heald, 1986).

At this point one is tempted to compare the Gisu concept of manhood with others in East Africa. As indicated above, many equally extol martial virtues, but in the modern era not all of these have feared male violence in the same way. The Kikuyu are a case in point and, as a related Bantu-speaking people, their concepts bear direct comparison with those of the Gisu. For the Kikuyu the cardinal virtues of the warrior combine fierceness with restraint. *Urume*, the quality *par excellence* of the warrior (*injamba*), has evident affinity with the Gisu *lirima*, implying bravery, determination in the face of adversity and violent forceful action.[5] Men may shake with *urume*, a physical manifestation which is widely recognized among both the Bantu and para-Nilotic peoples of Kenya as a sign of courage and, more especially, battle-readiness. At the same time, the Kikuyu warrior was expected to display the virtues of identification and loyalty to his age set, and obedience and submission to the authority of seniors. Disciplined self-control thus emerges as a major theme in Kikuyu life, with a man expected to exercise restraint both in his use of violence and, indeed, in sex (Kenyatta 1938). In this gerontocratic social order, warriorhood was only part of a process of individual self-development, orchestrated by age-group status; circumcision marked only the beginning of the achievement of the full potentialities of manhood. In this respect, and in their military traditions, the Kikuyu appear similar to the Samburu discussed earlier. Speaking of the Meru, closely-related to the Kikuyu, Fadiman notes that the process of 'hardening' for a Meru warrior involved a whole series of ordeals and beatings, where a true warrior 'was expected to show neither weakness in the face of pain, nor resistance to those who applied it' (1982: p. 49). Indeed, he writes that most of the pain a warrior was expected to bear was inflicted by members of his own community. As with the Kikuyu, the warrior was part of a disciplined fighting force which came under the direction of elders.

In so far as these historically forged attitudes persist we may perhaps find clues to the different perceptions of the capacity of men for violence. From the previous discussion what emerges as a significant shaper of attitudes is age-set organization, traditionally absent in Bugisu. Among the Gisu named age sets were formed to include boys circumcised at the same time, generally every two years; such men were held to have special bonds with each other, a comradeship developed in the months of curing and presumably tested in the subsequent fighting. But such sets did not form standing corps of warriors, nor did they collectively progress through a series of set ranks based on age status. Thus, while self-discipline is a valued quality, it is not stressed to any

---

[5] I am grateful to Terezia Hinga for pointing out to me the similarity between the Kikuyu and Gisu concepts.

great degree and receives little institutional support. Rather than to age status and to the submission to the group and its leaders, the greater weight is given to the essential equality of all men, won on a kind of once-and-for-all basis through the ordeal of circumcision.

If rites of passage are regarded not only as transition markers but as transformational experiences, then the possible effects on individual consciousness, and indeed on character structure, loom large. It is then no longer sufficient to see initiation rituals simply as formal markers of status or as part of the regulatory mechanism whereby social classifications are maintained and social life made predictable and orderly. As Herdt comments, 'a narrow sociological paradigm no longer seems adequate' (1982: p. 480). Indeed, when the focus shifts to the individual then what has been revealed is the often paradoxical nature of the rituals, sometimes in conflict with secular values and deeply disturbing to the participants. The ethnography coming from New Guinea (Herdt 1982) vividly makes this point, with the male cults there designed to create fierce warriors based on a cruelty which is at variance with other values of community and domestic life, and creating their own poignant moral dilemmas. With the cessation of warfare in recent years some of these peoples have gladly abandoned their cults or the more repugnant aspects of them. The Gisu rites do not involve cruelty in the same way. The Gisu dilemma is perhaps most easily seen as a variant on the problem of what to do with the warriors when there is no war to fight. If they have adapted to the extent of expunging the more obviously bellicose connotations from their rites, these rituals still leave them defined as a nation of violent men if not as a nation of warriors.

REFERENCES

Belshaw, D. G., Brock, B. and Wallace, I. 1966: *The Bugisu Coffee Industry: an economic and technical survey.* Report for International Bank for Reconstruction and Development.

Fadiman, J. A. 1982: *An Oral History of Tribal Warfare: The Meru of Mt. Kenya.* Ohio: Ohio University Press.

Geen, R. G. et al. 1975: The facilitation of aggression by aggression: evidence against the catharsis hypothesis, *Journal of Personality and Social Psychology*, 31(4), 721–6.

Geertz, C. 1974: From the native's point of view: on the nature of anthropological understanding. *Bulletin of the American Academy of Arts and Science*, 28(1).

Girard, René 1977: *Violence and the Sacred.* Baltimore and London: Johns Hopkins University Press.

Gluckman, M. 1963: *Order and Rebellion in Tribal Africa.* London: Cohen.

Gluckman, M. (ed.) 1964: *Closed Systems and Open Minds: the limits of Naivety in Social Anthropology*. Edinburgh and London: Oliver and Boyd.

Heald, S. S. 1974: *Homicide among the Gisu of Eastern Uganda with special reference to the killing of witches and thieves.* PhD thesis, University of London.

_____1982: The making of men: the relevance of vernacular psychology to the interpretation of a Gisu ritual. *Africa*, 52(1), 15—36.

_____1986: Witches and thieves: deviant motivations in Gisu society. *Man*, 21(2), 65—78.

Herdt, G. H. 1982: *Rituals of Manhood: Male Initiations in Papua New Guinea*. Berkeley, Los Angeles and London: University of California Press.

Homans, G. 1941: Anxiety and ritual: the theories of Malinowski and Radcliffe-Brown. *American Anthropologist*, 43, 164—72.

James, W. 1884: What is an emotion? *Mind* (9), 188—205.

Kaplan, R. M. and Singer, R. D. 1976: Television violence and viewer aggression: a re-examination of the evidence. *Journal of Social Issues*, 32, 18—34.

Kenyatta, J. 1938: *Facing Mount Kenya*. London: Secker and Warburg.

Konecni, V. J. and Ebbesen, E. B. 1976: Disinhibition versus the Cathartic effect: artifact and substance. *Journal of Personality and Social Psychology*, 34(3), 352—65.

La Fontaine, J. S. 1969: Tribalism among the Gisu. In P. H. Gulliver (ed.), *Tradition and Transition in East Africa*. London: Routledge and Kegan Paul.

Leach, E. R. 1958: Magical Hair. *Journal of the Royal Anthropological Institute*, 88(2), 147—64.

Malinowski, B. 1945: *Magic, Science and Religion*. Glencoe, Ill.: The Free Press.

Ocaya-Lakidi, Dent, 1979: Manhood, warriorhood and sex in Eastern Africa. *Journal of Asian and African Studies*, 134—65.

Radcliffe-Brown, A. R. 1952: *Structure and Function in Primitive Society*. Glencoe, Ill.: The Free Press.

Richards, A. I. 1956: *Economic Development and Tribal Change*. Cambridge: Heffer.

_____1967: African systems of thought: an Anglo-French dialogue. *Man*, NS, 2, 286—98.

Rosaldo, M. 1980: *Knowledge and Passion: Ilongot notions of self and social life.* Cambridge: Cambridge University Press.

Rosaldo, R. 1980: *Ilongot Headhunting 1883—1974: A study in Society and History.* Stanford: Stanford University Press.

Sargant, W. 1957: *Battle for the Mind: a Physiology of Conversion and Brainwashing.* London: Heinemann.

Schacter, S. and Singer, J. 1962: Cognitive, social and physiological determinants of emotional state. *Psychological Review*, 69, 379—99.

Scheff, T. J. 1977: The distancing of emotion in ritual. *Current Anthropology*, 18, 483—505.

Solomon, R. C. 1984: Getting angry: the Jamesian theory of emotion in anthropology. In R. A. Shweder and R. A. Levine (eds), *Culture Theory: Essays on Mind, Self and Emotion*, Cambridge: Cambridge University Press.

Southall, A. W. 1960: Homicide and suicide among the Alur. In B. Bohannan (ed.), *African Homicide and Suicide*, Princeton: Princeton University Press.

Spencer, P. 1965: *The Samburu. A study of Gerontocracy in a Nomadic Tribe.* London: Routledge and Kegan Paul.

—— 1970: The Function of ritual in the socialization of the Samburu Moran. In P. Mayer (ed.) *Socialization: the Approach from Social Anthropology*, ASA Mono 8, London: Tavistock.

Turner, V. 1967: *The Forest of Symbols: aspects of Ndembu ritual.* Ithaca: Cornell University Press.

Twaddle, M. 1969: Tribalism in eastern Uganda. In P. Gulliver (ed.), *Tradition and Transition in East Africa*, London: Routledge and Kegan Paul.

Watson, P. 1980: *War on the Mind: military uses and abuses of psychology.* Harmondsworth: Penguin.

5

Images of Cannibalism, Death and Domination in a 'Non-Violent' Society

Joanna Overing

THE 'PIAROA BOMB'

For the Piaroa, a jungle people who dwell along tributaries of the Orinoco in Venezuela, all death is caused by murder through sorcery, with sorcerers of foreign tribes usually judged as guilty of this murder. Punishment is drastic and carried out through the means of what modern Piaroa young men once referred to in jest as 'the Piaroa bomb': a powerful revenge magic that causes the total destruction of the community of the murderer and the massacre of all of its inhabitants. After an adult Piaroa's death, the members of the victim's family take certain parts of the deceased's anatomy — the right index finger, the skin from the underside of the right foot, fingernails, toenails and teeth — to a powerful Piaroa shaman, who then performs the complicated ritual of revenge. The shaman makes several packages each containing a mixture of the anatomical parts combined with various violent poisons. The resulting potion is so deadly that the participants are very careful not to touch any of it during its processing. A basket of the poisonous packages, attached to a long cord, is hung over a specially built wooden construction. The other end of the cord is held by members of the deceased's family during the two days that the shaman chants over the packages, giving them their force by blowing his words into them. Lying on the ground near the family are a number of

The fieldwork upon which this paper is based was carried out in 1968 and 1977 with M. R. Kaplan, to whom I am deeply indebted in general. The research in 1977, upon which much of the chapter is based, was financed by the SSRC Grant HR 5028, Central Research Funds of the University of London, London School of Economics Research Funds, and the Institute of Latin American Studies Travel Funds.

sharp utensils, such as knives, axes, machetes — all items that can be used for killing, but which are never implemented by the Piaroa in physical reality. Nevertheless, the presence of the utensils at the ceremony states the family's clear intention to avenge the death of their relative through violent means.

There are many versions of the bomb's force, one being that the shaman in his chanting transforms the potion into the Tapir/Anaconda supreme deity in his form as anaconda. The transformed packages are placed in the hollow of several trees, the number determined by the strength of the devastation sought. They are then lit by fire, and it is thus through smoke that their force is carried to the murderer's village. The anaconda upon his arrival at the village passes into the murderer's body, consumes him and then moves on to his relatives and other members of the village, eating them one by one. When the burning trees in the avenging village fall down, an earthquake completes the destruction of the foreign village.

If the murderer is known by the family of the deceased and access to him is possible, a less drastic revenge can be enacted where only the guilty one is killed. Some left-over food of the murderer is fed to a stinging ant; upon finishing the food, the ant travels into the stomach of the murderer to complete the meal, after which it travels to the heart, eats it, and the murderer of course dies.

For the Piaroa all killing is a form of cannibalism, although indirect, and all death a process of being eaten. While disease is not necessarily caused by cannibalism, it nevertheless is always violence inflicted upon one — a twirling stone in the head, a blow-gun dart or arrow in the stomach, a stone blocking the arteries, a fish-hook in the throat. It is also always a process of being eaten. During the cure, the body becomes a virtual battleground. The patient's stomach, transformed into a jaguar by the shaman, joins other curing forces also called into the patient, to devour the forces and spirits of disease which have taken wilful habitation within the body. The stakes of the cannibalistic battle are high — the life or the death of the stricken one.

The Piaroa themselves never kill through what we would classify as physical violence. For a Piaroa to commit murder by means of his or her 'own hands' would be unthinkable: to do so would be viewed as a fairly direct act of cannibalism which would have a disastrous effect on the killer. Such a kill is equivalent to having eaten the victim and the murderer would immediately die of *surípu*, a disease where the stomach and the intestines fill up with the eaten one, with death coming at their defecation. To murder, one must act indirectly by sending a surrogate eater within the quartz stones one sends through sorcery to the victim. It should be mentioned that Piaroa shamans are (in)famous in the region of the Middle Orinoco for their considerable skills in sorcery and 'wizardry'.

THE RHETORIC OF PEACE AND THE RHETORIC OF VIOLENCE

The Piaroa ideology of violence and cannibalism is associated with a social state of extremely peaceful living. Piaroaland is a place almost totally free of all forms of physical violence, where children, teenagers, and adults alike never express their anger through physical means. Children are not physically reprimanded; spouses are not struck. The Piaroa are appalled by any display of aggression, much less physical aggression, and they place immense value upon personal moderation in behaviour (see Overing 1985a). Powerful as a shaman leader is perceived to be, he is also the knowledgeable teacher of the ethical values of individual autonomy, equality, and tranquillity. The more powerful the shaman leader, the more humble is his demeanour and personal comportment as a responsible man of political affairs. In the Piaroa view, they have eradicated coercion as both a political and social force within society. Their reasons for such eradication lead us to an understanding of the concurrence in Piaroa society of extraordinary images of violence and an equally strong rhetoric of peace through which the good social life is always equated with the tranquil one where individuals are neither coerced nor subjected to the aggression of kinsmen and neighbours.

Piaroa reasoning about violence forms part of a more general theory which disallows political coercion in everyday life. On the one hand the Piaroa associate violence with domination; and on the other they associate domination, together with coercion and tyranny, with the control and ownership of scarce resources. Scarce resources for the Piaroa, in their theory of materiality, are the cultural capabilities for transforming the earth's resources into food; it is therefore through them that human existence on earth is made possible. In Piaroa ideology the forces of culture are owned *today* by celestial gods, and it is they who give the Piaroa, as individuals, the cultural capacities for living on earth. No-one, no leader, no group, in this (human) world may own these scarce resources, an ownership which in the Piaroa view would allow for the coercive or violent use of them and which would entail, among other controls, the control over economic activity and its products (see below). As I shall explain, culture is perceived as a violent and poisonous force, and it is through the ethic of moderation and through an ideological stress upon the political autonomy of the individual that the violence of culture is overcome (see Overing 1985a). Violence suffered by the Piaroa today is in a large part inflicted by unruly beings and gods *of the mythic past* who are avenging their loss of cultural capabilities, which was to the gain of the Piaroa who still have access to them.

Whether Piaroa society can be labelled as a peaceful, violent, or indeed warlike society would be a muddled question: it is all of these things — though for a Westerner living within it, with Western beliefs about violence, life is very peaceful. The Piaroa, though, would see the answer to be as complicated as it is in fact for them. The Piaroa ethic of moderation is a decidedly anti-violent one, yet in disease and death the Piaroa suffer extreme violence thrust upon them. What is more, they themselves are capable of carrying out violence, and see themselves as doing so on a daily basis, against enemies of this and other worlds.[1]

Analytically, there are many types of violence — physical, supernatural, psychological, and ideological, to name but a few. All have a powerful effect upon the recipient, and it is not our expertise as anthropologists to compare the respective damage of each. Sorcery leads to physical harm as surely does the bullet; in both cases the result of the attack depends upon the skill and intentions of the marksman. What is obviously the case is that different societies are violent (and peaceful) over different things or are violent over the same thing for different reasons. Members of societies are taught culturally correct and incorrect ways of being aggressive. These are issues we can explore. Unlike Western societies, the Piaroa are not violent over possessions or women. They are violent over disease and death, for them the area of foreign politics. In the remainder of the chapter I shall discuss the 'what fors', 'whys', and 'hows' of Piaroa violence, which includes as well the question of 'with whom'.

CANNIBALISM, MORTALITY AND THE ORIGIN OF THE CULINARY ARTS

Cannibalism as an inherent characteristic of explanatory schemes of disease and death is not unusual in Amerindian societies. In a wide range of societies, in both the warlike and the peaceful, one finds the death process depicted as a relationship between predator and prey. Lizot writes of the aggressive Yanomami, neighbours of the mild-mannered Piaroa, that every death is for them conceived as a cannibalistic act, with death occurring when the soul has been eaten by a supernatural or human being (Lizot 1985: p. 3).[2] Lévi-Strauss in *The Raw and the Cooked* (1969) explores the cannibal function within South American myths in general, and notes that in them the acquisition of the culinary arts is often linked with the themes of cannibalism and the

[1] I have written elsewhere on the Piaroa multiple-world cosmology. See Overing 1985b.
[2] Also see the thesis by Albert (1985) on the rituals of 'cannibalism' among the Yanomami.

origins of mortality and disease in humankind (pp. 151—2, 296—7). Piaroa mythic episodes clearly link the acquisition of culinary arts with cannibalism. The means of using the earth's resources for food were violent in both origin and acquisition, and the unfolding of these events in battles of mythic time led to a certain kind of cannibalism, and therefore death, as a precondition of humankind's nourishment. Mortality became but the other side of the coin of civilized and social eating.

If one of the most original insights of Lévi-Strauss into South American mythology was that the repeated and consistent message is that the acquisition of the culinary arts — fire and cultivated food — brings in its wake the loss of immortality, there is also the message nesting there that the social state in itself entails mortality. They are linked messages, for always lurking in the playing out of social relationships is the danger that comes from the competitor relationship, from the potential fight over resources, whether human or food in kind. For the Piaroa, at least, all such competition is visualized as ending in the cannibalistic feast or in the danger of so doing. The idiom of cannibalism is therefore all-pervasive in Piaroa thinking about social relationships — whether about the relationships between gods, between gods and humans, between humans and animals, and finally between humans, as for instance between affines or between Piaroa and all other people (see Overing Kaplan 1984).

I shall turn now to myth and the Piaroa exegesis of it to show that social relationships in their origin were cannibalistic. The mythic cycle which I shall consider relates that gods and beings of the past, at the origin of time on this earth, fought over resources and the capabilities of using them. In so doing they viewed each other as fair game in the battle over food; domination over others meant eating them — the primary social relationship of mythic time was that between predator and prey. Thus it is not without significance that the most salient transformations of the two creator gods were those of the great predators jaguar and eagle hawk, who were respectively *Kuemoi* and *Wahari*.

I have written more extensively elsewhere (1982, 1984, 1985a) about the arch-villain of Piaroa mythic time, *Kuemoi* (the cannibal, the Master of Water and Night), and his son-in-law rival, *Wahari* (the Master of the Jungle and Light, and the creator of the Piaroa). Throughout mythic time these two great sorcerers and creator gods fought for the domination over, and the ownership of, each other's respective domains — water and land — and the products of them. Most culture, the means to transform the earth's resources into food, was the creation of *Kuemoi*. From the forces he brought to the earth's surface from his birthplace in water, *Kuemoi* created cooking fire, cultivation, and the powers of the hunt such as curare — the hunting powders of sorcery and fish poisons. He was also the father of cultivated plants.

Wahari, ever wanting culture, stole from *Kuemoi.* He was also the fisherman and as such ate from *Kuemoi*'s domain, just as *Kuemoi,* the hunter, stalked jungle beings from the land of *Wahari* for food. It is important to note that all beings of mythic time were human in form, be they cultivated plants, animals or fish, unless clothed in another form through transformation or acting out a mythic role in their form from the future, post-mythic time. Thus, all eating, by definition, was cannibalistic.

The predation, particularly of *Wahari* the benevolent creator god, was not without its ambiguity. He married Maize, who was the daughter of *Kuemoi,* and from her received the art of cultivation. He also married Morokoto, a large fish. *Wahari* therefore married women from the very domains from which he ate. The theme of danger and predation are evident in his marriages, especially in that to Maize. He captured her with a swirling lasso of thorns, and she, in turn, although his prey was also a predator of *Wahari.* Her womb was a trap for jungle beings, created thus by her father: *Kuemoi* filled her womb with piranha and other lethal fish to kill his daughter's jungle lovers and therefore satisfy his hunger. *Wahari* carefully cleansed the womb of Maize before attempting sex with her. The Piaroa do not explicitly make the link between sex, eating, and predation. The theme, however, is structurally obvious both in mythic associations and in the symbolism linked both to hunting[3] and to relationships of affinity as played out in everyday life (see Overing Kaplan 1984 and below).

The creator of culture, *Kuemoi,* was the hunter and the violent predator of mythic time. Too unsociable to form such an enduring alliance as a marital tie, *Kuemoi* rapes his own daughter rather than, as did *Wahari,* capture a spouse from the category of prey. With respect to the domain of the jungle, *Kuemoi* was steadfastly intent upon eating from it. The crystal box in which dwelt all his powers was called 'the box of domination and aggression', and contained inside it was the jaguar and the terrible light of the jaguar's eyes, which enabled *Kuemoi* to be a hunter of the night. He created jaguar as his hunting 'dog' to help kill his prey, the jungle beings. And, as his creation, the jaguar also became his own transformation. Ever on the mad attack of beings of the jungle — and *Kuemoi* was always violently crazy — he created all dangerous and biting animals and all things poisonous in this world for jungle beings, a category that includes the Piaroa themselves. These venomous and attacking animals, poisonous toads, the vulture, the crocodile, dangerous fish, biting insects, snakes, and so on, are classed together as '*Kuemoi*'s thoughts' and are included as his possessions within his crystal box of powers.

[3] The Piaroa hunting charms, a product of *Kuemoi,* lure (seduce) the animals to the hunter.

Also in his crystal box of domination were the powers for culture. These powers were both wild and poisonous, for they were created by *Kuemoi* through the wild forces given to him in the form of poisonous hallucinogens by his father, the supreme deity. They included the deadly weapons of the hunt, the fire for slash-and-burn agriculture,[4] and the fire for transforming meat and plants into edible form.[5] In short, they are — and this is in a certain sense much of what culture is for the Piaroa — *the weapons and tools for the cannibalistic process*, the means by which resources are captured and processed for eating, the means by which the predator captures and processes his prey. Moreover, as the name for *Kuemoi*'s crystal box of power indicates, the Piaroa associate the ownership of these forces with violence and domination.

The artefacts owned by *Kuemoi* and coveted by *Wahari* were poisonous and contact with them led to madness, so evident in the mad state of *Kuemoi* who owned and handled all poisonous culture (see Overing 1985a). *Wahari* spent much of mythic time attempting to transform his spoils into tamer, more efficacious forces for their safe use by jungle beings. He did not always succeed in this latter task and was therefore frequently maddened by the poisonous culture of *Kuemoi* (Overing 1985a). What is more, this culture he stole was in the main no other than the means by which to cannibalize the beings of his own domain, the jungle, and therefore beings he was supposed to protect.

In the end, *Wahari* claimed jungle beings as his prey. Maddened by *Kuemoi*'s culture, *Wahari* presented a great feast to which all jungle animals and large fish were invited. As its finale, he transformed them into their animal/fish (edible) form and stole the beautiful ritual music of the animals from their sacred homes beneath the earth. Soon after this event both *Kuemoi* and *Wahari* were killed in violence.

At the end of mythic time the wild forces of culture, which caused so much havoc on earth, were taken from earth and their earthly owners by the celestial *Tianawa* gods and housed in crystal boxes beneath the waterfalls within their ethereal temple. Nowadays the gods give the gift of culture to the Piaroa, but cautiously in order that peace and not violence is the result of its use. The shaman, through wizardry, flies to the celestial home of the gods to

---

[4] See Lévi-Strauss (1969: p. 151) on the relationship between the origin of slash-and-burn agriculture, the burning down of plant life, and the cannibalistic process.

[5] It is not clear in the myths whether *Kuemoi* or *Wahari* was responsible for the origin of cooking fire, as opposed to fire for the agricultural process. The latter was clearly *Kuemoi*'s creation, and fire had its origin within the lake of *Kuemoi*'s birth. *Kuemoi* had two heads, one for eating meat raw, the other for eating meat cooked. Yet *Wahari* accuses him of (improperly) eating meat raw.

receive as a gift capabilities for culture, which he brings back to individual Piaroa in bounded form, contained within 'beads of knowledge' (see Overing Kaplan 1982; Overing 1985a). No individual should take within himself or herself more than he or she can handle. I have written elsewhere about the dangers caused by unmastered culture within one (see Overing 1985a). Unmastered culture is especially dangerous for the shaman, who incorporates within himself more forces than the layman: it is he who can become mad and in this state cannibalize others through sorcery.

It is because the Piaroa today receive cultural capabilities from the *Tianawa* gods that they also suffer the violence of disease and death. They suffer firstly because culture is poisonous and they sometimes take too much of its poisonous forces within themselves. But secondly, they are ever threatened, especially with disease, because their advantage, their access to culture and thus to 'civilized eating', was lost to most beings of mythic time. These beings wish to avenge their loss, and they do so by cannibalizing Piaroa victims. Disease and death as cannibalistic processes are described in the following section.

RECIPROCAL CANNIBALISM:
THE RELATIONSHIP OF PREDATOR AND PREY

In Piaroa theory, they are in a relationship of reciprocal cannibalism with animals and fish, and to a lesser degree with fowl and plants. With fish, most fowl, and plant food the relationship is one of exocannibalism, for members of these categories are not 'of a kind' with the Piaroa. With jungle animals, on the other hand, who in contrast are 'of a kind' with the Piaroa — classified with them as '*dea ruwa*', 'beings of the jungle' — the relationship is the disturbing one of 'endocannibalism'.[6] Although I do not stress the point below, it is especially over the latter relationship that the Piaroa elaborate theory and ritual. In terms of daily culinary activity, the Piaroa face no strong existential dilemma in eating fish and plants: fish and plants, both in origin from the domain of water, are in a symbolic relationship of affinity to the Piaroa.[7] Thus it is *logically*, if not morally, proper to eat them: one marries,

---

[6] It is a relationship of 'symbolic' cannibalism, because the Piaroa do not relate to the animals through kinship terms. The reason they give is the obvious one: they eat them, and therefore cannot be in a kinship relationship with them (Overing 1985b).

[7] See Overing and Kaplan 1982; Overing 1985b. The large fish and some birds do give disease to the Piaroa, but 'lesser' illnesses, such as sore throat or skin rash.

eats, and is aggressive toward those of the domain different from that of self.[8] Jungle animals, however, are symbolically 'kin' to the Piaroa, and as such a forbidden category in classificatory logic for the purposes of sex, eating, and aggression (see Overing Kaplan 1984). Endocannibalism is but a step away from incest.[9]

The Piaroa say that animals and large fish — and to a lesser degree, birds and plants — give them disease. A Piaroa contracts disease through contact with the animals: stepping on faeces or urine, smelling their odour, or eating their flesh contaminates. Disease, as I have noted above, is a process of being eaten. Animals and fish are predators of their predators, thereby avenging both their position as prey and also a yet greater treachery. It was *Wahari*, the creator god of the Piaroa, who was responsible for the edible condition of animals and fish. He was moreover responsible for their cultureless present-day state: he stole their 'thoughts', ceremonial knowledge, from them.

One of the most important tasks of the Piaroa shaman leader is the seemingly innocent task of maintaining the fertility of his territory (Overing Kaplan 1975), of performing the increase ceremonies which keep the jungles and the rivers filled with game. The Piaroa view these rites as the most dangerous task of wizardry, and rightly so; for the great shaman in these rituals performs a mimetic re-enactment of *Wahari*'s treacherous act when he transformed his human jungle neighbours into food (see Overing 1985a). The animals and fish live as humans in their sacred homes of creation beneath the earth, and the shaman in bringing them up to terrestrial space transforms them into edible and cultureless animal/fish form. The flutes played by the men during the great increase ceremony are those that the shaman has stolen from the animal homes beneath the earth. The lyrical sounds of the flutes become songs telling of the triumph of men in attaining a predator relationship with the animals.[10]

Through his nightly chanting the shaman protects the Piaroa from the fifteen or so diseases that the animals, fish, some birds and plants give the

---

[8] See Albert's (1985) description of the Yanomami for a variation on the same theme.

[9] In their nightly chants the Piaroa shamans transform the flesh of animals into the 'safe' vegetable food, that is, they transform it from the incestuous category of 'kin' to (marriageable) 'affine' (Overing 1985b).

[10] I am using the term 'men' purposefully: Piaroa women cannot see these flutes. The men in playing them for the women are flaunting their triumph over the animals, yet keeping the secret of its treachery from the women. This is a radically different version of the 'sacred flutes cult' from that normally described for Amazonia where the men stole culture (flutes) from the women and, in the cult, display their present-day domination over women.

Piaroa to avenge their loss of humanity and consequent edible state. These prophylactic and curing recitations are given to the shaman by the celestial *Tianawa* gods who own the crystal boxes of culture, and become therefore a critical aspect of the shaman's cultural capability and knowledge. The greater portion of any chant is made up of lists, lists of what the Piaroa call 'names' — the names of the gods, the diseases, the animals. From the lists of names of the diseases we learn that each disease is named first of all as the product of its guardian 'Grandfather' and as the possession of its 'Master' (*ruwang*), and is given a multitude of attributions to describe its action. These attributions are so elaborate that (to give an example) a partial analysis of the disease paranoia, 'go around, fall down' (*k'erau*) would have to take into account its characterization as an emanation from the bird *orokoko* (nightjar); its constitution as a field of powers of madness between mountain peaks, as a red face paint, as whirling translucent chips of wood, as an insect in the victim's head, as the sap of trees, as the soul in human and animal form of the animal who sent it, as the 'sweat' of the sky, as the 'rust' of the sun; and as comprised of both the diseases, paralysis (*hurae*) and 'monkey's urine madness' (*k'irau*), while remaining distinct from either of these.[11]

Very generally, we can distinguish six categories of gods, spirits or beings with which the shaman is involved when curing:

1 the *Tianawa* gods who give him the words of the chants and whose powers are the source of the shaman's own power;
2 the *Tianawa* gods who participate directly in the curing process in their terrestrial transformations and whom the shaman supplicates for aid in his chanting;
3 the earth and water spirits, known as the Masters of Land and Water, who send disease, and the spirits of the animals who give disease;
4 the thunder and sun gods who also send disease;
5 gods of mythic time who guard the specific disease and order the animal to send it, and finally;
6 the sorcerers, theoretically from other lands, who might be responsible for sending the disease.

The two most important guardians of disease, called in this role the 'grandfathers of illness' (*tà'domu Waràwa*), are the Masters of Land and Water: *Re'yo*, the 'Master' and the 'Grandfather' of all jungle animals, and *Ahe Itamu*, the 'Master' and the 'Grandfather' of fish. They are responsible

---

[11] See Overing, J. and M. R. Kaplan (1986) and Overing (1985a) on the disease *k'erau* and *k'irau*.

for sending the diseases (the 'culture lost') of the animals and the fish to the Piaroa. Neither animal nor fish can order its own disease to be sent; for neither has *ta'kwarü* (life of thoughts) or *ta'kwakomenà* (responsibility and volition) to do the deed for themselves.[12] The other powerful beings who send the diseases of fish and animals are the Thunder gods and the Sun gods who also, as guardians of disease, are called 'Grandfathers of Disease'. They, with the Earth and Water Spirits, are owners of disease, and therefore also called the 'Masters of Disease' (*Ruwatu Waràwa*). When the Piaroa kill an animal these powerful spirits can order the spirit of the animal killed — the *ta'kwa ruwang* of the animal, its 'master of thoughts' and as such a direct reference to a culture lost — into the body of a Piaroa to eat it. The 'Masters of Disease' themselves join the spirit of the animal to work with it there: together they both cause and become a part of the disease.

Through his nightly chanting, the shaman combats these forces of disease for his community. Periodically during his singing he blows the words of the chant given to him by the *Tianawa* gods into a container of water and one of honey. In the morning, the adults drink of the water while the children take the 'blown' honey; when the liquid goes into them, so too do the words of the shaman's chant which contain within them the forces to fight disease. In his chanting, the shaman has supplicated the 'Masters' and the 'Grandfathers' of disease not to send disease; with the help of the Tianawa gods, he has transformed the animal to be consumed into vegetable, rendering harmless the process of eating for his community, a step toward preventing the eating from being an act of cannibalism — or, at least, endocannibalism.

As further precaution against disease, and also for its cure, the shaman calls upon a special set of *Tianawa* gods who travel down to earth transformed as predators — as puma, jaguar, eagle hawk and wasp. They help by entering the victim in their predator form to do battle there with the spirits of disease: they eat them. Thus, the Piaroa say that when one drinks of the water into which the shaman has blown the words of his chants, one's stomach is transformed into jaguar, a predator of the spirits of disease.

Aside from the general guardians of disease (*Re'yo* and *Ahe Itamu*, the Thunder and Sun gods), each of the fifteen or so diseases has its own 'Grandfather' and 'Master' specific to itself (Overing Kaplan 1982; Overing and Kaplan 1986). The 'Grandfather' of a specific disease sends the disease to a victim only upon the command of a human sorcerer. As a result, the disease is a much more serious one than if sent by the general guardians of disease alone: the patient can die. Indeed, the Piaroa consider the sorcerer's

[12] They lose 'intentionality' (*ta'kwakomenà*) in the transformation process.

quartz stones to be the source of all Piaroa death. The sorcerer asks the 'Grandfather' guardian of the specific disease to send both the disease's 'Master' and the disease itself into the sorcerer's quartz stone, which he then shoots into his victim.

The 'Grandfathers' of specific diseases are all gods who participated in mythic history and who, at the end of mythic time when the *Tianawa* gods took culture into their crystal boxes, lost access to the means of transforming the earth's resources for their own needs. For instance, the 'Grandfather' of boils is *Kuemoi*, the mad creator of culture and its first owner; the 'Grandfather' of stomach-ache ('arrow into the stomach') is *Hurewe*, the child born of the incestuous union between *Wahari* and his sister; the 'Grandfather' of blindness and eye diseases is *Buok'a*, the brother of *Wahari*; the 'Grandfather' of promiscuity ('monkey urine madness') is *Cheheru*, as the promiscuous sister of *Wahari* during mythic time, not in her present-day transformation as the *Tianawa* goddess of fertility.

The 'Masters' of specific diseases are small carnivorous creatures: the victim is eaten by the disease, just as when the general 'Masters' of disease and the spirit of the animals work together within a body, eating it. As an example, childbirth disease is sent by sorcery in the following way: *Ime*, white-lipped peccary in his human mythic time form as 'Grandfather' of childbirth disease, is asked by the sorcerer to send this disease inside his quartz stone; *Ime* then orders the 'Master' of childbirth disease, three eating lizards, into the stone which the sorcerer can send to his victim. The lizards then inhabit the womb of the victim, eating it — alongside the spirit of the animal.

To decide upon the correct cure when a person is ill the shaman must determine whether the disease has been sent by a sorcerer or by the general 'Masters' of disease. If from the latter, the shaman's chants should alone be sufficient to cure; however if the specific 'Master' of the disease has entered the victim within a quartz stone, the shaman must perform a withdrawal rite as well, removing the stone to save the patient.

In sum, in curing and preventing disease the shaman calls upon the present-day owners of culture, the *Tianawa* gods, to send their forces of culture — contained within their crystal boxes — into the domesticated safety of the shaman's 'beads of knowledge' (see Overing 1985a); so tamed, the shaman blows them into water which when drunk by the members of his community can do battle against the forces of disease that might enter into their bodies to eat. The forces of disease sent by the general 'Masters of Illness' are the gifts of revenge given to the animals for the culture they lost at the end of mythic time: or, in other words, disease is culture transformed while its cure is culture domesticated (Overing Kaplan 1982). The disease sent by the specific

'Grandfathers' of disease is another matter, and probably should be best understood as both remnants of wild culture that can enter society from the mythic past and as vengeance for culture lost.

THE EGALITARIAN POLITICS OF A DISCOURSE
ON PEACE AND VIOLENCE

The Piaroa place an extreme value upon 'the tranquil life' (*adiupàwi*), and proper maturity is attained by an adult only insofar as she or he achieves tranquillity in relationship with others on a daily basis (Overing Kaplan 1975; Overing 1985a). In contrast the Piaroa discourse on disease and death, eating and sorcery, is deeply violent: it is a discourse of predation, cannibalism, and revenge. Yet the two discourses, that of peace and that of predation, are not entirely separate but two related aspects in Piaroa thought of what is a typically Amerindian egalitarian political philosophy: this rejects any ownership of scarce resources that would allow for the coercive or violent use of them and that might entail political control over labour and its products (Overing 1986). In Piaroa understanding, the ownership of scarce resources — the knowledge and the power to transform elements of the world to fulfil human needs in society — leads, as in *Kuemoi*'s day, to an intolerable level of violence, competition, domination, and tyranny, or, in other words, to a state of existence inimical to the possibility of orderly social life. The benevolent *Tianawa* gods who today own poisonous cultural abilities do so to prevent its misuse, and *can* do so only because they themselves *do not use these abilities* to fulfil their own needs. They live an asocial life, isolated one from the next in separate compartments in their celestial temple. They do not eat, drink, sleep, or engage in sexual activity. They are without needs and therefore do not participate in the cannibalistic process to satisfy themselves. For this reason they have immortality — and can safely own culture. Social (human) need too easily leads, in Piaroa theory, to the misuse of cultural ability, as the history of the mythic past teaches.

The *Tianawa* gods own all sources of cultural abilities which allow for the transformation of the earth's resources, while Earth and Water spirits own the resources themselves. Neither the political leader, as such, nor the (political) group owns material resources in Piaroaland. Today the jungle and its products are owned by the Master of the Jungle, the great ogre of the Forest, *Re'yo*, while rivers and their products are owned by the Master of Water, the ethereal water spirit, *Ahe Itamu*. Together they are the guardians and ultimate owners of cleared gardens, and it is they who make garden land fertile. Gardens are cleared in the territory of the Master of the Jungle, while cultivated plants are in origin from the domain of water, Kuemoi's former territory. Thus *Re'yo* and *Ahe Itamu* have equal rights over gardens. Individual Piaroa who clear, plant, and tend a garden also own the products of their labour.[13]

Cultural forces domesticated within the person in his or her 'beads of knowledge' give one the capabilities for hunting, fishing, planting, cooking — or, in other words, the capacity to transform resources for use, that is, to create and use weapons for the cannabalistic process. Such capacities within one are labelled as one's 'thoughts' (*ta'kwarü*); in emphasizing the ability of the cultural person to have an effect, an ability to transform elements in the world, the Piaroa refer to the products of a person's garden as his or her 'thoughts' (*'a'kwa'*). A person can only own the product of a transformation caused by his or her own labour and allowed for by the individual capabilities taken within one from the gods; he or she can never own the land from whence it came. In Piaroa theory, they have eradicated dangerous coercion and domination, or their possibility, from the political process. No-one can order another's labour because that labour is private to the person; the capabilities for which the individual in which they dwell holds total responsibility. Competition over the resources of others or over another's abilities to use resources could in the Piaroa view lead only to intolerable violence.

Clearly, the Piaroa understand a major source of violence in human affairs — competition over resources and the powers for transforming the earth's surface to fulfil needs — and their political process is one that rejects even the possibility of the ownership of resources that would allow for a political domination based upon economic control over resources. On the other hand, the Piaroa are still suffering the violence of the past when life on earth was a battle for such control, a battle over the eating of others and therefore the aggressive domination of them, a process literally and not just symbolically summarized by *Kuemoi*'s crystal box of jaguar power. They pay for their privileged access to culture when they are cannibalized in retaliation for this privilege by those who in the past lost it. They are also in a relationship of

---

[13] A technicality: Piaroa distinguish sharply between products of the garden (individually owned) and products of the jungle (communally used). The former are conceived as the results of a transformational process enacted by the gardener, while meat jungle products belong more to the shaman leader than to the hunter. The shaman through wizardry transformed humans into animals. The hunter, then, gives his kill to the shaman who distributes the game equally within his local group. Plant food and other products gathered in the forest are likewise distributed equally by the gatherer to all members of the group. Such products have not been transformed through human capabilities.

reciprocal cannibalism with animals, and Piaroa shaman leaders must daily battle the great jungle and water spirits who punish those who endanger the life of their domains. The battles for domination over the use of resources are no longer between social humans, but between humans on the one side and earth and water spirits, gods of the mythic past, and transformed humans on the other.

Ever wary of the signs of arrogance that their own leaders might manifest, the Piaroa keep a sharp check on human power that dominates. Aggression on the part of the shaman leaders (both within one's group and within the political territory) is an indication that they have taken cultural forces, the means for the cannibalistic process, from the *Tianawa* gods beyond their individual control. The sanctions on such out-of-control behaviour are considerable (see Overing Kaplan 1975; Overing 1985a), and the disruptive leader must immediately demonstrate his sanity (Overing 1985a), diffidence, and controlled humility to retain political legitimacy. Such sanctions have no effect on leaders who are strangers. As a result, the human 'stranger' is always a potential enemy and therefore 'the Piaroa bomb', the cannibalistic retaliation for all Piaroa deaths.

Finally, the Piaroa discourse on cannibalism, very similar to that of their more overtly violent neighbours, the Yanomami, 'orders' relationships between groups and in doing so is a discourse forthcoming from a particular metaphysics about the nature of social life itself. This discourse (again, a typically Amerindian one; see Overing Kaplan 1984) centres on the danger and the necessity of the stranger to the perpetuation of the social group (also see Riviére 1984). Society exists only through the interaction of unlike entities and forces that are potentially highly dangerous to one another (Overing Kaplan 1984; Overing 1986). For the Piaroa and for the Yanomami (Albert 1985), it is the affine who is the dangerous and necessary 'other'. Such dangers for the local group are overcome by the Piaroa through a principle of 'perpetual reciprocity' between affines: the marriage exchange is based upon a principle of reciprocity carried out through the serial and multiple repetition of affinal ties within the group (Overing Kaplan 1975, 1984; Overing 1986). Through affinity, safe consanguinity is achieved (Overing Kaplan 1975). According to Albert, dangerous affinity within the relatively endogamous village of the Yanamami is nullified through ties of cannibalistic reciprocity a village has with its allies (classificatory affines) and its enemies. A village is in the relationship of endocannibalistic reciprocity with its allies and exocannibalistic reciprocity with its foes. Through elaborate ritual 'political cuisine', the 'affinal' allies consume in second mortuary rites the bones of the affines within the village — while enemies in warrior raids rid the village, through exocannibalism, of the affines' flesh. The village is thereby left as a 'safe' consanguineal whole and the village freed of its dangerous affinal forces. As with the Piaroa, to physically kill another human being leads to the incorporation of the victim's flesh within the murderer — the victim is 'eaten'. Unlike the Piaroa, the Yanomami who kills on a raid into enemy's territory avoids the murderer's death through a 'homicide ritual' that slowly rids the 'eater' of the decomposing flesh of his enemy's affine (Albert 1985).

For the Piaroa, classificatory affines are political competitors and as such potential cannibals, as well as potential brothers-in-law or fathers-in-law. In political battles between shaman leaders (always of different local groups), the 'other' is always classified as 'affine' and as *Kuemoi*, the cannibal; he is seen in hallucinatory vision *as Kuemoi* in his transformation as jaguar or anaconda — a predator of self and kinsmen. A secure relationship of safety can only be achieved with political competitors through repeated marital exchanges. However, actual deaths are usually attributed to the cannibalism of unknown enemies and not to that of competitors. Death is therefore caused by those with whom one is in the relationship of blatant negative reciprocity.

If one can say that Yanomami violence is a logical violence through which the danger of the flesh and the bones of one's affines is erased, violence for the Piaroa becomes even more abstract: the violence is one of category, and is with the 'unknown stranger' and cannibal, and not with the one who can in political fact steal your food or your people. The political competitor can do the latter;[14] however he is a potential and not an actual killer. The actual murderer is the factually 'empty', but semantically 'full' sign of the stranger cannibal, and this is the secret of Piaroa 'peace' in daily life.

REFERENCES

Albert, B. 1985: *Temps du Sang, Temps de Cendres: Représentation de la maladie, systeme rituel et espace politique chez les Yanomami du sud-est (Amazonie brésilienne)*. Thesis for docteur de l'université de Paris X.
Lévi-Strauss, C. 1969: *The Raw and the Cooked*. London: Allen Lane.
Lizot, J. 1985: *Tales of the Yanomami: daily life in the Venezuelan forest*. Cambridge: Cambridge University Press.
Overing Kaplan, J. 1975: *The Piaroa, a People of the Orinoco Basin*. Oxford: Clarendon Press.
———— 1982: The paths of sacred words: shamanism and the domestication of the asocial in Piaroa society. Presented at the symposium on 'Shamanism in Lowland

[14] Rivière persuasively argues (1984) that, through the political competition for followers, the leader in the Guianas is also acquiring labour power, and therefore food, for the group.

South American Societies', 44th International Congress of Americanists, Manchester.

_____ 1984: Dualisms as an expression of difference and danger: marriage exchange and reciprocity among the Piaroa of Venezuela. In K. Kensinger (ed.), *Marriage Practices in Lowland South American Societies*, Urbana: University of Illinois Press.

Overing, J. 1985a: There is no end of evil: the guilty innocents and their fallible god. In D. Parkin (ed.), *The Anthropology of Evil*, Oxford: Basil Blackwell.

_____ 1985b: Today I shall call him 'Mummy': multiple worlds and classificatory confusion. In J. Overing (ed.), *Reason and Morality*, London: Tavistock.

_____ 1986: Elementary structures of reciprocity: a comparative note on Guianan, Central Brazilian and Northwest Amazon socio-political thought. In A. Colson and D. Heinen (eds), *Themes in Political Organization,* Caracas: Fundacion La Salle.

Overing, J. and Kaplan, M. R. 1986: Wótuha. In *Los Aborigines de Venezuela*, 3. Caracas: Fundacion La Salle.

Rivière, P. 1984: *Individual and Society in the Guianas*. Cambridge: Cambridge University Press.

6

The Beauty of Violence: *Jidaigeki*, *Yakuza* and 'Eroduction' Films in Japanese Cinema

Brian Moeran

INTRODUCTION

This chapter considers three genres of Japanese film — the *jidaigeki* period drama; the *yakuza* gangster film; and pornographic cinema known popularly as 'eroduction' — and focuses on the interrelationships between violence, sex, death and beauty in Japanese society. At the same time, since many of the films discussed stem from works of Japanese literature, I shall also bring in one or two literary works in my exposition of this theme.

Japanese society is frequently described by anthropologists as being a society of harmony and group identification. At the same time, critics of Japanese film and popular culture have had occasion to comment upon the nihilism and violence often found therein. Since anthropologists dealing with Japan have rarely been interested in film, and since film critics are rarely interested in Japanese social organization, the paradox between an ideology based on harmony and a popular culture which makes much of unharmonious activities has rarely been addressed. Buruma (1984) has suggested that the sort of violence alluded to here provides an outlet by which Japanese society is made safer, and that the kinds of sadism, masochism, torture, and other forms of violence found in films and popular literature, are in effect mere fantasies of a people forced in their everyday lives to be gentle and meek. Violence is, in short, seen to be no more than a reversal of normal, everyday behaviour 'a direct result of being made to conform to such a strict and limiting code of normality' (1984: p. 225).

While there is clearly some truth in this argument, I feel that there is more to the explanation than a functionalist approach which argues that a society needs an alternative ideology in order that otherwise repressed feelings of aggression might emerge in some socially acceptable form. My own research suggests that violence in Japanese society cannot be separated from attitudes towards sex, death and beauty, and that all of these may be connected with concepts of time and space. Certainly, the Japanese do not introduce scenes of women having their bellies ripped open, or of men slashing one another to gory death, merely to show what their society might be like if people did not obey the principles of harmony and group commitment espoused by politicians, company directors and educationalists. They do so in an attempt to overcome, firstly, the concept of time, and secondly, that of space as represented by notions of self and other. By coming to terms with time, the Japanese are able to go beyond Western acculturation and return to a foetal sense of 'Japaneseness'. An awareness of what it means to be 'Japanese' simultaneously leads to an emphasis on group ideals and harmony in Japanese society and denies that there is any distance between 'self' and 'other'. In short, violence — together with sex, death and the appreciation of beauty — *is* a means towards supporting social ideals, but not quite for the reasons suggested hitherto.

JIDAIGEKI, YAKUZA AND 'ERODUCTION' FILMS

One of the characteristics of the Japanese film industry is that films are readily categorized into types, depending on their subject matter. Thus we find a distinction made between types of hero/heroine portrayed (e.g. the *hahamono* 'mother' films, and *tsumamono* 'wife' films); between films depicting certain groups in Japanese society (e.g. the *rumpenmono* 'vagrant' films, *taiyōzokumono* 'sun tribe' youth gang films, and *sararimanmono* 'salary man' films); between differences in historical settings (e.g. *Meijimono*, Meiji Period films (1868–1912), and *Taishōmono*, Taisho Period films (1912–26)).

The most obvious historical distinction is that drawn between *gendaimono*, 'modern' films, and *jidaigeki*, 'period' films. *Jidaigeki* refers to all films whose stories take place prior to the Meiji Restoration in 1868 and which therefore deal with Japanese society prior to its Westernization. *Gendaimono* refers to all films whose action takes place after the Meiji Restoration. It is, therefore, Japan's official break with feudalism and its first contacts with the West which mark the dividing line between 'period' and 'modern' films.

The *jidaigeki* themselves subsume a further subdivision, known as *chanbara*. Whereas *jidaigeki* can range in time right back to the Heian Period (794–1185) or even earlier, *chanbara* deal almost exclusively with the Tokugawa Period (1603–1868). This distinction is not, however, entirely based on historical periods. Many — but not all[1] — film critics regard *jidaigeki* as serious art, in which directors attempt to discover what is of unique value in Japanese history, and how this uniqueness should be preserved. In these films, we find that social norms are frequently questioned, as heroes are made to work out for themselves what it is that they should believe and how they should live. *Chanbara*, on the other hand, are usually seen as little more than escapist entertainment — mere morality plays which do not question the *status quo*, but unthinkingly accept it (cf. Moeran 1985). In this respect, *chanbara* form what Mellen (1976: p. 116) refers to as 'the touchstone of authoritarian art'.

The *jidaigeki*[2] probably went through their golden age in the two decades before the Pacific War. It has been suggested that one reason for their popularity then lies in the fact that the past was seen as less threatening an arena in which to discuss social problems. Directors could avoid being seen — by either the military regime or by the film companies — as dissidents, if they set their plots in a dim and distant past. At the same time, it seems unlikely that these ploys fooled their audiences. In this way, political authority, the market and the general public were all satisfied. Attacking present-day society by means of the *jidaigeki* genre was a form of ritualized dissent in a society which frowned upon open criticism (Mellen 1976: pp. 85—6).

This searching in the past to answer problems of the present did have its unexpected results. The pre-war military government did not regard the *jidaigeki* as much of a threat to the social order; yet the post-war American Occupation Forces tried to get rid of the genre because they thought it too chauvinistic and militaristic. The Americans were not, however, very successful in this and the *jidaigeki* came back into fashion in the mid-1950s — at a time when the Japanese were going through an economic boom and were, at the same time, beginning to turn back to their old traditions in a renewed identity crisis. Ironically, perhaps, American disapproval of the period films led to Japanese directors concentrating their attention on the *yakuza* genre, in which gangsters acted as modern-day samurai, behaving according to feudal values, and bringing each film to a rousing climax with bloody sword-play and dagger-throwing. We thus find in the *yakuza* genre the

---

[1] Anderson and Richie (1959: pp. 59—62) clearly would not agree with the distinction (based on Mellon [1976]) between *jidaigeki* and *chanbara*, for they regard the former as mere 'escapism' and consider the golden age of *jidaigeki* to have occurred in the two decades prior to the Pacific War.

[2] I shall use the term '*jidaigeki*' for the genre as a whole, since I do not wish to make what would amount to aesthetic judgements on the quality of the films discussed in this chapter.

whole gamut of Tokugawa period values re-emerging in present-day industrial society.

Part of the emphasis on the production of *yakuza* and *jidaigeki* lies in the situation in which the Japanese film industry found itself in the 1950s. Not only were production costs rising, but so were admission charges. Television was booming in popularity and, as a result, attracting more and more advertising. In order to combat all this, in 1952 the cinemas began showing double features, and major companies found that they were being required to turn out approximately one feature a week to keep the cinemas supplied. The fastest method of production, of course, was the action picture in which a series of films could be produced with the same sets, costumes and even actors (Anderson and Richie 1959: p. 245).

Kyoto rapidly became the centre for the production of *jidaigeki*, and Tokyo that of *yakuza* films, of which something like 1500 were made in the decade lasting from the mid-1960s to the mid-1970s (Tucker 1973: p. 127). In an attempt to attract a wider audience, which was rapidly decreasing because of the popularity of television, film directors stuck to the idea of limited plots characterized by violence and bloodshed. From the *yakuza* films developed a whole range about 'discontented youth, school drop-outs, drug addicts and tormented young love . . . Narcotics, prostitution, extortion and revenge became the staple diet. Studios went to extreme lengths to capture the market in these films, some even using ex-gangsters as stars' (Tucker: p. 123).[3] In the mid-60s, two thirds to three quarters of all films produced were of the *yakuza* type. By the 1970s, the same percentage of films made in Japan were 'eroductions', or 'pink' films. These started out as low-budget one hour films in which out-of-work models, actors, and even volunteers took part. They were immensely successful, if only because television could not show such erotic scenes and hence were unable to compete with them.

At the same time, the *yakuza* films became highly charged with sexual elements, so that we can see in the development of these three genres of Japanese film — the *jidaigeki, yakuza* and 'eroduction' — the emergence of a form of popular culture which emphasized both sex and violence. One example from many can be seen in Masumura Yasuzō's *The Red Angel* (1966), where the erotic development of a young woman is closely tied up with her experience as a nurse in a field hospital, and with her confrontation with the horrors of violent and bloody death.

---

[3] One of the foremost producers of *yakuza* films, Taoka Mitsuru, is himself the son of a powerful gangland boss, Taoka Kazuo, who was killed by a rival gang in 1981.

VIOLENCE, SEX, DEATH AND BEAUTY

One aspect of violence in Japanese films is the extent to which, in both the *jidaigeki* and *yakuza* genres, killing seems to go on for the sake of killing and details of slaughter are lovingly observed. Long before *The Wild Bunch*, Japanese directors were filming slow-motion shots of flesh exploding under the impact of bullets, and they also developed somewhat gruesome forms of make-up and special effects. We can see limbs being cut off and bodies hewn in two, and make-up artists have now developed a technique whereby a sword will first appear to slash a man's face before — two or three seconds later — a razor-like cut will open up and the victim's blood begin to flow (Tucker 1973: p. 112).[4]

Some critics, such as Anderson and Richie (1959: p. 318), are not so impressed with the technical mastery of Japanese film makers in their portrayal of violence.

Pointless killing is one of the main features of the Japanese film . . . the feeling of the cheapness of life is inescapable . . . Japanese films also tend to accentuate the attendant gore. Gushing blood, open wounds and the like abound . . . There are also all kinds of torture and various varieties of suicide. Often the violence goes beyond the bounds of plot necessity.

This view is shared by Mellen. Bloodshed pervades the *chanbara*, she says, quite independently of any rationale in the plots, which act as occasions for violence in much the same way as in pornography films they act as occasions for sexuality. 'In *chanbara* the charge, arousal, and catharsis derived from the gore and blood-letting are equally orgasmic. The violence of the *chanbara* is a sexual surrogate and also an emblem of sensuality in a repressed culture' (Mellen 1976: p. 118).

While I shall return to the relationship between repression and violence later on, we should note here that sex has always figured strongly in Japanese art and literature, and that a number of visual and poetic metaphors have been adopted into the semiotics of Japanese film (for example, the transience of life and youth seen in the falling of the cherry blossoms; mountain waterfalls signifying passion; the Buddhist notion of impurity seen in the clouds of dust

---

[4] Some of the emphasis on visual effects in Japanese films may be due to a tendency for the Japanese to depend on the eye, rather than the ear, when it comes to aesthetic sensibility.

surrounding so many of Kurosawa's battle scenes, and in Ichikawa Kon's *The Harp of Burma* [1956] with its opening epitaph: 'Blood red are the soil and peaks of Burma').

In art, we find that many of Japan's greatest artists did work which we in the West might well label 'pornographic'. Pornography was widely prevalent and goes back to tenth century drawings known as *wara-e*, which depicted monks and abbots indulging in all sorts of sexual activities (Buruma 1984: p. 55). Erotic pillow books used to be given to young brides as early as the Heian Period, even though it is only in recent post-war decades that young people have been seen holding hands — let alone kissing — in public.[5] Other artists indulged in sadism. The woodblock print artist Kuniyoshi, for example, and his pupil Yoshitoshi, portrayed women being tortured — as did the Edo Period artist, Ekin.

The relationship between sex and death is a frequent feature of Japanese literature, where we find parallels with Bataille's notion that eroticism is the joy of life pushed to the point of death (Bataille 1965) — the union of *eros* and *thanatos*. Tanizaki Junichiro, for example, in his 1962 *Diary of a Mad Old Man (Futen Rōjin Nikki)*, describes the way in which his hero — like many others in this author's work, a foot fetishist — feels his blood pressure rise whenever his daughter-in-law allows him to lick her feet.

The thought of really dying did frighten me. I tried to calm myself down, telling myself not to get excited. The strange thing is, however, that I never stopped sucking her feet, I couldn't stop. The more I sought to stop, the harder I sucked, like an idiot. Thinking I was going to die, I still kept on sucking. Fear and excitement and pleasure came in turns. (quoted in Buruma 1984: p. 49)

This theme is echoed in another of Tanizaki's novels, *The Key (Kagi)*, made into a film directed by Ichikawa in 1959 (and titled in English *The Odd Obsession*). The hero has a stroke while making love to his wife, who (in the film) then tempts him once more by stripping in front of him — enough to raise his blood pressure and cause him to die.

---

[5] The first kiss on Japanese film was screened on 23 May 1946 in two films which opened on the same day: Chiba Yasuki's *A Certain Night's Kiss (Aru yo no seppun)*, and Sasaki Yasuki's *Twenty Year Old Youth (Hatachi no seishun)*. Public reaction centred on such questions as: was it commercial or artistic motivation which prompted the filming of a kiss? Was there any sexual meaning in a kiss? Was a kiss 'Japanese' or not? Was a kiss hygienic or not? (Anderson and Richie 1959: p. 176). Kyō Machiko was 'the first actress to have public attention drawn to her sex appeal' (1959: p. 232) in the early 1950s; Yamamoto Satsuyo was the first actress to appear on the screen nude, in 1956.

Another modern author to describe the relationship between sex and death in a number of works was Mishima Yukio. In *Patriotism* (*Yūkoku*), based on the 26 February 1936 Incident, in which a number of important political and military figures were murdered by army rebels, Mishima describes a lieutenant who did not take part in the assassinations and who decided to commit suicide rather than have to take action against those of his friends who had participated. As he lies on a mattress waiting to make love to his wife for the last time, he thinks about the whole affair:

Was it death he was now waiting for? Or a wild ecstacy of the senses? The two seemed to overlap, almost as if the object of his bodily desire was death itself. But, however that might be, it was certain that never before had the lieutenant tasted such total freedom. (quoted in Buruma 1984: p. 165)

Here we have echoes of Kabuki theatre where a favourite theme is that of lovers dying together — something which is seen by the Japanese as the supreme form of sexual ecstasy. The choice of death is, in an ordered society, perhaps the only moment in which an individual can attain true liberation.

Mishima is, in fact, one of Japan's more interesting modern writers in that he acted out in real life what he frequently alluded to in his fiction and essays. By committing the samurai's ritual act of *seppuku*, Mishima forced the Japanese to consider — if but briefly — the meaning of death in a modern society whose major premise is that it is best to live as long as possible (Mishima 1977: p. 27). Before disembowelling himself in the headquarters of the Japanese Self-Defence Force, he shouted down from the balcony to those assembled below:

Have you studied *Bu*? Do you understand the way of the sword? What does the sword mean to a Japanese? . . . I ask you. Are *you* men? Are you *bushi* (warriors)? (quoted in Scott-Stokes 1974: p. 47)

In this context, one of Mishima's more interesting works is *The Way of the Samurai*, his commentary on the early eighteenth-century work on this theme — *Hagakure* (*Hidden Leaves*) — by the Nabeshima clan retainer, Yamamoto Jōchō. Concerned that modern Japanese society was slipping into an 'age of performing artists', in which baseball players and television pop stars were the only people to get public attention, Mishima objected to the fact that human beings had ceased to be 'total human personalities' and were 'reduced to a kind of skilled puppet'. What one should do, he claimed, was 'live beautifully and die beautifully' (Mishima 1977: pp. 21—2).

Mishima cites the *Hagakure* as a splendid example of 'a living philosophy

that holds life and death as the two sides of one shield' (p. 42). In it he
discovers for himself the *Hagakure*'s notion that:

The way of the samurai is death. Human life lasts but an instant. One should spend it
doing what one pleases. In this world fleeting as a dream, to live in misery doing what
one dislikes is foolishness.

The morality of the samurai — and, of course, of the *jidaigeki* and *yakuza*
films — is a supremely male view of morality.[6] Indeed, the values of the
yakuza gangsters are essentially a reassertion of patriarchal supremacy (Mellen
1976: p. 126) in a society which has gradually become more 'feminine' in its
ways, with Westernization and peace (cf. Mishima 1977: p. 18). Here, what I
wish to point to is the fact that morality in the *Hagakure* is determined by
aesthetics. 'What is beautiful must be strong, vivid and brimming with
energy. This is the first principle: the second is that what is moral must be
beautiful' (1977: p. 84). There is a nice circle of ideas here in which beauty
= strength = death = morality = beauty.

Death is seen to be one of the purest acts man can carry out. And the
emphasis here is on manliness. In many respects, it is the relationship
between man and man, rather than between man and woman, which is the
focus of much of Japanese literature and popular culture. In such epic tales as
the story of the *Forty Seven Rōnin*, who avenged the death of their feudal lord
and then committed suicide, we find that emotional involvements with
women are ignored. As Nakane (1970: p. 71fn.) has pointed out, in the
feudal period men were so bent on devotion to their masters that they had
very little time left to consider women. Not only this, but this kind of
'samurai mentality' still permeates modern Japanese life.

In both the *jidaigeki* and *yakuza* films, we find a male-centred world in
which the only meaningful relationships are those among men (Mellen 1976:
p. 126). We find a kind of 'homosexual chivalry' based on death. Movie heroes
often 'perish together in a splendidly suicidal last stand against an impossible
majority of enemies. Often this orgasmic finale is the only time one sees them
looking happy' (Buruma 1984: p. 129). This, too, is the stock image of the

---

[6] As will be discussed below, in Japanese film and literature there is a close association
between masculinity, beauty and the exaltation of death, on the one hand, and femininity,
torture and sexuality, on the other. One question which has not been addressed in this
chapter, but which merits consideration, is whether in Japan, as well as elsewhere, there is not
'some half-suppressed desire to place the blame for all forms of violence on women' (Girard
1977: p. 36).

kamikaze pilot who smilingly plunges his plane in its steep dive to destruction.

This cult of death is closely connected with youth, for 'death is the only pure and thus fitting end to the perfection of youth' (1984: p. 131).[7] This may explain, perhaps, why the Japanese like to keep their trees from growing by clipping them into miniature shrubs (*bonsai*); or why they see the cherry blossoms as a fleeting moment of purity, prior to the growth of leaves; or why they have cultivated the concept of *bishōnen*, androgynous youths, who by the very fragility of their beauty remind us of impermanence and death; or why Mishima can write that the higher, spiritual emotion for a Japanese is love of one man for another.

In other words, death is here the prevention of ugliness, and in this respect it is almost the reverse of the kinds of dualities discussed by Needham (1973). Certainly, in Japan, none of the concepts of death, sex or violence discussed here can be dealt with in terms of neat oppositional categories. Death is, for Mishima, 'an image . . . beyond which there exists a spring of pure water, from which tiny streams are continuously pouring their pure waters into this world' (Mishima 1977: p. 100). Here one cannot help comparing the *jidaigeki* or *yakuza* films with such rituals as the Spanish bullfight (cf. Marvin in this book), where the death of the bull at the hand of the *matador* functions as a kind of purification.[8] In many films, the death of the samurai or gangster hero is just as inevitable and serves much the same purpose (cf. Buruma 1984: p. 171).

This notion of purity comes up once more in pornography and 'eroduction' films where torture is seen by some Japanese critics as a kind of 'purification ceremony'. Usually the victims in these films are women and, according to Shinto and Buddhist beliefs, women are basically impure because of the association of menstrual blood with pollution. Their sexuality, however, can be purified through rape and, in the eroduction films, we find that victims are such innocent symbols as uniformed schoolgirls, nurses, or newly married housewives, who almost invariably become attracted to their rapists — and by

---

[7] My colleague, David Parkin, who was kind enough to read through and comment on an earlier draft of this chapter, has drawn my attention to the fact that there is a parallel between the cult of death and youth in Japan and the killing of the divine king before his powers wane in certain African kingdoms.

[8] Clearly, the comparison could be taken much further. The linking of violence with sex, death and beauty is immediately reminiscent of the work of authors like García Lorca and Hemingway, as well as such writers as Sade, Genet and Camus. The 'aestheticization' of violence would appear to be a characteristic particularly common in both French and Japanese modern literature.

this attraction reveal their inherent impurity (1984: p. 59).[9] At the same time, when intercourse takes place in most of these films, the man remains more or less fully clothed, while making use of such penis substitutes as whips, candles, pistols and shoe horns. To some extent this probably reveals a Japanese male anxiety of masculine inadequacy, and it is interesting to note that women in films — and in art in general — are frequently depicted as mother figures who end up comforting their aggressors once the latter confess their fear of sexual impotence. Women are seen to be the physical, and men the spiritual sufferers (1984: p. 61).

This might seem like an inconsistency, but the relationship here between men and women is, I would argue, logical. On the one hand, it seems as though rape defines women as 'bad', as having some innate sexual desire which is aroused by their being ravished. And yet, on the other, we find that women comfort their lovers, and become the good wives and mothers (*ryōsai kenbo*) that Japanese society expects of them. We thus end up with a nice structuralist formula along the lines of:

$$\text{male sexual excess} : \text{male sexual privation}$$
$$::$$
$$\text{female impurity} : \text{female purity}$$
$$\text{(as whore)} \quad \text{(as mother)}$$

This can be seen more clearly, perhaps, in the following diagram:

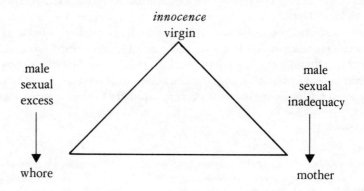

One point to be made about sex in general in Japan is that, from early times, it was the 'play' (*asobi*) involved in courtship or visits to brothels which was seen to be exciting, rather than the act of intercourse itself. Thus we find aristocratic men of the Heian court peering through fences, trying to catch a brief glimpse of their loved ones, or exchanging melancholy poems with women whom they had perhaps seen but briefly in the shadows of a tree-lined garden. Much later on, in the Edo Period, men went to the 'floating world' (*ukiyo*) of Yoshiwara, the pleasure quarters of Tokyo (old Edo), and there dallied with courtesans who would entertain them with singing, dancing and any number of childlike games. Thus, 'human passion and its physical expression were not controlled by an abstract moral code, whether of chivalry or sin, but by aesthetics, by decorum for its own sake. Love was a kind of art for art's sake, an exquisite piece of theatre' (Buruma 1984: p. 78). In Japan, love and death, sex and violence, end up as works of art. Indeed, in the case of gangsters, their bodies *are* works of art, for they sport 'tattoos, painfully carved on their skins from the neck to the knees — sometimes even to the ankles. One can imagine their capacity, indeed their gluttony, for pain' (p. 184). It is hardly surprising in this context to find that the craft of making swords has also been regarded as little short of a fine art in Japan. Aesthetics ends up not simply as the ritual purifier, but as a delineator of the means by which such purification will take place.

NIHILISM? OR THE CONQUERING OF TIME AND SPACE?

If it is more on aesthetic, than purely ethical, grounds that the heroes of the *jidaigeki* and *yakuza* films are to be judged, we must also take account of the fact that they are engaged in trying to resolve a conflict of ideals brought on by Japan's modernization over the past century. Traditionally, Japanese society has been organized according to a set of beliefs which emphasizes the subordination of individual interests to those of the group to which she or he belongs, and which stresses that action should be according to the ethical code of *giri* and *ninjō*, socially contracted dependence and human spontaneity. With modernization and Western influence, however, this set of beliefs has come to be questioned, even though out-and-out individuality is still seen as a social threat (Moeran 1984a).

It is not surprising to find that one form taken by individualism in films is that of nihilism, where all traditional beliefs are rejected and a doctrine of the purely negative is espoused. Richie (1982: p. 188) remarks that:

Perhaps because Japanese society is so oppressive, liberation can take the extreme form of total nihilism. Nihilism as a course of action certainly began after the repressive Tokugawa government attained control. Collective big business in Japan still retains many features of that feudal period, and perhaps as a consequence the attractions of nihilism remain. Even in a picture such as *Samurai Rebellion* . . . the sheer joy of negation (killing people, destroying houses) can be seen as at least a part of the motivation for the action.

Again:

In films such as *The Pornographers* . . . the director (Imamura Shōhei) is really celebrating a completely amoral, vital, and overflowing rejection of Japanese collective beliefs. (p. 188)

While the first nihilistic heroes of the cinema emerged in *jidaigeki* as early as 1927 (Anderson and Richie 1959: p. 137), Richie argues that the new post-war nihilism was brought on by the fact that by the 1960s Japan had become an affluent and leisure-oriented society which ignored the traditional values based on a Confucian work ethic (Richie 1982: p. 190). Both the *jidaigeki* and the *yakuza* films which continued — on the surface at least — to portray in modern form the 'soul of the warrior', made use of the past as a means of coming to terms with the present. In this respect, many directors set their films in the past — not to praise or exalt a set of feudal values, but 'rather to uncover a route of escape from the rigid, restrictive, if compelling, definition of what it means to be a Japanese — a code which has been damaging to the individual and demeaning to the national dignity' (Mellen 1976: p. 59). To some extent, then, they share with Mishima 'the idea that a return to the traditions of old Japan, when it was a primitive island insulated from the rest of the world, would allow a revitalization of the culture' (1976: p. 10).[10]

What is of interest here is that in Japan every new 'religious' creed appears to have brought in its wake a spate of pornography and/or violence. The tenth century *wara-e* drawings of monks and abbots indulging in various kinds of sexual activities were produced soon after the rise to power of Buddhism. The next major stage in pornography production was during the Edo Period when neo-Confucianism was adopted and imposed by the ruling shogunate. Now it

---

[10] Here again, there is ambivalence, in that nihilism offers the individual an almost frightening liberation, while she or he is at the same time oppressed by feudal values. It is, therefore, difficult to talk of death and violence in terms of clear-cut oppositions which tend to offer the mind an easy theoretical escape from what is in fact a complicated existential 'reality'.

is Westernization and an essentially Christian morality to which Japan has to some extent succumbed as it pursues its quest for perfection in the system of industrial capitalism.[11] This point ties up with Girard's argument that it is religion which keeps man's violence within bounds — religion being defined as 'that obscurity that surrounds man's efforts to defend himself by curative or preventative means against his own violence' (1977: p. 23).[12]

The sense of nihilism that arises from the clash of two differing systems of thought is also connected with the long-felt Japanese sense of transience, or impermanence (*mujō*). We have already seen this underlying the idea of purity of youth, and in Mishima's notion (a notion shared by a long line of Japanese writers from Lady Murasaki onwards) that the world is but a fleeting dream. In aesthetic terms, this transience has been alluded to as *mono no aware*, or the pathos of things, whereby beauty is linked with sadness at the natural evanescence of our lives and of the world in general.

Above all, the idea of impermanence suggests the fragility of time and it is time, I would suggest, which lies at the heart of this strange quartet of violence, sex, death and beauty. Again, it is Mishima who makes the point:

> Time changes human beings, makes them inconsistent and opportunistic, makes them degenerate or, in a very few cases, improve. However, if one assumes that humanity is always facing death, and that there is no truth except from moment to moment, then the process of time does not merit the respect we accord it. (1977: p. 43)

It seems to me that everything about the *jidaigeki* and *yakuza* films is an attempt to stop time. On the surface, this is obvious. *Jidaigeki* are period dramas whose plots take place entirely in (pre)feudal Japan. The present is

---

[11] The way in which women fall in love with their rapists in modern pornographic films, mentioned earlier, could in some respects be seen as a metaphor for Japan itself, as — over the centuries — it has adulatingly adopted each new wave of culture from, first, the Asian continent and now, the West.

[12] Girard (1977: p. 115) has argued further that there are both 'good' and 'bad' forms of violence, and that violence is 'good' when it is sacrificial. At the same time, he suggests (p. 93) that a destructive cycle of violence can only come to an end when it is directed against a surrogate victim. While Girard's argument centres on, and is illustrated by, classical mythology, I think it is possible to argue that — in the case of Japanese society — the 'surrogate victim' is in fact Westernization. Violence in Japan is, therefore, directed towards maintaining Japanese values. In this respect, it does not operate 'without reason' (p. 46) so much as *against* reason, for these values are ultimately concerned to go beyond the comprehensibility of logic and the mind (as we shall see below). 'Good' violence is sacrificial because it brings about selflessness, and selflessness is harmonious in that it maintains group ideals.

116   *Brian Moeran*

thus collapsed into the past. At the same time we should note that, in both the martial and aesthetic arts, it is the principle of selflessness which is extolled.

Here the influence of Zen Buddhism is, of course, very strong. The practitioner of an art is invited to be at one with the object she or he produces. In Japanese folk craft (*mingei*), to take but one example, it is by identifying with the object through direct perception (*chokkan*) that one is supposed to appreciate beauty (cf. Moeran 1984b). Similarly, in swordsmanship, the samurai seeks to lose all consciousness of his self, to be 'without heart' (*mushin*), to be at one with his surroundings. The famous Edo Period swordsman and painter, Miyamoto Musashi, has written about this in his *Book of Five Rings*:

The Book of the Void. By void I mean that which has no beginning and no end. Attaining this principle means not attaining the principle. The Way of strategy is the Way of Nature. When you appreciate the power of nature, knowing the rhythm of any situation, you will be able to hit the enemy naturally and strike naturally. All this is the Way of the Void. (Miyamoto 1974: p. 44)

This notion of selflessness demands that man go beyond his thinking self and intuitively grasp a spiritual nothingness which is beyond dualities of good and bad, right and wrong, beauty and ugliness. In this respect, it can be said to be anti-language. Yet language does in many respects make us aware of time (cf. Bloch 1977: p. 283). In Japan — and doubtless in many other societies, too — the appreciation of beauty, the sexual climax and the attainment of selflessness when face to face with death, are all moments when language is driven from man's mind and time is conquered. It is only at such moments perhaps that the Japanese can overcome the irrevocable march of history, only then that they can solve the inherent conflict between individual desires and group constraints. And, at the same time, the conquering of time becomes the conquering of space between self and other. In short, violence is a kind of 'communitas'.

REFERENCES

Anderson, J. and Richie, D. 1959: *The Japanese Film: art and industry*. Tokyo: Tuttle.
Bataille, G. 1965: *L'Erotisme*. Paris: Minuit.
Bloch, M. 1977: The past and the present in the present. *Man (N.S.)*, 12, 278—92.
Buruma, J. 1984: *Behind the Mask: on sexual demons, sacred mothers, transvestites, gangsters and other Japanese heroes*. New York: Pantheon.
Girard, R. 1977: *Violence and the Sacred*. Baltimore: Johns Hopkins Press.
Mellen, J. 1976: *The Waves at Genji's Door*. New York: Pantheon.

Mishima, Y. 1977: *The Way of the Samurai*. New York: Pedigree.

Moeran, B. 1984a: Individual, group and *seishin* — Japan's internal cultural debate. *Man (NS)*, 19, 252—66.

———— 1984b: *Lost Innocence: folk craft potters of Onta, Japan*. Berkeley and Los Angeles: University of California Press.

———— 1985: Confucian confusion: the good, the bad and the noodle western. In D. Parkin (ed.), *The Anthropology of Evil*, Oxford: Basil Blackwell.

Nakane, C. 1970: *Japanese Society*. Berkeley and Los Angeles: University of California Press.

Needham, R. (ed.) 1973: *Right and Left: essays on dual symbolic classification*. Chicago and London: University of Chicago Press.

Richie, D. 1982: *The Japanese Movie*. Tokyo: Kodansha International.

Scott-Stokes, H. 1974: *The Life and Death of Yukio Mishima*. New York: Farrar Straus and Giroux.

Tucker, R. 1973: *Japan: film image*. London: Studio Vista.

7

Honour, Integrity and the Problem of Violence in the Spanish Bullfight

Garry Marvin

> From long habit they either see not, or are not offended by those painful
> and bloody details, which most distress the unaccustomed stranger,
> while, on the other hand, they perceive a thousand novelties in incidents
> which, to untutored eyes, appear the same thing over and over again. . . .
> A thousand delicate shades are appreciated in the character and conduct
> of the combatants, biped and quadruped.
>
> Richard Ford 1855: p. 99

THE BULLFIGHT AND 'VIOLENCE'

In many societies, violence and violent events fascinate; they both attract and
repel, and they tend to produce powerful emotional responses in those who
witness them. This seems especially true where the events are public spectacles
in which human beings or other creatures can be injured or killed. In this
chapter, I shall examine the communicative and expressive dimensions of the
apparently violent acts which constitute an essential part of the complex
ritual drama of the bullfight — a spectacle in which human performers
perpetrate the death of an animal, and themselves stand to be the victim of

I should like to thank Bob Davis, Henk Driessen, Margaret Kenna, Brian Moeran and David
Riches, for I profited greatly from their comments, criticisms and suggestions for re-
writing. In particular, I thank Richard Fardon, who painstakingly read through and
commented on an earlier draft of this chapter.

that animal's attack.[1] The bullfight is an event in which the emotional responses generated are very great — and conveyed in it is an important sense of what it means to be human in the ambience of Spanish society and culture. When a professional commentator states that, 'In the bullfight the Spaniard has found the most perfect form for defining his human quality' (Campos de España 1969: p. 137), he comes close to grasping its fundamental significance. But of equal importance in the event is the confrontation of death itself, a point that is remarked by Federico García Lorca, the Andalusian poet and dramatist, who reflects that, 'Spain is the only nation where death is the national spectacle' (1980: p. 1108).

The centrality of the bullfight in Spanish culture is suggested in the very name by which it is known: *La Fiesta Nacional*[2] ('The National Feast', i.e. the national celebration). Since the mid-eighteenth century, when it began to assume its present form, the bullfight has been regarded, by both Spaniards and foreigners, as quintessentially Spanish. The event's significance is emphasized not only in the fact that it is seen as appropriate for marking important religious and secular occasions, but also by the way in which its

---

[1] Throughout Spain there are a variety of events which feature the confrontation of humans and bulls, and it should be emphasized that I shall be concerned here only with the formal, professional bullfight — the *corrida de toros*. The structure of, and the processes within this event are the same throughout Spain. However, there are important differences in people's level of interest in the bullfight, and in their responses to the event, in different regions of Spain. For example, in Galacia, Asturias, Catalonia and the Basque country, there is less enthusiasm for the bullfight than in Castile or Andalusia. There is also an enormous difference in the response to styles of performance as between an audience in Seville and one in Bilbao. It is therefore important to stress that my work on the bullfight is based on fieldwork — of two years' duration — in and around Seville, in Andalusia (the region of southern Spain). Andalusia has a very distinctive culture, and I would not wish to argue that all aspects of my interpretation of the relationship between the bullfight and Andalusian culture apply equally to other regions.

[2] Although the term, *Fiesta Nacional*, would be understood by all Spaniards to refer to the bullfight, and many newspapers head their bullfight section with this term, it is again necessary to emphasize that the event is more popular in some regions than in others. An intriguing question concerns the process by which the formal professional bullfight, with its rigid separation of audience and performers — which was an important celebratory form in many parts of Spain — was raised to the status of *Fiesta Nacional*. In part, this probably involved the event being 'exported' to some regions as a standardized spectacle. That said, it is important to emphasize that the bullfight is pan-Spanish (certainly, no other event is so labelled), and is not simply an aspect of regional culture, as certain dance and song forms are. The way in which the bullfight has been manipulated by various political movements, as a symbolic device to emphasize 'Spanishness' is not something which can be dealt with here.

120   *Garry Marvin*

central figures have become folk heroes, lauded in the work of creative artists, and in which its imagery and symbolism have permeated Spanish language[3] and thought.

For an outsider, the most obvious fact about the bullfight is that men deliberately weaken, wound and kill a large animal before an approving audience. Much of the action is undoubtedly disturbing to the non-Spaniard; indeed for many people, the immediacy of being a witness to physical harm, to an intentional spilling of blood, and to a killing (i.e. destruction), identifies the bullfight as a 'violent' event. However, these features are not the focus for performers or audience. Indeed, the Spanish term *violencia*, although an apparent cognate of the English 'violence', seems to be inappropriate for referring to the various acts of which a performance consists.[4] *Aficionados* (fans) who were asked if the bullfight involved violence would inevitably respond in terms of whether it included acts of cruelty, in spite of the fact that my questions never mentioned *crueldad* (cruelty). This reflects Spanish perceptions of the way foreigners link violence, cruelty and unacceptable behaviour in the context of the bullfight. It is certainly significant that when discussing the bullfight amongst themselves, or writing press reports about it, Spaniards do not independently invoke the word, violence.

The anthropologist's concern is, of course, not to dwell on the ethical matters relating to events which some people find disturbing. It is, rather, to *understand* — in this case, a culturally-acclaimed ritual in which a man risks injury and death, attempting to control and kill a wild bull in a public arena; it is to grasp how such an event can come to be so central to the celebration of

---

[3] See Cossío (1978: pp. 235—42) for a list of bullfight terms and expressions which have entered daily Spanish usage.

[4] The term *violencia* is less frequently used in Spanish than is the term 'violence' in English. Although it is possible, in Spanish, to speak of events or actions as being *violento*, this is not common; in my experience the term is more often used to refer to the emotional state of a person. Indeed, the primary definition of *violento* given by the dictionary of the Royal Academy is of something 'out of its natural state, condition or form'. María Moliner, in her *Diccionario del uso Español*, writes that *violencia* may be used of something which happens, or is done, with roughness or abruptness, and with extraordinary force or intensity. But she, too, emphasizes that it is more often employed to describe either the condition of a person not in a normal state of mind, or actions performed by a person contrary to their natural disposition. In the context of describing an emotional state, the English terms 'intensity', 'rage' and 'fury' could also be used to translate *violento* or *violencia*. Definitions which emphasize both force and unnaturalness, and which perhaps give a feeling of the unacceptable, offer a reasonably accurate sense of how, in my experience, Spaniards use the term. Since there is no concept of the matador (bullfighter) acting as a result of an unnatural or disturbed mental state, the terms are unlikely to be used to describe his actions.

various important occasions. However, during the search for the indigenous meanings, I do not believe the anthropologist can escape important analytical issues about the concept of violence itself.

As is evident in the discussions in this book, the term 'violence' has a problematic status. How are acts of violence to be identified? What are the moral implications when the researcher labels specific acts as violent? By what right may anthropologists address by means of 'their' sense of violence, activities which the participants do not label or see as such? In everyday Anglo-Saxon usage, 'violence' carried negative moral connotations (identifying the behaviour concerned as unpleasant, unacceptable, illegal and disturbing), and it is therefore vital that the dangers of ethnocentrically using the term be recognized. Certainly, the difficulty — even the impossibility — of producing a single definition of violence which might hold good for all cultures may be accepted (as David Parkin points out in this book, violence is not a nomothetic category). Yet, for all this, I do not think it possible to abandon our own sense of the term altogether.

The salience of the term 'violence' relates to the problem of initially identifying a class of social actions for anthropological analysis. In my view, Anglo-Saxon anthropologists will inevitably be guided by Anglo-Saxon usage here. In my everyday world, human actions which involve the deliberate infliction of harm on others are normally seen as 'violent'. As an anthropologist, the enquiries I first make of the (violent) practices of another society will be framed by the classifications implied by my concept: the fact that people in that society seem to be performing actions which come under the purview of this concept will have drawn my attention to them in the first place. This said, my professional responsibility is then to interpret the actions in a way which transcends my own categories and moral concern, and beyond this, to relate them analytically to certain broader cultural values to which the members of this society subscribe. To give an example, an Englishman hitting his wife and a Yanomamö Indian husband hitting his, will, to most people, be similar events — examples of interpersonal violence. And in terms of the physical actions and results, this perception is probably justified. However, for the anthropologist the pertinence of such an identification is as a starting point for analysis. Research into Yanomamö society will eventually reveal that, for Yanomamö husbands and wives, wife-beating has a quite distinct meaning which crucially often does not have perjorative connotations (cf. Heelas 1982. p. 52, for the ethnography of the Yanomamö Indians of the Brazilian-Venezuelan border, see Chagnon, 1968). There are evidently parallels in this respect as between Yanomamö wife-beating and the Spanish bullfight.

To consider the bullfight as incorporating acts of violence, then, is not to prejudice the analysis. It is rather a prerequisite for opening it up for investigation; it is a means to prepare questions designed to understand why people engage in it, why it takes the form that it does, and what meaning it has for the actors. The use of the term 'violence' in what follows reflects the concept's importance in this regard.

VIOLENCE AND ORDER

To understand the meaning of the bullfight, the relationship between man and bull which evolves during the course of a performance must be examined. This relationship centrally involves the infliction of physical harm on the animal and the risk of severe injury to the man. A key to the examination may be found not least in the responses of those attracted to watching the performance. Certainly, the actions which constitute a bullfight are regarded by both performers and audience as necessary, acceptable and appropriate to the event. An initial framework for the enquiry is offered through discussion of an important theoretical issue relating to the study of violence in human society. This issue concerns the connection between violence and aggression.

The terms 'violence' and 'aggression' are often used interchangeably, without much thought being given to the relationship assumed between them. 'Violence' is sometimes used to refer to an emotional state, though more usually to describe behaviour itself. Where it is the latter, such behaviour is commonly attributed, at least in part, to the 'aggressive' mental state of the perpetrator of the acts concerned. Thus the understanding of violence becomes dependent on an explanation of the causes and results of the psychological status of individuals and their idiosyncratic motivations. I find this position problematic in general, and certainly I could not discern anything in the bullfighters I knew and watched every day, which would suggest that they were in an aggressive frame of mind. There is no indication that they regarded the bull which they had to kill with any more hostility than do slaughtermen (I knew many of them as well) who kill dozens of animals daily: there was no sense in which bullfighters were venting anger during the course of a performance. Left unexamined in psychological reductionist explanations is the specific nature of the violent act itself. Thus, with the bullfight, such explanations fail to deal with the cultural specificity of the event. They fail to account for the stereotyped nature of the violence, the fact that it occurs only on certain occasions and that there are special rules, canons of aesthetics and norms of expected behaviour which structure it. It is certainly difficult to imagine how such a complex cultural phenomenon could have developed from, and been sustained by, the aggressive 'condition' of the performers.

In the bullfight, then, what is emphatically not seen is an outburst of aggressive behaviour, anger or hostility on the part of the performer, which has as its aim the destruction of the bull by any means possible. Events or acts labelled as violent are often treated as being disorderly, or disruptive of the social fabric, but this is certainly not so in this context. It is clear that violent acts *can* be orderly; they may occur in set, regular and acceptable ways in controlled circumstances, and moreover there may be culturally or socially specific responses to them. To give an example: a boxing match and a street brawl both involve people hitting one another with fists, but the events are essentially different in terms of their respective modes of organization, and in terms of the responses of witnesses. And just as in the boxing match there are particularly strict rules governing the process of the event, so in the bullfight the matador and his assistants may not destroy the bull in any manner they choose. In both events, the rules are in fact designed to supervise order; they define and limit the nature of the contest. For the conduct of the bullfight, there is indeed a most elaborate protocol. And from the audience in the arena, comments of censure are certainly forthcoming when there is any deviation from what it stipulates.[5] Punishment from the bullfight authorities may also be expected if the offence is of sufficient seriousness. In short, as the drama of destruction unfolds, control by man on bull is gradually imposed, and in violence, order is expressed (Marvin 1982: pp. 319ff., pp. 349ff.).

THE BULLFIGHT AS RITUAL

The violence in the bullfight is instrumental in the sense that the weakening of the bull through the use of various lances, sharpened darts and capework makes it possible for the man to kill it. It is also instrumental in that thrusting a sword into the animal does kill it. And indeed each bullfight produces six

[5] All bullfights are governed by the *Reglamento de Espectaculos Taurinos* (latest edition 1962), a document of 138 legally enforceable articles produced by the Spanish government. These articles regulate all aspects of the event, except the actual style of performance in the arena. The 'unwritten rules' are those general ideas relating to style, aesthetics, and as to what constitutes a proper performance, which are held by members of the audience and the performers. Of course, not all people judge styles or evaluate performances in the same way, and there will be differences of opinion as to the status of these 'rules'.

dead bulls ready for the butcher. But to see the event simply as a slaughtering process hardly leads one to understand it. The bullfight is essentially a ritual event, and as with most rituals there is no simple relationship between means and ends. The bull will be eaten and therefore must be killed, but a wild fighting bull is difficult to kill with a sword: in terms of efficiency it would be far easier to lean over the fence and shoot it — but the event would then be a very different one. In fact, what is important in the bullfight is the *manner* in which the killing is carried out; it is the 'process' of the killing which gains the matador prestige. An emphasis on process is, of course, at the basis of many types of contest in human social life. In a duel, for example, although each of the contestants aims to kill their opponent and thus triumph, if one of them pulls a pistol when the agreed weapons are swords, the outcome can constitute neither a victory nor a defeat. To kill while following the rules of the contest is acceptable; to kill in any other way would be dishonourable, unacceptable and akin to murder. To look at 'violent' actions in purely utilitarian terms is to miss their most significant aspect — their communicative and expressive function. In the rest of this chapter I consider exactly what is being communicated and expressed in the bullfight. My analysis draws on material collected in Andalusia, Spain's southernmost region.

John Corbin (in this book) shows that in Andalusian culture there is a fundamental concern with what it means to be civilized (i.e. fully human); Andalusians are careful to behave in ways which will demonstrate this quality (see also J. Corbin and M. Corbin, forthcoming). Corbin's interpretation is closely aligned with the general appreciation of 'civilization' given by Norbert Elias, which refers to the 'social quality' of people, and which implies a process in which people are actively involved:

Every particular characteristic that we attribute to it [civilization] . . . bears witness to a particular structure of human relations, to a particular social structure, and to the corresponding forms of behaviour. (Elias 1978: p. 59)

I have used this approach elsewhere (Marvin 1982) and argued that, in terms of Andalusian culture, the bullfight is highly 'civilized', for it embodies values which are central to the ethos of this culture. It is impossible to deal with all relevant values in the context of a single chapter. So I simply wish to suggest here that the bullfight, consisting of a highly structured contest between two *males* acted out under the critical gaze of the public, makes sense when interpreted as a transposition into dramatic ritual form of key values associated with the way in which men in Andalusian communities are expected to behave, and regulate their relations, one with another. Specifically, I maintain that the event may be understood only in terms of a culture in which men are expected to be rigorously competitive in defence of their masculine self-image. In Andalusia, this competitiveness is discharged through the idiom of honour and reputation.

HONOUR AND THE MEANING OF THE BULLFIGHT

Anton Blok argues that the full analysis of codes of honour in the Mediterranean countries must be set in a context of the structures of social control and political power, and the levels of state formation in the region (Blok 1981). He suggests that ideologies of honour develop in conditions where effective state control is at a low level — where people who need protection have to resort to self-help because they cannot rely on the agencies or agents of the state. One of the key elements in the Mediterranean codes of honour is self-reliance: an individual against whom an affront is directed must deal with it directly using his own resources. When damage is done to a person's honour he cannot redeem it by seeking redress through the institutions of the state. To do this would be to appeal to an alien system and, in any case, does nothing to remove the stain on his social character — nor does it allow the person to repair his standing vis-à-vis the person who insulted him. What is at stake in the competitive relations between men in such a system is 'reputation' — which is something that is accorded to an individual *by others*. The individual must act in such a way that others judge him to have behaved correctly. Bourdieu captures the essence of such ideas when he summarizes the preoccupation with honour, thus:

The point of honour is the ethic appropriate to an individual who always sees himself through the eyes of others, who has need of others in order to exist, because his self-image is inseparable from the image of himself that he receives back from others. Respectability . . . is essentially defined by its social dimension, and so must be won and defended in the face of everyone. (1979: p. 113)

Anthropologists working in Mediterranean countries have pointed out that the concept of honour is often represented in terms of the physical person (see especially Pitt-Rivers 1965: pp. 25—9), and that there is an emphasis on demonstrating the physical integrity and strength of the male. This is important, for as Pitt-Rivers points out, 'The ultimate vindication of honour lies in physical violence' (1965: p. 29). In the extreme case, the final proof of superiority is that the individual is able to take the life of another. However, this *is* the extreme case, since most threats and challenges to honour and reputation may be dealt with in less drastic ways. In comparison with other areas of the Mediterranean,[6] in Andalusia, the idea of showing willingness to resort to physical violence is subject to rather less elaboration. (This, I think, is representative of Spain in general.) Nonetheless, the potential for violence remains, and it follows that what a man needs in others is that they take account of his readiness to respond with force to a serious challenge. They must know that he simply will not back down and lose face.

The bullfight can be understood in terms of such values. The action in the arena reflects the ideal behaviour of men when great difficulty faces them. Situations where they are forced to confront other men in a public place epitomize this difficulty. The matador has traditionally been regarded as the epitome of masculinity — as having in abundance those qualities most admired of men in this society. In the bullfight, although the confrontation is between man and animal, rather than man and man, the bull effectively constitutes a challenge from a difficult, dangerous and powerful male. If the matador is able to meet the challenge successfully, he gains prestige and status, and vindicates his claim to be a true man. Failure brings insult, ridicule and a loss of reputation.

What is clear, then, is that the bull in the arena occupies a structurally similar position to that of a man who poses a threat to the reputation of another. As Bourdieu points out (1979: p. 105), a notable aspect of challenge and response in terms of honour is that a man need — indeed ought — only respond to the challenge of an equal. It is therefore important to emphasize that in the bullfight the animal against which the man must pit himself is regarded as a worthy opponent and thus constitutes an acceptable challenge. The Andalusian's image of the character of the Spanish fighting bull is highly developed and the animal's qualities much admired. The bull is an imposing and threatening figure in the arena — a large, aggressive, wilful and dangerous male which is extremely difficult to control. To confront the challenge posed by this creature, to control it, dominate it and finally kill it is a triumph indeed.

Whilst the reputation of an ordinary man is continually under scrutiny in the give and take of daily life, the bullfight is distinctive, for it is a test of masculinity which is artificial and elaborately constructed, and which engages 'special men'. But it follows that the bullfight amounts to *the* occasion for a man to display masculinity and to offer proof of himself in public. Although the matador is judged as a performer, this is inextricably linked with his personal qualities as a man. He is not an actor in the sense of a theatrical actor

---

[6] See, for example, Blok (1974), Black-Michaud (1975), Campbell (1974) and Hertzfeld (1980).

playing a part; he does not have to conceal himself. He *is* a matador — and, as such, plays himself. All men should be willing to defend their honour, but the matador is prepared to go beyond the normal and test himself in extreme circumstances. He puts himself into a position of extraordinary precariousness where, should he fail to live up to expectation and is nervous or cowardly in front of the bull, he risks insult and ridicule, and thus loss of honour and a sullied reputation. And if he is unable to master the situation he also plainly risks injury or death. To become a matador is a voluntary decision, and to choose to be in the arena is also voluntary; once there, the matador cannot, without losing face, back down from the challenge.

In Andalusian codes, the ability to destroy a human opponent physically constitutes a supreme victory; yet people rarely resort to such measures. Indeed, the *act* of fighting is strongly devalued in this culture (I elaborate on this shortly). However, as Driessen shows (1983: p. 129), men certainly communicate their *potential* for violence, and thereby display their capacity and willingness to resist encroachments by other men. This invites a closer examination of the bullfight where, contrastingly, physical violence is *overtly* the key element in the relationship between matador and bull. It importantly transpires that there is absolutely no notion that matadors ought to be aggressive and physically strong men. There is no admiration of them as athletes and no corresponding sense of a cult of the body associated with them;[7] they simply do not have to be highly trained or muscularly developed. A reputation as men of violence, such as Blok reports of the Mafia (esp. 1974: p. 181) and Hobsbawm of European bandits (1969: p. 28), is not something which is associated with matadors. And what is highly significant in terms of the relationship of violence between the man and the bull is that the matador does not have to attack an 'other'. The matador is not the instigator; he merely responds to that other's attack. The aim indeed is not even to put an end to the attack — for the matador has encouraged it. Instead, it is to withstand the attack. As the matador perpetrates acts of violence on the animal, there is therefore no sense that he is defending himself. And when he finally kills his opponent, this is seen as neither attack nor defence. Rather, what *is* important is that the matador confront, withstand and direct the physical force of his opponent.

---

[7] Although there is no cult of the body or of athleticism in respect of the bullfight (in fact, some commentators even see too much physical training as potentially damaging to the spirit of the event), there is often a humorous contrast drawn between the usually lithe, graceful body of the matador and the somewhat more rotund figures of the *picadors* (mounted assistants), and the occasionally overweight older *banderillos* (foot assistants), who look somewhat foolish in their tight costumes.

In a good performance, then, there is a contrast between the composure of the man and the ferocity of the animal. The animal, and not the man, is the aggressor. The man uses a cape to protect himself, but only so that the charging bull is directed as closely as possible to his body, so that a demonstration is given of nerve, courage, skill and control. By facing the charging bull calmly, by bringing it to him and then making it go where he chooses, the matador, refusing to succumb to the threat of violence which the animal poses, demonstrates his mastery of the situation. The appropriate state for a true man is thus dramatized.

In Andalusian culture, competitive masculinity, in which one man seeks to impose his will on another, is typically expressed in terms of a sexual imagery — the central feature of which is that male power emanates from the testicles. Those who are weak, unassertive or cowardly are said to lack *cojones* (testicles) and to be *manso* (a tame or domestic animal, which here connotes meekness and unassertiveness); the full masculinity of such men is denied. The association of assertiveness and wilfulness with the possession of testicles also applies to animals, and male animals of various kinds are castrated (in itself, an act of violence) as part of the domestication process, which makes them docile and manageable. It is significant that the fighting bull is not castrated and is therefore, in the terms of the imagery, fully male. This, combined with its strength, power and size, contributes to its worth as an opponent. The matador's gradual domination (and ultimate destruction) of the bull, in which he bends its will to his own, constitutes, both at the symbolic and behavioural level, an emasculation of it — just as in a conflict between men.

The wider social connotations of the competitive masculinity of everyday life are also captured in the bullfight. A first point in this regard is the socio-spatial context of the event. The bull is brought from the countryside, the world of nature, to an urban centre, a place of culture and the domain of civilized people, and it is then brought into confrontation with men in a specially constructed public arena. In Andalusian culture there is a strong differentiation between public and private space and, as in many cultures, there are expectations of appropriate behaviour for men and women with regard to this division (Corbin 1981). Public space is very much associated with men; it is the place for them to assert themselves. The bullfight is effectively an accentuation of this. The very name of the edifice in which it takes place, the *Plaza de Toros* (literally the 'Place of Bulls'), is significant here. In Spanish, *plaza* is a town square, and in villages and small towns the main *plaza* will be the focus of public social life (see Lopez Casero 1972). In the town square and the bull-ring, then, similar processes of evaluation take place. As in daily life in Andalusia, where people observe and comment on the behaviour and character of others and allow or deny them honour, status and prestige, so in the bullfight the audience responds in a similar way: as onlookers they provide a highly critical vocal commentary on the matador's masculinity and reputation.

A second point is that Andalusian gender roles mean that in daily life men are 'on stage' — they are *expected* to present themselves in public places, where they should interact with other men. On such a stage they are alternately actors and audience in a daily drama in which their masculine self-image, and the reputation it implies, is held up to public scrutiny. The bullfight may be understood as involving a transposition of the establishment and preservation of masculinity from the daily realm of human social intercourse onto something resembling a theatre stage where professional performers attempt to demonstrate these qualities in more arduous circumstances. To a certain extent, the matador is an Everyman figure, in that he has the qualities which each man ought to have. Ordinary men are therefore able to identify with him — yet he is also more than an ordinary man, so there is interest in seeing him do what ordinary men cannot. Yet at the same time, the bullfight is a special event which, for the audience (although not for the performers) is set apart from daily life. Competition between men in everyday life is potentially damaging to the delicate web of social relations, especially if physical violence is involved. However, in the bullfight, the audience is able to contemplate a spectacle of highly competitive maleness in a stylized and ritual form. The fact that one of the contestants is an animal allows for the incorporation of acts of violence which would be intolerable in a contest between men. However worthy an opponent, the bull is still only an animal and may be treated in ways in which it is impossible to treat a fellow human being.

THE AESTHETICS OF THE BULLFIGHT

The bullfight is an institutionalized conflict which involves certain necessary acts of violence in which an animal is caused harm and suffering. But neither performers nor audience attend to these acts and their effects as a source of interest and pleasure. In contrast to the material considered by Brian Moeran in this book there is no aesthetic of violence; it cannot be stressed enough that Andalusians do not enjoy witnessing an animal suffering. Indeed, in an important sense there is no concern at all with what happens to the animal. This is often interpreted as callousness by outside observers, for whom the inclination is to focus on the injury done to the bull. This they find shocking; they are unable to see beyond it. What underlies the misunderstanding is the fact of different cultural perceptions of the relationship between humans and animals. Where the relationship between humans and animals is perceived as close, one would expect people to be upset by the killing of an animal in a public spectacle. In Andalusian culture, however, human and animal realms are treated as entirely separate; there is little anthropomorphization of animals. Thus, although the fighting bull is much admired and respected, the sole reason for its existence is for it to be killed in the arena; there is no empathetic concern for its welfare. Even so, what Andalusians tolerate as acceptable forms of violence and ways of treating animals has changed greatly during the history of the bullfight. Present-day *aficionados* say that they find the idea of the use of swords and cutlasses to hamstring the animal, packs of dogs to attack it, and gunpowder charges implanted in its flesh — all of which occurred in earlier bullfights — disagreeable, unpleasant and unacceptable. Such a change in emotional response may be understood in terms of the 'civilizing process' (Elias; see above) in European societies, part of which involves alteration in the social standards of affect (which includes such feelings as shame, repulsion and perceptions of what constitutes cruelty).

For performers and audience, the aesthetics of the bullfight are perfectly in tune with the social values which the event ritually dramatizes. What is of primary concern is how the *matador* comports himself as he faces the bull. All notions of beauty, of appreciation of style, and indeed all aesthetic judgements, are based on the relationship between the man and bull, as mediated by the cape. The man must be brave and stand his ground in the face of the charging bull, but this is not enough. Simply to stand there, and do nothing, would be regarded as suicidal foolishness and would earn no praise from the audience. What is important is the way in which the man uses his body and cape to direct the charge of the bull. The matador should remain still, and should attempt to bring the bull close past his body in a smooth curve; the impression should be given that the speed of the animal is regulated by the movement — ideally, the slowest possible movement — of the cape, or of the *muleta* (the small red cloth used in the last part of the performance).

Aficionados look for a graceful, harmonious relationship between man, cape and bull, and for a balanced linking of one pass with another in such a way as to achieve a flowing performance (for more detailed discussion of styles of performance, see Bollain [1968] and Marvin [1982: pp. 352—6]). Hemingway's notion of 'grace under pressure' is extremely important for grasping the aesthetics of the bullfight. Thus, the beauty of the event is not simply that of visually pleasing movements — as, for example, may be seen when the matador is in training. Rather, it is the fact that these movements are intimately connected with the danger involved in bringing the bull under control. The great matador, Domingo Ortega, says in a short book on the art of bullfighting:

> ... it must not be forgotten that one is not dealing with a ballet in which the aim of the visual aesthetic is everything, but that bullfighting has a fixed end [i.e. the domination of the bull] ... to make passes is not the same as the art of bullfighting. (1950: p. 14)

In this way, the matador must work to control the unpredictable animal, and make it charge in the way he wants it to, and he must adapt his style and performance to take account of the difficulties and threat posed by each individual bull.

Since it is what the *man* does which is the critical aspect of the bullfight, excitement and appreciation do not come from witnessing the destruction of an animal. The killing is, of course, acceptable and necessary, but judgements about the nature of that killing are always made in the context of what constitutes a proper performance. Correctly performed, the killing of the bull is the most dangerous and risky part of the performance, for the matador must lean over the horns of the bull to place the sword between the shoulder blades. Judgements of the style of killing will be based not only on the efficacy of the sword thrust, but also on the commitment of the matador, as indicated by his closeness to the bull. The matador who makes a bad job of killing because he is concerned with his own safety will be condemned as an *asesino* (murderer), that is, as a socially unacceptable killer. The focus here is not on the animal — not on the fact that it is suffering a slow death. Rather, it is on the fact that the man has failed to behave in the correct manner and fulfil his obligations as a matador. Just as there are notions of honourable and dishonourable ways of treating opponents in inter-human contests, so there are with regard to this event.

That it is the matador's performance — and not the animal's death itself — which is the central spectacle, is evident in the perception of the sword, the means by which death is delivered. To kill a fighting bull with a sword is both difficult, and, if performed correctly, unquestionably dangerous. Yet the sword is significantly not thought of — as it would be in other contexts — as a weapon. Crucial in this regard is that the sword may not be used as a means of defence or attack: the matador may certainly not use it to weaken the bull prior to killing it. Although the sword is used to put an end to the contest, the skill involved in wielding it is regarded as more akin to that of the slaughterman than of the fencer.

Andalusian views on the physically destructive aspect of the bullfight may be further clarified by drawing a contrast with their perceptions of boxing.

Boxing — an institutionalized combat between men before an audience — is viewed with distaste by most of my informants. They cannot understand how men are willing to humiliate, or be humiliated by, another man in a physical struggle in public. Andalusian perceptions of what constitutes civilized behaviour may be recalled again. Being civilized involves emphasizing the cultural part of man, and controlling or being distanced from, the more animalistic side. The event of boxing is described through the words *pelear* and *luchar*, which may be directly translated as 'to fight'. Fighting is associated with an aggressive frame of mind, and such a resort to physicality and direct bodily contact is considered as bestializing. Consonant with this is the important point that the term 'bull*fight*' is strictly unsuitable for translating the Spanish name for the event in that it misrepresents the relationship between man and bull. In Spanish, the event is *la corrida de toros* ('the running of bulls'). For Spaniards, there is no sense of men fighting — as engaging in physical struggle — with the bull. Direct contact between the two is considered to be absent. Humans may be brought into close proximity with animals, but this is in order that they may ultimately establish superiority and distance over them. To be civilized is to establish a 'proper' relation between animal and man — between nature and culture.

For both sides in this event, injury and death feature strongly, and this has claimed the attention of many foreigners. But these aspects of the bullfight are not emphasized by Spaniards. Right up to the moment of performance, a matador may well be concerned about the risk of injury, but those with whom I spoke expressed more concern about how they would be treated by the crowd. If questioned, *aficionados* and performers will agree that the danger of death is always there, but this is no more than something that hovers in the background. The death or injury of a bullfighter is unpleasant and disturbing, and forms no part of what *aficionados* expect to see in the arena. It is true that there are cases where matadors who have been killed are glorified (most famously this occurs in Lorca's *Lament for Ignacio Sanchez Mejias*), but there is no sense that it is specifically the death on the horns of the bull which is celebrated. The matador should always triumph over the threat of death, and it is therefore not fitting that he be killed in the arena — that is the place for the bull to die. Matadors are, in fact, rarely killed, but they are often injured. And the wounds are regarded as evidence of mistakes; they indicate the price that has to be paid when the bull is allowed to get the better of the man.

There is, however, considerable interest in how both man and bull comport themselves both in the face of possible injury and pain, and in actual suffering. Judgements focus on how they respond to pain, and on whether they are able to overcome it in order to carry on acting in an appropriate manner so that the performance might continue. The matador is not expected to 'succumb to violence'; to do so is, in an important sense, an indication of being controlled by the bull — a reversal of the proper relation. However, having committed the mistake which allows the bull to control the relationship, the matador can still gain the admiration of the audience if, in his adversity, he exercises self-control, and demonstrates a willingness to stay in the arena. If he is not too badly injured, he will certainly be expected to overcome the pain and complete the performance before returning to the infirmary. Matadors who are badly injured sometimes have to be forced out of the arena by their assistants, to the audience's acclaim. The reaction to the severe goring and subsequent death of the great matador, Francisco Riverra 'Paquirri', in 1984, provides an unfortunate, but superbly enlightening example of the ideal behaviour of a matador when obviously suffering pain. The media, professional bullfighters, *aficionados* and members of the public were effusive in their praise for his bravery, self-control and calmness — a calmness which extended to offering quietly words of advice to the doctors who were treating him. People interviewed about the event more than six months later were still awestruck by his resilience in this extreme circumstance, and many were able to repeat verbatim his last words to the doctors and his assistants — words that indicated his exemplary fortitude and courage.

CONCLUSION

This paper began with a commonsense Anglo-Saxon definition of violence. This definition involved the notion of the deliberate infliction of physical harm, and the idea that the rendering of such harm is, in some significant sense, unacceptable. While the minimal Anglo-Saxon definition allows us to isolate a set of actions for analysis, the interpretation of the meaning of such actions for people who subscribe to different cultural values is highly problematic. I suggest that much of the difficulty of analysis turns on the nature of the *reaction* evoked by violent acts, both in those perpetrating them, and in those witnessing them. So far as direct interpersonal violence is concerned, the reaction seems to be mediated by perceptions of the 'other' who suffers the violence. The notion of 'suffer' is significant here. To follow a point introduced earlier, violent acts may well be found disturbing because of the empathy, or concern, felt for the pain or distress of the 'other'; the greater the degree to which the 'other' is close to the witness's sense of self, the greater is the concern. The conception of the 'other' and the associated ideas of appropriate treatment for that 'other' is therefore plainly critical. If the 'other' may be distanced, or can be categorized as something, or someone, to whom such concerns need not apply, or who is regarded as having no sense or feeling, then the degree to which perpetrator and witness are disturbed by the acts being witnessed will be reduced. At least to some extent, politicians, soldiers, executioners, jailers, torturers, assassins, surgeons, slaughtermen, football hooligans, hunters and anglers all engage in such 'distancing'. The salient point, however, is that anthropologists, too, are witnesses. The danger is that their own cultural perceptions and distancing procedures will colour their analysis.

Even though the term *violencia* is rarely used in Spanish, Spaniards plainly have a strong sense of the acceptable and unacceptable uses of physical force against others, and a central issue is clearly the status of the 'other' and the circumstances in which such actions occur. Thus acts which have traditionally been condemned as unacceptably inflicting harm are contraception, abortion, rape, suicide and murder, all of which in essential ways violate and threaten the Andalusian sense of self (Corbin 1981). Matters of human life and death should be left to the will of God. Animals are, in contrast, regarded as subject to human will. They are conceptually distanced from human beings, and the way they are treated is not governed by notions of *humane* conduct.

The Anglo-Saxon focus on the bullfight, as an event whose central feature comprises the infliction of physical harm and injury on an animal in a public spectacle, and as a source of amusement and excitement, is liable to distort the meaning it commands for the performer and for the Spanish audience. Part of the Anglo-Saxon experience of the 'civilizing process' has involved the closing of the distance between the animal and human worlds. This has included a change in attitude to the use of animals in public entertainments and sports, to the manner in which animals are kept in captivity for public viewing and to the conditions in which they are raised for food and in which they are slaughtered and consumed. The identification of human and animal has indeed become so close that certain groups now argue for 'animal rights' in terms similar to the advocacy of 'human rights'. With the change of perception which makes animals 'like us', it is hardly surprising that public spectacles or entertainment which involve deliberately inflicting injury on them are seen as violence. The central argument of this chapter is that activities which strike members of one society as violent (and which are judged accordingly) may be conceptualized and evaluated quite differently by members of another society. Lorca's enthusiasm for the bullfight as an art form and as a 'most civilized spectacle' (1980: p. 1105) will not easily be understood by the Anglo-Saxon observer, who will initially regard it with repugnance — as violent, cruel and barbaric. Even when told that, for Spaniards, the bullfight is 'the most perfect form for defining the human condition', his or her moral qualms may well remain. But they should be mitigated in the knowledge that there are different cultural definitions of being human, being male, and being civilized.

REFERENCES

Black-Michaud, J. 1975: *Cohesive Force: feud in the Mediterranean and Middle East.* Oxford: Basil Blackwell.

Blok, A. 1974: *The Mafia of a Sicilian Village, 1860—1960.* Oxford: Basil Blackwell.

—— 1981: Rams and billy-goats: A key to the Mediterranean code of honour. *Man,* 16, 427—40.

Bollain, L. 1968: *El Toreo.* Sevilla: Editorial Catolica Española.

Bourdieu, P. 1979: The sense of honour. In *Algeria 1960: essays by Pierre Bourdieu.* Cambridge: Cambridge University Press.

Campbell, J. K. 1964: *Honour, Family and Patronage: A study of institutions and values in a Greek mountain community.* Oxford: Clarendon Press.

Campos de España, R. 1969: España y los Toros. In Carlos Orellana (ed.), *Los Toros,* Madrid: Orel.

Chagnon, N. 1968: *Yanomamö: The fierce people.* New York: Holt, Rinehart and Winston.

Corbin, J. R. 1981: *Symbolic Deaths.* BBC Open University Arts Foundation Programme.

Corbin, J. R. and Corbin, M. P. (forthcoming): *Urbane Thought: class and culture in an Andalusian city.* Aldershot: Gower Press.

Cossío, J. M. 1978: *Los Toros,* 2, Madrid: Espasa-Calpe.

Driessen, H. 1983: Male sociability and rituals of masculinity in rural Andalusia. *Anthropological Quarterly,* 56, 125—33.

Elias, N. 1978: *The Civilizing Process.* Oxford: Basil Blackwell.

Ford, R. 1855: *A Handbook for Travellers in Spain.* London: John Murray.

Heelas, P. 1982: Anthropology, violence and catharsis. In P. Marsh and A. Campbell (eds), *Aggression and Violence,* Oxford: Basil Blackwell.

Hertzfeld, M. 1980: Honour and shame: problems in the comparative analysis of moral systems. *Man,* 15, 339—45.

Hobsbawm, E. 1969: *Bandits.* London: Weidenfeld and Nicolson.

Lopez Casero, L. 1972: La Plaza, estructura y procesos en un pueblo de la Mancha. *Ethnica,* 4.

Lorca, F. García, 1980: *Obras Completas.* Madrid: Aguilar.

Marvin, G. R. 1982: *'La Corrida de Toros': An anthropological study of animal and human nature in Andalusia.* University College Swansea, PhD thesis.

Ortega, D. 1950: *El Arte de Torear.* Madrid: Revista de Oriente.

Pitt-Rivers, J. R. 1965: Honour and social status. In J. R. Peristiany (ed.) *Honour and shame: the values of the Mediterranean,* London: Weidenfeld and Nicolson.

8

Fighting in an
Australian Aboriginal Supercamp

David McKnight

INTRODUCTION

This chapter examines fighting in an Australian Aboriginal community on Mornington Island, northern Queensland, the largest island of a group collectively known as the Wellesley Islands (see map 1). Before 1914, when a mission was founded there, the sole occupants of Mornington Island were the Lardil. Close by to the south-west, separated by a narrow channel, lies Denham Island and the Forsyth Islands, the traditional territory of the Yangkal who also occupied a small strip of the mainland coast. To the south-east of Mornington Island are the South Wellesley Islands, the territory of the Kaiadilt. Before coming into contact with European Australians there was only sporadic contact between the Kaiadilt and the neighbouring mainlanders, and such meetings as they had with outsiders, Aboriginal or European, were often violent — and frequently ended tragically for the Kaiadilt. To the south and east of the Yangkal mainlanders were the Yulkul who inhabited the coastal area and hinterland from Point Parker to Nicholson River. In the early 1860s, Burketown was founded about twenty miles from the mouth of Albert River and was mainly a port for the cattle stations in the Gulf area. Although Burketown was (and is) small, it exerted a shattering influence on neighbouring tribes. Alcohol, opium, disease and social disruption all took their toll. Many Yangkal visited Burketown, and so did a few Lardil men and women, but the Lardil for the most part remained outside its fatal attraction. It was not until 1914, when a Presbyterian mission was founded on Mornington Island, that the Lardil came into continuous contact with European Australians. As we shall see, by the time of research, the Lardil had been joined by the Kaiadilt and by the remnants of both the Yangkal and the

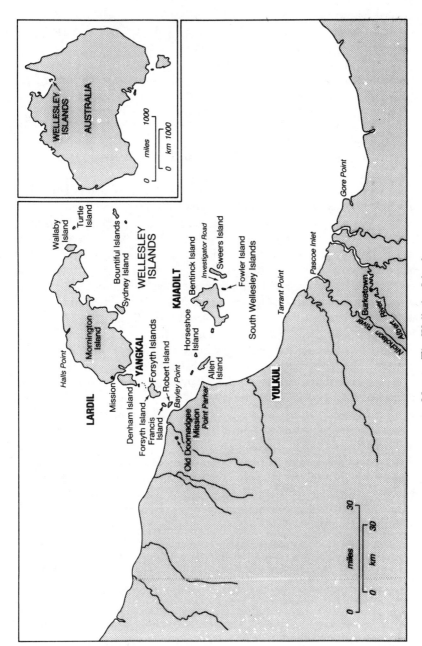

Map 1 The Wellesley Islands

Yulkul. Some of the effects of this contact and tribal admixture are discussed
in what follows.

About twenty years ago, in 1966 — virtually on the first day of my
fieldwork on Mornington Island — I heard a commotion in the village. I
remember naively and breathlessly running to record what it was about,
concerned that all would be over before I arrived on the scene and my only
chance of witnessing a public altercation would pass. A woman asked me why
I was hurrying; when I told her she laughingly remarked that I would see
many fights. She was quite right. During my three years of fieldwork on
Mornington Island hundreds of fights occurred.[1] Indeed, fighting appeared to
be the main social activity. At one period I calculated that there were several
arguments every day with antagonists angrily trading harsh words; every day
there was usually one fight; each week there was at least one brawl involving
a couple of dozen people; about once a month there was a mêlée involving at
least a hundred people; and every once in a while there was a tremendous
upheaval which involved most of the community. A mêlée or upheaval was
usually followed by a period of calm, as if everyone had been drained of
aggressive emotions. I had little previous experience of Australian Aborigines
and after I got over my initial surprise about so much fighting I accepted it as
a way of life and became quite blasé about it. In fact, eventually I became so
used to violence that I often failed to record that a fight had occurred. Or I
would cryptically note: 'Fight today among the Roberts.' 'The Escotts and the
Roughseys were quarrelling.' 'Pompey threw some boomerangs — must find
out why.' 'A big brawl at the ridge.' But before my senses became dulled by
over-familiarity I made a close study of fighting and the possible reasons for
the violent clashes. And even after my study was completed, and I had turned
to other matters, I would return to the subject from time to time. It seemed
very odd to me that there *was* so much fighting.[2] Odd because the people were
polite, friendly, warm-hearted and good-humoured; many seemed to go out of
their way to be nice to me. Yet in an argument they would be suddenly
transformed into aggressive, swearing and dangerous antagonists. Both men
and women were spirited fighters. I was often in the thick of the brawls — not
fighting, but recording. My escape from injury was not solely the result of my
agility and cowardice but undoubtedly resulted from the fact that people often

[1] My main period of fieldwork on Mornington Island was in the years 1966—8. Additional
visits were made in 1970, 1972, 1975, 1977 and 1985.
[2] The bulk of my material on fighting was collected before the Mornington Islanders
obtained regular access to alcohol. I plan to examine the consequences of alcohol in a
separate publication.

stood in front of me ready to block flying objects, and because recently acquired Aboriginal friends and relatives would vehemently threaten that if anybody hit me they would be killed. Naturally it was comforting that people were concerned about my well-being — but I really did not expect to suffer any injury, at least not on purpose. At the time I thought that the threats made on my behalf were melodramatic, but looking back I now realize that they helped to ensure my safe stay in the field.

It was a common sight to see men walking about with a bundle of boomerangs and a club. Most people regard boomerangs as hunting implements, and so they are, but on Mornington Island they are mainly used for fighting. There are three types — the full returning boomerang, the heavy hunting boomerang, and the hooked boomerang. The edges of all three types are sharp and can cause severe cuts. The full returning boomerang may be thrown at an opponent from a distance of only a few yards. The thrower twists his wrist so that the boomerang either flies straight at his opponent or else comes from the side at a slight angle. It is a dangerous weapon because it can easily break a limb or penetrate the skull and kill. An astute fighter can block it with another boomerang, or with his club or a stick. The heavy hunting boomerang is larger, heavier and curved in an arc; in fights it is usually thrown from a greater distance than a full returning boomerang. It is difficult to block because of the unpredictable way that it skips and bounces off the ground. The hooked boomerang is particularly dangerous and is only used for serious fighting. Its erratic flight makes it difficult to block. The hooked end is pointed and it can give a bad gash. The principle of a hooked boomerang, so I was told, is that when an opponent attempts to block it the hook may catch his club and swing around and hit him. A fighting club (*murrkuni*), or *nulla nulla* as it is widely known in Australia, is made out of heavy hardwood. It is about three or four feet long and about two or three inches in diameter, tapered at both ends, one end usually roughened to ensure a good grip. It is normally wielded with both hands and serves as a defensive or offensive weapon. Thus it can be used to block a boomerang or any flying object, or to bash an opponent. A common defensive posture, particularly at night when it is difficult to spot flying objects, or when one is outnumbered, is to kneel on one knee and hold one's boomerang and club crossed in front of the body. In using a club one tries to smash an opponent's fingers, or break his arm or leg, or render him senseless with a stunning blow on the head. Many people had smashed or broken fingers and a few were missing a finger or a joint. Scars were prolific too, but some of these were the result of self-inflicted mourning cuts.

In addition to boomerangs and clubs, people would use spears, axes, and indeed any cudgel that they could lay their hands on in the heat of a fight.

Occasionally a rifle appeared on the scene, but normally this was only a threatening gesture, for the rifle was usually held in one hand and a cartridge in the other. As a precaution the Superintendent had banned 0.303s and other rifles of greater calibre than 0.22 — the type normally used for hunting. Inserting a cartridge in a rifle was similar to 'hooking' a spear, i.e. inserting one's spear in a spear-thrower. A spear-thrower increases the accuracy, speed, distance and force of a throw. One of the criteria that the Mornington Islanders used for judging the seriousness of a fight was whether or not spears were hooked. But spears used in any manner would invariably provoke the women to cry out in alarm. Rocks and stones were sometimes thrown, particularly by women; in the middle of a brawl they might also throw sand and dirt, thus temporarily blinding combatants. Women rarely used boomerangs but most of them would pick up a club, a stick, or occasionally an axe, and a few were formidable fighters. I witnessed women suffer awesome blows over the head and, although bleeding profusely, still showing plenty of fight. Women in their anger, or as a display of anger, would perform a dance which consisted of a rapid in-and-out motion of the knees and a stomping of feet; at the same time they would make a high-pitched trilling sound. The general impression was that they had lost all control of themselves and that they were likely to cause someone grievous harm. For my part I found this aggressive display extremely intimidating. Sometimes when engaged in this display a woman would thrust a stick between her legs. The sexual symbolism was not lost on the Mornington Islanders; people likened this display to the act of coitus and it was claimed that it urged men to continue fighting. Seeing a close relative being injured a woman could be so overcome by sorrow she would strike herself on the head with a club or a rock. There was very little kicking, biting or gouging. I did record one instance of a man having part of his ear bitten off but this had happened years before my fieldwork. I witnessed some severe injuries with people suffering broken limbs, being knocked unconscious, and being cut badly enough to need many stitches. The injured had their wounds attended at the mission hospital but in severe cases they were flown to the hospital in Mount Isa by the flying doctor service. Nobody was killed while I was in the field in 1966—8, but people were frightened that this would happen and they recalled past cases when it had — the most recent being, I believe, in the 1930s. (As it turned out their fears were justified, for since the mid-1970s there have been several deaths connected with fighting and alcohol.)

Let me pause for a moment and make an initial attempt to place the fighting in perspective. When discussing a subject within the confines of one chapter there is always the possibility that readers may mistakenly conclude that very little else happens. So perhaps I should stress that life was not all high drama and many other activities such as singing, dancing, hunting and fishing, also took place. I should also mention that there was much vitality and *joie de vivre* among the Mornington Islanders. For myself, despite the occasional bad patches that every fieldworker experiences, I have thoroughly enjoyed living with them, as my frequent field trips might indicate. A point that needs to be stressed is that some Mornington Islanders, particularly the older people, publicly expressed concern about the high incidence of violence. Many of the fights that I witnessed appeared more ferocious than they really were, and they were essentially boomerang-waving or club-banging affrays during which the antagonists aired their grievances. But that was only being wise after the event, for one could seldom predict what course an argument would take. At times blows were pulled, so not as much damage was inflicted as could have been. Often, however, blows were not pulled but, as people were adept at dodging and parrying, they normally managed to escape injury. Not everyone was a fighter but this did not prevent them from having their say in the arguments. A fight was not the inevitable end of an argument; nor did every fight end in injuries; neither was every injury a serious one. Given the frequency of fights, however, there *were* many serious injuries. When the fighting had degenerated into a riot the Mission Superintendent was usually called to intervene. It says something for his strength of character, and perhaps for the power of white authority, that his unarmed presence usually had a calming effect. The Mornington Islanders held him in high regard and wanted no repetition of what had happened to the first missionary who was murdered in 1917 while touring the northern part of the island. If the Superintendent thought that the fighting was completely out-of-hand he occasionally called on the assistance of the Burketown police. (At one period, about 1975, the Presbyterian Board of Missions in Sydney became so concerned about the situation that, on making a new appointment, they chose a man whom they thought could do something about controlling the violence — he was an experienced soldier. Once or twice the fighting became so violent and widespread that a plane-load of policemen had to be flown in to quell matters.)

As I said, I was puzzled by the fighting, and in particular why there was so much of it. But first I should point out that fighting is not peculiar to the Mornington Islanders, for as I later learned from visiting other communities in Northern Queensland, particularly Aurukun in Cape York Peninsula, where I spent a year, that fighting was endemic elsewhere.[3] And from my

[3] Fieldwork at Aurukun was carried out in the years 1968, 1970, 1972, 1981 and 1983. During my fieldwork at Mornington Island and Aurukun I made brief visits to Doomadgee, Mount Isa, Karumba, Burketown, Weipa and Cairns. In all these places violent clashes occurred among the Aborigines. The incidence of violence at Aurukun is comparable to what I witnessed at Mornington Island (McKnight 1982).

reading of the literature it is clear that it is common in most Australian communities — though I hesitate to say that it is common in all Aboriginal communities. Second, it is not a new phenomenon that has only occurred since the advent of European Australians. It is, however, quite likely that the incidence of fighting has increased because of European influence and I shall return to this point.

My genealogical data and case histories clearly demonstrate that before the mission was founded (1914) fighting occurred among the Lardil and people were sometimes speared to death. This was also the case for the neighbouring tribes. The Kaiadilt had a reputation for fierceness. According to Tindale's findings, in 1942 the Kaiadilt population had reached a peak of 123 but it rapidly fell to about seventy (Tindale 1962). There were a number of reasons for this population decline. In the latter half of the 1940s there was a long period of drought followed by an exceptional high tide. These natural events caused a shortage of food and fresh water. Some deaths occurred because of malnutrition and accidental drownings. Moreover, there was murderous inter-clan strife over women and scarce resources. Because of these calamities the Kaiadilt elected to emigrate to Mornington Island in 1947—8; by the late 1960s their population had increased to about ninety. On Mornington Island they were camped (and I have chosen my word carefully) near the beach and formed a separate residential group and were largely endogamous. There were many outbreaks of violence among the Kaiadilt, and rumours that one or two accidental deaths in the recent past had not in fact been accidental. There were some clashes involving Kaiadilt and other Mornington Islanders but these were largely individual and family affairs; I never witnessed any tribal fights between the Kaiadilt and the others — perhaps this was so because the Kaiadilt were wary of their numerically weak position. There were a few cases of Aboriginal police taking advantage of the weak position of the Kaiadilt and treating them rather roughly. On the whole, the other Mornington Islanders had a healthy respect for the fighting abilities of the Kaiadilt, and recognized them as industrious and steady workers — nevertheless they had a low opinion of their social worth and viewed them as wild. Whenever the Kaiadilt were fighting among themselves the other Mornington Islanders would moralize about their wildness and savagery, just as outsiders were apt to criticize the Mornington Islanders for their violent behaviour. It is only since 1969 that there have been some marriages with the Kaiadilt.

Before the mission was founded there were fights between the Lardil and the neighbouring Yangkal, though not always on a tribal basis, and between the Lardil and mainlanders. I recorded cases of Lardil being killed by 'wild men' (*murrukumen*) from the mainland. There were instances of fighting between the Kaiadilt and the neighbouring Yulkul mainlanders when the Kaiadilt camped on Allen Island. Traditionally, contact between Kaiadilt and Lardil was very rare — the short expanse of sea, about twenty miles, being too dangerous for regular communication on their flimsy mangrove rafts. This is not the place to discuss the history of the Kaiadilt but I may mention that in the 1920s and 1930s the missionaries, in their endeavours to make the mission economically self-sufficient, had developed a *bêche-de-mer* fishing industry. Occasionally, on the fishing expeditions to the South Wellesley Islands, they came into some contact with the Kaiadilt who proved to be very elusive. Most accounts of the Kaiadilt since they were first contacted by Flinders in 1802 have remarked on their elusiveness (Flinders 1814: p. 137). To give the Kaiadilt their due it seems that they were mostly the recipients rather than the perpetrators of violence when contact occurred with outsiders. In the mid-1930s the *bêche-de-mer* fishing industry came to an end and there was even less contact with the Kaiadilt. However, in 1941 some Mornington Islanders set out to Burketown on the mission launch to pick up supplies and stopped at Allen Island for water. They were attacked by two Kaiadilt men who had temporarily escaped there with their wives and children, in all, thirteen persons, to avoid the fighting on Bentinck Island.[4] They killed one Mornington Islander, and captured and raped one woman. An expedition was organized by the Queensland police and the Kaiadilt men were arrested, jailed in Burketown (where one of them, perhaps both, mutilated himself by cutting off a testicle), and eventually sent with their families to Aurukun, a Presbyterian Mission on the west coast of Cape York Peninsula, a few hundred miles from the Wellesley Islands.

Other incidents could be cited, but I think I have given enough to show that, formerly, intra-tribal fighting occurred not only among the Mornington Islanders but among the neighbouring tribes, and that there were violent clashes between some of them. Thus the fighting that I witnessed was certainly not a new phenomenon. However, I should also mention that, traditionally, inter-tribal contact extended to inter-marriage, trading, ritual gatherings and ordinary visiting.

---

[4] In this particular episode several Kaiadilt were drowned while attempting to make their way, by raft, from Bentinck Island to Allen Island. There are, incidentally, a few large rock fish-traps on Allen Island which indicates that it was sometimes occupied for long periods and was not solely a temporary haven.

LARDIL TRADITIONAL LOCAL AND SOCIAL ORGANIZATION

Let me quickly sketch the traditional local and social organization of the Lardil.[5] Before the mission was founded the population of Mornington Island was approximately 230. There were some thirty-four patriclans. Each of these clans was identified with a small area of land consisting of a strip of coast and some hinterland. Some clan areas had a strip of coast of several miles while others had a strip of coast of only a few hundred yards. When a clan died out their land was normally cared for by a neighbouring clan or by someone who had affiliations either with the deceased members of the clan or with their clan area. The main economic benefits that a clan enjoyed were rights to certain pieces of dugong (a large sea mammal) and sea turtle, both highly prized foods. Despite the mystical ties and economic rights it would appear that the clan area was in most cases an identity area and was not regarded as a place where the members were supposed to gain a living or live permanently or even most of the time.[6]

There were four cardinal areas, consisting of the northern people (*jirrkurumbenda*), the eastern people (*lilumbenda*), the southern people (*larumbenda*), and the western people (*balumbenda*). In each cardinal area there were several favourite camping sites and two or three clans, sometimes more and sometimes less, would camp for varying periods here. Geographical moieties, windward and leeward, divided the island into two. By and large, the

[5] I must emphasize that the traditional local organization was no longer operative when I was in the field. My reconstruction is based on such data as informants' accounts, case histories, genealogical data, records about where people were born and where they died, where their country was located and where they habitually lived, location of camp sites and cartographical information (e.g. recording boundaries and place names), as well as from what I observed on camping expeditions.

[6] Clan members had spiritual ties with their country and most important was the belief that in their own country they were normally safe from *markiri*. The subject of *markiri* is complex and cannot adequately be described in a few sentences, but because of the exigences of space I am forced to make an attempt. Briefly, *markiri* (*mar* = hand; *kiri* = wash, bathe) is a mystical sickness which results primarily when land food and sea food are mixed. The two types of food should not be eaten together. The offender is believed to be attacked by the mythical Rainbow Serpent (*Thuwathu*) or its local manifestation. As a precaution against *markiri* people should purify their hands before going into the sea or eating sea food, and they should purify their hands after coming out of the sea before collecting or eating land food.

windward moiety consisted of the southern part of the island, and the leeward moiety consisted of the northern part of the island. Identification was, and is, rather flexible, for I recorded a few cases of southern (windward) people identifying with the leeward moiety. These anomalies were not regarded as important. There was never any doubt about which moiety a person belonged to; I noticed that even children knew their moiety identity. These groups played a part in the major brawls and in competitive dancing displays.

Using a broad brush, the traditional local and social organization was basically a matter of small patriclans who identified with a small area in which they had certain economic rights and spiritual ties. In a few cases a clan was large enough and possessed an area with sufficient resources to have enabled them to be independent had they so chosen, but this was the exception rather than the rule. In any event, clan land was not the exclusive property of a clan, for land belonged to everybody — for the most part, people had the right to forage and travel wherever they pleased. The trespassers-will-be-prosecuted complex, so often reported for other tribes (e.g. Aranda, see Strehlow 1947 and 1970), was not characteristic of the Lardil. Neighbouring clans often camped together. At times, members of several clans (probably seldom more than thirty people) within a cardinal area would form a base camp at one of the favourite camping sites. The composition of these camps seems to have been quite fluid but people tended to stay within their cardinal area, even though they had a right to forage in other cardinal areas. Traditionally there was conflict between the cardinal areas so it was not always safe to put one's rights into practice. There were, however, many marriages between the cardinal areas, so people had close relatives in different areas who would have warmly welcomed them. Occasionally, because of some ritual reason (e.g. initiation ceremony) and/or because of rich seasonal foraging (e.g. water lilies and some types of fish), a large number of people, perhaps a hundred or more, would assemble for short periods.

VIOLENCE IN THE PAST

In the past, before the mission was founded or before the mission hegemony was established, there was certainly violence among the Lardil. Indeed, some people were known by nicknames derived from injuries received in a fight, and they became so identified by their nicknames that their real names were often forgotten. No-one took offence over their nickname, or if they did they never showed it. One man was known as *bunjimurrkunimen*, i.e. hit on the back of the neck with a club; another man was called *jamiyaru*, i.e. speared in the foot; another was known as *dumawangalku*, i.e. hit on the back with a boomerang; one woman was known as *kuwawangalku*, i.e. hit in the eye with a boomerang.

Traditionally some types of fighting were hedged in with rules and rituals which undoubtedly helped to prevent them from becoming too serious. In a ritualized fight, i.e. a 'square up', opponents performed their totemic dances as they approached each other. First, they threw light spears from a distance, which were less dangerous than heavy killing spears. As they came closer they threw their boomerangs. And finally they clashed with their clubs. It was the rule (and still is) that as long as a fighter is holding his weapon he may be struck, and this is so even if he is lying half-stunned on the ground. It was also the rule that if a man dropped his club, or if it was struck out of his hands, then he should not be hit. In the formal fights there were always middlemen, or blockers, who were closely related to both sides. They blocked the spears and boomerangs and parried the blows for both parties. Although the combatants may have been eager to grapple with each other they took care not to hurt the middlemen. The role of the middlemen was solely to defend and never to attack, even if they were hit accidentally. This is the case still, and I sometimes witnessed angry antagonists vainly trying to run around the middlemen to get at their opponent. A fight could be brought to an honourable end with one of the fighters holding his club above his head, thus placing himself in a vulnerable position. In this case his opponent was expected to give the upraised club a symbolic hit. I witnessed such behaviour on several occasions and significantly most of them involved older men.

A 'square up' always occurred as part of the mortuary ceremonies, or when it was decided that two groups would formally meet to settle their differences by fighting it out. The meeting of the two groups would normally take place at a salt pan or at some level ground; here they would face each other for battle. Older initiated men with their weapons stood on the sidelines or walked between the two groups and exhorted the people not to be too violent. Spears and boomerangs were thrown at will in an unorganized fashion, and then the two groups rushed at each other. Needless to say, people did their best not to hurt close relatives on the opposing side. Normally, as soon as someone was seriously injured or killed the battle would stop. Ideally, in the evening the two groups danced together, thus indicating that hostilities had ceased. An old woman recounted her experience in one 'square up' where many people were injured. She struck another woman with her digging-stick and broke her leg. She was immediately overcome by shame and sorrow for what she had done, for they were good friends. Bursting into tears, she helped her injured friend off the battle ground.

At times a raid was made by one group against another because of some trouble over women, or in revenge for a death brought about by sorcery or otherwise.[7] The raiding party consisted only of men. These raids were usually surprise attacks at night and the express intention was to kill one of the enemy. Men had a right to refuse to participate in a raid if it was directed against any of their close relatives, and people had a right to warn their relatives of an impending raid. I recorded cases when this happened.

In addition to these types of fights I recorded instances of unregulated and unformalized fights when people were seriously injured and killed.

CHANGES IN LOCAL AND SOCIAL ORGANIZATION

The traditional local and social organization had considerably changed by 1966 when I began my fieldwork. The mission had been established for over fifty years. The population of Mornington Island had been augmented by the Kaiadilt and the tribal remnants of the Yangkal, Yulkul, Karrawa, Wanyi, as well as one or two representatives of more distant tribes. The total population was approximately 600. In the 1920s, the police and the Protector of Aborigines had begun to send waifs, orphans and people whom they thought were unable to cope with life on the mainland, to Mornington Island. Families were broken up and scattered. Hence some people ended up having relatives in a number of missions, settlements and fringe towns. Many of the newcomers were 'half-caste' children whose mothers were Aborigines and whose fathers were white Australians and, in some cases, Chinese. Perhaps the authorities meant well, but it was an unsettling experience, in both senses of the word, for those involved. Middle-aged people vividly described to me the anguish they suffered as children when they were forcibly separated from their parents, especially their mothers, whom they never saw again, or only years later when they were dying. Boys and girls were placed in separate dormitories and educated by the missionaries. Normally, older girls could only leave the dormitory by getting married. The missionaries were intent on making

[7] Elsewhere (McKnight 1981) I have examined Lardil sorcery beliefs and practices. Briefly, sorcery is directed against people outside one's clan, particularly classificatory brothers and affines. Sorcerers among the Lardil are invariably men, but both men and women may be victims of sorcery. I should stress here that fighting is only part of the general picture of conflict and violence. There is an intricate connection between fighting and sorcery, as is indicated by the general term for sorcery, i.e. 'spearing in the bush.' Many of the Mornington Islanders were constantly on guard against sorcery, and many accidents, deaths, and general misfortunes were attributed to it. People were locked in a vicious circle, for fear of sorcery and sorcery accusations brought about anxiety, conflict and fighting, which in turn resulted in fear of sorcery.

Christians out of the children — that is to say, Presbyterians. The missionaries were determined to create a gap between the generations for this made it easier to influence the younger generation, and they succeeded only too well in this. By the time I arrived, children, teenagers and many young adults (with the exception of the Kaiadilt) spoke neither Lardil nor any other Aboriginal language fluently, if at all. I daresay that many readers would be inclined to heap criticism on the missionaries for this unfortunate state of affairs. It was certainly a strange situation when missionaries could exercise such control over a society — even to the extent of raising the children — when in their own society, i.e. among European Australians, they did not possess such power. Nor were they, as far as I am able to determine, particularly trained to exercise such power. However, had it not been for the missionaries there would have been very few Aborigines left on Mornington Island or in many other parts of Queensland. Furthermore, the missionaries — at least, some of them — stoutly defended the land rights of the Aborigines against mining and cattle interests even before this cause became a popular issue. Indeed, the Mornington Islanders were fortunate to have a mission. To be sure, they could have been more fortunate, but in the historical period that we are dealing with, a more fortunate situation did not exist — certainly not in Queensland.

In 1954 the dormitory system was phased out, partly for economic reasons and partly because the Victorian values which had brought about its formation were no longer fashionable. Hence, when I was in the field, all the Aborigines lived in a village community about half a mile from the mission compound. Most dwellings were made out of bush timber and covered with corrugated iron; some were no more than pieces of corrugated iron and tarpaulin. There were, however, several more substantial dwellings consisting of two rooms and sometimes boasting verandahs, but even these dwellings did not possess any amenities. Water was obtained from one or two wells and a few public taps. On the whole, the dwellings were hot and stuffy in the dry season, and damp in the rainy season. Many of the flimsier dwellings were often wrecked by cyclones. They were frequently overcrowded and lacked privacy. Although to many outsiders the living conditions seemed poor, one must nevertheless bear in mind that the Mornington Islanders spent most of their time outdoors. And in the 1970s, when the Government provided better accommodation, many people initially refused to move out of their ramshackle homes.

The layout of the village was never systematically planned, either by the missionaries or by the Aborigines. It simply developed over the years in an *ad hoc* fashion. This gave the village an interesting appearance avoiding the drab inflexibility of some other settlements, where a type of grid system prevailed. Sometimes brothers resided side by side, in other cases brothers had dwellings in different parts of the village; clansmen were either clustered fairly close together, or scattered throughout the village; in some cases a man lived with his affines while in other cases he stayed as far away from them as possible. People complained that this scattering of countrymen was not right and that people who belonged to the same area should all live together. Despite this criticism, one could still discern something of a pattern. The Kaiadilt were camped on the beach in the southern part of the village, i.e. in the direction of their country; the mainlanders and the northern people tended to reside on a ridge on the northern side of the village whereas the southerners tended to reside on the southern side of the village. A rather meandering line could be drawn through the village separating windward in the south from leeward in the north.

What we have is a permanent supercamp quite unlike anything that the Aborigines had experienced in the past. In one small area, covering about two square miles, there are all the Lardil — eastern, western, northern, and southern, as well as windward and leeward — plus remnants of the Yangkal and mainland tribes, and the Kaiadilt. Not only is there the traditional conflict between the various Lardil groups, but also the conflict between the tribes plus, among all tribes, an undercurrent of conflict between Aborigines of full descent and Aborigines of mixed descent. Added to this is the superimposed authority of the missionaries and the Queensland government on people who not long ago had been free of outside control and who now had to follow rules, customs and laws, many of which were quite contrary to their traditional values. There were Aboriginal councillors and policemen whose job was to enforce, whether they knew it or not, the dictates of white Australians. Thus we have a situation where people have their children taken out of their hands and educated to the demands of a foreign social order, where men who were used to running their own affairs, and who had been a political force in their tribe, have had their power taken away from them. The situation was exacerbated by factors such as the loss of authority and power of the older generation, demographic changes which *inter alia* entailed larger families and a shift in the overall age structure, clashes over traditional values and new values, and, most important, an increase in population density and relational density. It is to these matters that I now wish to turn. But before doing so I should like to make a few points about loss of culture and values. When I was first in the field in 1966 there were many men and women who had been young adults or children when the mission was founded in 1914. Naturally enough, they did not forget their language as soon as they cast their eyes on the missionaries. Nor did they immediately discard all their traditional values. Furthermore, many people who had been born after the mission was established were little affected by the missionaries. It was not until the 1930s that the missionaries established their hegemony. And as there were usually only three or four missionaries it was impossible for them to brainwash everybody completely. The changes wrought by the missionaries were not all of the same degree, nor were they of the same pace, nor was everybody equally affected. Many values remained undisturbed (for example, those relating to the avoidance of affines) because the missionaries had no knowledge of their existence. The missionaries were successful in prohibiting polygamy, at least formally. Yet in matters of religion, where one might think that they would have been pre-eminently successful, they failed completely to rid people of their beliefs (and practices) about sorcery. Many of the religious teachings of the missionaries had surprisingly very little impact. When the Mission was taken over by the Queensland Government in the mid-1970s church attendance rapidly declined.

CHANGES IN THE SOCIAL ORDER

I mentioned the experience that many mainlanders, and Aborigines of mixed descent, had suffered by being forcibly sent to Mornington Island. But they were not the only ones to undergo a dormitory childhood, for the Lardil children were also placed in the dormitories. The result of this is that when they became adults and had children of their own they had little experience of family life; consequently some parents found it abnormally difficult to rear children. (I even overheard some Mornington Islanders claim that it was the missionaries' job to raise children.) And the children in turn suffered because they were not properly socialized for their role in life — whatever that was supposed to be. In addition, because of the medical and health care provided by the missionaries and the flying doctor service, women had much larger families than formerly and they found it very difficult to cope with so many children. Children were frequently allowed to fend for themselves, though the mission took care that they did not suffer from malnutrition, and they ran about much as they pleased. (This situation may not have differed very much from the traditional pattern, for it is common practice among Australian Aborigines not to impose much discipline on children.) In some ways the mission was caught in a 'no-win' situation. If they took control of events and made certain that the children, the elderly and the sick were well fed and cared for, then they were likely to be accused of paternalism. But if they did not do this, then they were likely to be accused of hard-heartedness, exploitation and of only being concerned with the people's spiritual welfare and not with their physical well-being.

Husband and wife often came into conflict with each other, and with other families, over the behaviour of the children. Fathers were much more indulgent than mothers and when an exasperated mother slapped her child the father was quick to take the child's part. I would frequently overhear one parent complaining about the children's behaviour while the other parent staunchly defended them. And even when the other parent agreed, the first parent was liable to do an abrupt about-turn and defend the children. But when middle-aged and elderly people talked among themselves about the young people they were apt to grumble that they could neither hunt nor work. Obviously this grumbling stemmed, at least in part, from the stress and strain of coping with a changing world. And one may also interpret such grumbling as an attempt by the elderly to enhance themselves at the expense of the younger generation. In some cases, the complaints were arguably not without justification. But I hasten to add that some young people, particularly among the women, could certainly be regarded as competent and dependable workers.

The last ceremony of initiation had occurred some fifteen years before I was in the field, thus this traditional method of the older generation imposing their authority and power over the younger generation was lost. What was also lost, for the younger generation, was all the sacred knowledge associated with initiations. Consequently, in addition to not learning their tribal language the young men also lost the opportunity to learn the languages, namely the hand language and the *Demiin* language, associated respectively with the first initiation (*luruku* i.e. circumcision) and second initiation (*warama* i.e. subincision). As a matter of interest here, I may mention that for about a year after the first initiation the initiate was required to communicate only by the hand language (*kangka marlda*; *kangka* = speak, *marlda* = hand) and normally he was forbidden to speak Lardil. The hand language contains hundreds of signs. After the second initiation the initiate was taught the other auxiliary language, *Demiin,* which interestingly enough possesses several click consonants and other unusual sounds which do not occur in Lardil nor, I believe, in any other Australian Aboriginal language. The *Demiin* language classifies the world differently from the Lardil language. One consequence of the failure of the young men, and quite a few middle-aged men, to be initiated was that spiritually they were not regarded as real men, but as boys.

When it came to matters of power and physical force, the older men were outnumbered and they were up against physically stronger opponents. The older men could do little more than grumble among themselves and ridicule the ignorance of the younger generation. Here lies a fatal flaw, for by ridiculing the younger generation they unwittingly widened the generation gap, since ridicule is one of the traditional values or sanctions which has survived intact. It is ironic that it is among the values, in the changing situation, that the Mornington Islanders could well have done without. In the past, ridicule was a powerful weapon which forced people to conform, but its potency depended on there being only one body of knowledge and one social order. When the older people used this traditional sanction the younger generation simply turned to European values and prided themselves on a knowledge of everything white, and regarded the old people as ignorant *myalls*, i.e. bush people who speak no English and who are unfamiliar with the customs of white Australians. They turned to a materially more powerful culture, one which had far more political power and force than the elders. For did not the elders themselves succumb to this power? And did not the elders also covet European goods? The young people would say such things as: 'Everything has changed. Money talks nowadays.' They justified many of their actions on the grounds that what they were doing was the white man's way. Many of them became almost completely uninterested in what the older generation had to say and the older generation found themselves with a body of knowledge that few wanted except the visiting anthropologist and some other outsiders.

Although the young people placed high value on most European things, many of them were nevertheless often unable to cope with the values and practicalities of European life. Young men obtained jobs as stockmen on the mainland cattle stations and young women went into domestic service. However, some of them acquired the habit of not finishing their contract and they would walk off the job poorer than when they began. There are several reasons why this happened. Their values and socialization were such that they had become used to being pampered by their family, and doing, or more exactly not doing, as they pleased. They were not always well trained for their jobs and sometimes they were not suited for a particular job, a matter which, needless to say, is not peculiar to the Mornington Islanders. Some of the young people were not able to tolerate criticism. This last point is closely associated with the traditional value that one should not criticize someone's work for this causes ill-feeling and may lead to a fight. Such a value was certainly not conducive to working for white Australians. When young people walked off the job they normally received sympathetic support from their close kin. However, some of the older cattle men grumbled that many of the younger men could not cope with hard work and with being absent from their relatives for long periods.

Women were also placed in a difficult position. Middle-aged mothers had to contend with unruly adolescents who frequently quarrelled and fought with them, and embroiled them in their battles. Some women found it difficult to feed their older children, who were at an age when in the past they would have been contributing to the family larder. In some families, some of the older youths had become what could be regarded as untrustworthy and selfish, for as soon as their mother was out of sight they would raid her meagre hoard of food. In a way they were following traditional practice, for, in the past, food was not normally saved. But it is one thing to act like this when all the family were hunting and gathering, and another when the family live in a village, hunt at week-ends, and purchase much of their food supply and modern hunting equipment out of low wages and welfare benefits. Many young people had produced children without getting married. In itself this was no bad thing, but they were not all taking responsibility for their offspring. A heavy burden was falling on grandmothers who not only had to care for their own children but also their grandchildren. In the village one could see clusters of small children gathered around camp fires being fed damper (a type of bread which is very filling but not particularly nutritious) and tea by their grandmothers. Sometimes there were quarrels between grandparents and parents over care of the children.

FIGHTING IN THE VILLAGE SUPERCAMP

One of the customs of the Lardil and other Mornington Islanders is, when they think they have been wronged, to create a scene. They do not shout out all their grievances all the time, though one might be forgiven for thinking that some of them do. They tend to hoard their complaints and then kick up a fuss when they think they have plenty to complain about. I often heard people airing their grievances to all and sundry, complaining about people who think they can do as they please, who never hunt, who won't work, know nothing, carry tales, urge others into trouble, break tribal laws, fornicate indiscriminately, think that the speaker is a myall, and so on. At this stage names are not necessarily mentioned, but normally people know who is being referred to and they may or may not shout back and say what is on their mind. Eventually voices rise to an angry pitch which carries far. Cries of '*Merri. Merri.*' (Listen. Listen.) can be heard as others try to discern who is shouting and what the 'growl' is all about. The Mornington Islanders regard it as quite proper for people to air their grievances. But the very act of airing grievances, no matter how justified, is likely to fuel conflict. Practically all fights begin with an airing of grievances, but not all airing of grievances result in a fight — it might just end in 'tongue bashing' or 'growling'. In the next stage one of the opponents may pick up a club or a cudgel and start banging against the corrugated iron frame of their dwelling (or even better, somebody else's), which creates an aggressive noise that can be heard throughout the village. In their anger, or as a display of anger, men would bite the handle of their spears.

(Teeth are often used as a tool or a vice. When making a spear men heat the handle and often straighten it by gripping it with their teeth and pulling the handle down with their hands.) Interested people begin to approach, if they have not already done so. By the time the banging starts at least one of the antagonists has worked himself or herself to such a pitch that they start destroying any object that they can. Pots and pans may be kicked and heaved all over the place, glass louvres are smashed, and even the store rations may be strewn on the ground. Somewhere at this point of the destruction of things voices rise to a shrill crescendo as the antagonists swear at each other in earnest. Swearing is one of the actions which is likely to trigger off a fight. Men, particularly initiated men, feel duty-bound to thrash a woman if she swears at them. Swearing at an opponent's mother, actual or classificatory, or telling someone to *datha ngama*, i.e. fuck (your) mother, or calling a man *ngama daan*, i.e. mother fucker, normally results in a violent reprisal. Invariably the antagonists make derogatory comments about the size, colour and shape of each other's genitals. Sometimes an opponent is accused of being 'bony'. To be bony is to be in ill health and is associated with death, for in death only the bones are left. (No one takes exception to being called fat, for to be fat is to be strong and healthy.) Old fights and scandals are sometimes raked up and other people are drawn into the conflict. Kin and affines come rushing up to see what is happening and whether their help is needed. Normally, providing that one is not fighting them, one can depend on the assistance of one's parents, older children, siblings, maternal relatives, brothers-in-law, sisters-in-law, cross-cousins, etc. Children excitedly scream '*Baya! Baya!*' (Fight! Fight!) and rush up to view the spectacle. In no time there is a big mob involved, with people swearing and shouting such things as: 'Where's my uncle?' 'Countrymen!' People work themselves up to a high pitch and by doing so this pumps up the adrenalin and dulls the pain of most blows.

Fights vary in their severity, how long they last and how many people are involved. Much depends on the relationship of those involved; sometimes they quickly flare up and as quickly die down; sometimes they cause deep-lasting enmity and at other times they are immediately forgotten and the antagonists weepingly embrace one another and call each other by their kinship term. Sometimes they may go on for an hour or so, or for the best part of the day, or even for a few days, flaring up every once in a while. Subsidiary fights may become more important than the main fight, as the fighting spreads like a bush fire throughout the village. Sometimes a particular fight is only a feint in order to draw in a third party who is the person that one of the fighters really wants to grapple with. When somebody is injured there may be a lull in the fight as relatives rush to give aid and carry away the wounded. On other occasions an injury may draw in even more people who are determined to avenge their kin. People may withdraw to have their wounds attended or they may be exhausted from fighting. For these and other reasons a fight may dwindle to an end with no clear winner or loser. The antagonists may return to their homes where throughout the day or night they shout abuse at each other, daring the other party to come and fight. Veiled threats or not-so-veiled threats of sorcery are sometimes made. Thus somebody may say, 'We'll see about that', or 'My *kaku* (mother's brother) is behind me' (i.e. My mother's brother will get you with sorcery), or even more explicitly, 'I'll sing you' (i.e. I'll get you with sorcery). Then all of a sudden the fighting may erupt again.

People fight for many reasons. They fight to pay off old scores, and over the children's behaviour, competition for the opposite sex, suspicions of adultery, accusations of sorcery, because they think they have been ill-used, and so on. But these are matters that people fight over, and in themselves they do not explain why there is fighting or why there is so much fighting. To what extent a cultural view about fighting affects its occurrence is a debatable point. People may condemn fighting and regard it as unworthy of human beings, yet these views need not accord with their practices. However, it would not be surprising to find that fighting is common in a society where it is culturally regarded as natural and as an expected form of behaviour. Indeed, one would be surprised (at least I would) if it were otherwise. In any event, the Lardil and members of other tribes on Mornington Island are far from being aghast when fighting occurs — indeed they expect that people will attempt to use violence as a form of self-help, to right wrongs, and to enforce their rights. They, and many other Aborigines, apparently regard violence as a feature of human nature and its expression no bad thing (see Stanner 1969). Violence, or the threat of violence, is normally countered with violence or the threat of violence. From what I observed, the Mornington Islanders act as if they have the right to do what they please and as if they will do so unless they are forcibly prevented. Young men in particular appear to seek violent clashes in order to establish who is the better man, i.e. who is the better fighter. Besides the possibility of severe injuries, many young men seem to enjoy the confrontations. They do not seek to hide their injuries. Quite the contrary in fact, for they often tie a piece of cloth on the outside of the leg of their trousers to draw attention to the fact that they have been hurt. Physical size does not seem to be taken into consideration, for even when fighting with their fists quite small men fearlessly trade blows with big men. Fist fighting has its ritual component just as stick fighting. Rolling up one's trouser legs, even when one is only wearing shorts, is the first sign of willingness to fight. The antagonists start by shadow boxing from some distance away — ducking, weaving and feinting — urging their opponent to come closer and disdainfully dancing in and out. To the observer the scene is at first not without humour, but often hard blows are exchanged and one of the fighters may be badly hurt. The defeated youth usually runs home to collect his weapons and so the fight escalates.

Fist fighting is an innovation that the older men disdain, as they well know that in a fist fight they are not a match for a young man. In any event, the older men are used to fighting with wood and, unless old age has considerably weakened them, they can hold their own with boomerangs, clubs and spears. A large physique and brute strength are not necessary for an accomplished traditional fighter. More important are skill, agility and quick reflexes, plus a few tricks learnt through the years. Hence an older man fighting a young man with traditional weapons has a very good chance of holding his own or winning. But once old age weakens a man he no longer has the strength to ward off blows, or to deliver a strong blow, or to throw a boomerang or spear with accuracy. In this case, he is no longer a power to be reckoned with. All that he can do is to shout ineffectively from the sidelines while younger men and women fight it out. And nowadays this aptly reflects his political power — mere shouting from the sidelines.[8]

The relationship between ideal child-rearing practices (along with childhood experiences) and both ideal and actual adult behaviour is, of course, a complex issue. Exigencies of space prevent a detailed examination of this double helix, so only a few bald observations can be offered. Although I do not hold that the violent behaviour of the Mornington Islanders can be attributed simply to their childhood experience, nevertheless there is some connection and it is plain that the aggressive behaviour of children and adults is all of a piece. Children are continuously exposed to violence and they soon learn to regard violence as a way of life. Initially when I observed children screaming and crying when their parents were involved in fights I thought the children were terrified. I eventually learnt that I had misinterpreted their reactions, for they in fact often enjoyed the spectacle. This was borne out by people's comments and by the children's animated and carefree accounts. Most children seemed to have strong egos and they would stubbornly assert themselves. They were apt to strike out when thwarted. They frequently threw tantrums, smashed things and took sulk (*bunme*). The children fought each other and took sides in the traditional windward and leeward manner — even my five-year-old son was recruited. *The* childhood game was throwing tin lids at one another which the children blocked with sticks, or else they rolled the lids on the ground and tried to hit them, using their sticks as spears. Another favourite game was to place a glob of mud on the end of a switch and fling it at dragonflies. Needless to say these games are excellent training for hunting and fighting. Interestingly enough, the two come together, for almost all the best hunters are the best fighters. Participating in adult fights, with a weapon, is one way of demonstrating that a youth is a man. I witnessed this transformation a few times and I was impressed by how sudden and complete the transformation could be.

POPULATION DENSITY AND RELATIONAL DENSITY

The supercamp that the Mornington Islanders live in nowadays is quite different in area, population size, age structure and composition from their traditional camps.[9] The people are aware of these differences. The elderly, in particular, would marvel at the number of children, and claimed that they had never seen so many of them. Occasionally they would ask children who their parents were, in order to be certain about their relationship with them. Complaints about the number of people, the higgledy-piggledly residences and smoke from camp fires, were frequently made. Although I cannot be certain about the exact figures I think it is safe to conclude that, in the past, camps were normally small both in area and population size, and the people who habitually camped together were closely related. Occasionally, larger groups camped together, but only for short periods. It is certain that the whole Lardil tribe never camped together, and no one ever suggested that they did. It would in fact have been economically impossible for them to do so. But nowadays the whole tribe is together permanently in one supercamp, along with members of other tribes. As a consequence, not only is the population density high, but so is the relational density.[10] In a society like our own not everybody in a

---

[8] Fighting plays an important part in the politics of marriage. I intend to examine this topic in detail in a monograph.

[9] Ideally one would like to calculate the area and population size of traditional camps and contrast this with the village supercamp situation. Regrettably my data are not firm enough for such exact calculations.

[10] Originally I used the term social density for relational density. But as Durkheim also employed the term social density with a somewhat different meaning, I decided, in order to avoid any misunderstanding, to substitute the term relational density. For Durkheim, social density is mainly a matter of population concentration. Thus the greater the concentration of population in a given area the greater the social density (Durkheim 1984: pp. 200–3). I am not concerned here with population numbers or population density *per se*, but the number of social relationships in a community which result from a particular type of kinship system, which may be referred to as an all-embracing kinship system, where each person calls everybody else by a kinship or affinal term and has specific rights and duties towards them. Two societies may have the same social density (in Durkheim's use of the term) but they may differ radically in their relational density.

neighbourhood, or an estate, or a block of flats, is related to one another and indeed most people do not know each other. The situation in the Mornington Island supercamp is quite different. Each person is related to everybody else and calls them by a kinship or affinal term and *ideally* behaves towards them accordingly (i.e. acknowledges a duty to give them help or resources, as occasion demands). Thus each person has some 600 relationships, and there are, all told, approximately 359,400 relationships (600 × 599 = 359,400).[11] This high relational density places a heavy strain on relationships and on the social system as a whole. And even if these figures are scaled down by, say, 100,000, on the grounds that relationships between small children are not particularly demanding or load-bearing, we are still left with over a quarter of a million relationships. To place these figures in perspective, if we accept that the average population size of a traditional camp was 30 (which I think is a generous figure) then the relational density would have been 870 relationships (30 × 29 = 870). For the benefit of readers who are not familiar with the kinship and marriage systems of Australian Aborigines I should point out that classificatory relationships can be just as binding and load-carrying as actual genealogical relationships. Distant classificatory relationships are not watered-down versions of actual or close kin and affinal relationships. A consequence of the distinction between population density and relational density is that crude comparisons based in terms of population density can be grossly misleading. For two societies may have the same population density but they may differ greatly in the crucial factor of relational density.[12] Clearly we should be wary of comparisons of population densities between Australian

[11] Mention should be made of Frederick Rose's material on the Aborigines of Groote Eylandt, Northern Territory. Rose published 221 tables, one for each person, which *inter alia* shows the relationship of each person with everybody else (Rose 1960: pp. 247–467). For various reasons some tables are incomplete, but, all told, Rose recorded some 25,000 relationships. Rose estimated that the Aboriginal population, in 1941, was approximately 300–50 and the population density was approximately one person to three square miles (p. 12). In contrast, the Lardil population density in 1914 was approximately one person to one and a half square miles.

[12] I should like to make some additional points about relational density, for I do not believe that this concept has been isolated elsewhere. Relational density has a bearing on Morgan's famous distinction between classificatory kinship systems and descriptive kinship systems (Morgan 1871). It seems to me that these two systems may entail different psychological or emotive consequences. In a society with a classificatory kinship terminology one has many relatives in a particular category. For example, there are many women whom a man calls 'mother', and no matter how old a man may be there will always be women whom he calls 'mother'. In contrast, in a descriptive kinship terminology there may be only one woman who is called 'mother', and normally she is one's genetrix. Once this woman dies a man is motherless. However, as is well known, in some descriptive systems, such as our own, a

Aborigines and agriculturalists. For although, as it has often been pointed out, agriculturalists have a higher population density, nevertheless they may have a lower relational density. This point should also be taken into account when comparing Australian Aborigines with other hunting and gathering societies.

I would argue that the high population density and, more importantly, the high relational density of supercamp life, are factors which contribute to the incidence of violence. I camped in the bush on many occasions with Mornington Islanders. These camps rarely consisted of more than 20 people and often a lot less. At the beginning of the school holidays there were usually a few large camps, which were probably similar to the traditional base camps, but they soon dwindled as people split off and formed smaller camps. The campers were usually closely related. Each social unit, which was often a family (a man and his wife and unmarried children), had their own camp fire with enough space between them so that they were not cheek-by-jowl. If there were several older youths or bachelors present they normally camped together, which accords with accounts about traditional camping arrangements. On these camping trips people would exclaim how wonderful it was to be in the bush with just close kin, away from all the fighting, eating proper bush food, drinking really good water, and so on. All would adamantly declare their intention of not returning to the mission. But before long because of a shortage of supplies (mainly sugar, tea and tobacco), or sickness, or a desire to take back some bush food to a relative, etc., they would troop back. Significantly, on all the camping expeditions that I was present, I did not observe any overt violence. At times there were disagreements but they did not develop into fights. It would therefore seem that the Mornington Islanders can handle conflict when camps are small and members are closely related, but conflict erupts into violence when camps are large and many people are

---

number of genealogical relationships may be terminologically conflated into one category. Hence more than one person may be called by a particular term, e.g. 'aunt' and 'uncle'. But a descriptive system is not, and probably cannot be, all-embracing, as a classificatory system may be. It would seem that every all-embracing kinship system has a classificatory kinship terminology. A society with a classificatory kinship terminology has a greater relational density than a society with a descriptive kinship terminology. There are, however, other matters to be considered. A classificatory kinship terminology does not in itself entail rights and duties, nor the degree of rights and duties. The more rights and duties involved in a relationship, the heavier the relationship; and the fewer rights and duties involved in a relationship, the lighter the relationship. Finally I can only mention here that, following Durkheim (1893/1984) and Fortes (1969), a distinction may be made in terms of moral density.

distantly related. Additional support for this conclusion comes from the fact that the violent conflicts of the past that people recalled were almost invariably against outsiders, i.e. against members of other clans, or people outside their cardinal area, or between windward and leeward, or against other tribes. The serious fights that I witnessed in the village supercamp were against these same outsiders.[13]

Pertinent to my conclusion are the early reports about the occasional large assemblages among Australian Aborigines. In various regions several tribes would congregate to take advantage of the rich food resources that occurred every few years. A famous instance was the gathering of seeds from the bunya trees (*Araucaria bidwillii*) by the Brisbane tribes, in southern Queensland. 'At the prospect of an abundant yield, tribes would gather from a distance of upwards of a hundred miles to feast upon the bunya. The visit usually terminated with a battle' (Mathew 1910: p. 94). The usual violent outcome of these and other large assemblages indicates that the traditional social organization and forms of social control could not contain conflict at this level and neither, perhaps, were they expected to.

CONCLUSION

The answer to the question that I have so often asked myself in the field, i.e. why is there so much fighting, obviously lies in a number of factors. Fighting was endemic among the Lardil and other tribes on Mornington Island even before they came under mission control. There were violent clashes between the Lardil and Yangkal as well as with the neighbouring mainland tribes. Violence occurred among the Kaiadilt and there were violent clashes with outsiders. Granted that the Kaiadilt had suffered from an unprecedented concatenation of events, nevertheless it is surely significant that their social

---

[13] Professor Peter Worsley informs me that during his fieldwork on Groote Eylandt in 1952–53, fighting very rarely occurred. The Aboriginal population in that period was approximately 450. The low incidence of fighting may reflect the fact that the Aboriginal population was ethnically and culturally homogeneous, certainly more so than on Mornington Island; the people kept more of their traditional culture (e.g. unlike the Mornington Islanders they retained their language); and the population density and relational density were less than on Mornington Island. The Groote Eylandt Aborigines resided in two distinct supercamps. One was secular and was developed by Frederick H. Gray. The other was religious and was founded by the Church Mission Society. The Mission supercamp was established in 1921, but there was little real contact between the missionaries and the Aborigines until the mid-1930s (Worsley 1954: pp. 263ff.).

breakdown occurred at a time when their population density and relational density were at their peak. In the past the general picture of fighting among the Lardil appears to have been as follows. Most violent fights occurred outside the clan, and killings rarely occurred between members of a clan or other close kin. Both men and women fought and both men and women were killed, but men were the lethal fighters for they had the killing implements, that is, spears, boomerangs and clubs, and all killings were done by men.[14] I know of no case where a woman killed another woman or man. Traditionally, within the tribe there was a history of violence between different cardinal areas, and between windward and leeward moieties. To some extent fighting was controlled by rituals, rules and the role of middlemen, but this did not prevent severe woundings and killings.[15] Sometimes fighting was in the form of a duel, a formal 'square up' between two men or two groups in order to end hostilities; sometimes fighting consisted of a raid on a distant social group, or another tribe where rules seem to have been cast aside; and sometimes it was an unplanned and unorganized clash between two or more people. Fighting was an expected and accepted method of standing up for one's rights and exerting political influence.

The local and social organization of the tribes was disrupted after the mission was founded in 1914. This process occurred over a period of a couple of decades as the mission extended its influence in economic, religious, political and educational matters. A village supercamp developed near the mission which was quite unlike anything that the Aborigines had experienced in the past. Not only was the whole Lardil tribe, with their various factions and groups, camped in one place, but so were the Yangkal and remnants of several mainland tribes, and eventually the Kaiadilt. It was, to put it in popular idiom, unreal. The composition of the supercamp in itself goes far to explain why there has been so much fighting on Mornington Island. But there were also other factors at work. Within each tribal group, and for the supercamp as a whole, there were changes in the age structure. This came about in two ways: from children and young people being sent to Mornington

---

[14] Men are not only killers with spears but also killers with sorcery. Taking a broader view we discover a common theme in *markiri*, sorcery and fighting, viz. all three are highly xenophobic.

[15] Elsewhere (McKnight 1982: p. 507) I have briefly examined the part that nomadism and semi-nomadism may play in the incidence of violence. Suffice to say that although in the past Mornington Islanders shifted camp in order to avoid conflict and although, whilst I was in the field, people sometimes moved their dwellings (literally tore them down), or took their family and camped on the beach, or visited their clan area, these actions were nevertheless not particularly effective, for there was still much violence.

Island from the mainland; and from an increase in the birth rate as well as a decrease in the infant mortality rate. As a result the elders were heavily outnumbered by young people. The missionaries purposely created a generation gap by *inter alia* separating the children and young people from the old people, teaching them new values, and forbidding initiations and polygamy. These devices undermined the authority of the elders and when they attempted to use traditional sanctions (e.g. ridicule) many of the young people simply turned their backs on them and ridiculed them in turn. This situation did not happen all at once, not all traditional values were rejected, and neither did the young people accept all the new cultural values offered or imposed by the missionaries. But there were enough changes to create a split between the generations.

The presence of Aborigines of mixed descent, who identified with the missionaries and with things European, exacerbated matters. It seems that it was particularly through them that the missionaries sought to introduce and consolidate fundamental changes. This was accomplished partly by giving them more responsibilities, with the self-fulfilling expectation that they would be more capable than Aborigines of full descent. There has been, perhaps as a result of this favoured treatment, conflict between Aborigines of mixed descent and Aborigines of full descent. In addition, such was the ill feeling of many Lardil against mainlanders (of full descent as well as mixed descent) that they frequently claimed that the mainlanders did not belong to Mornington Island and that they should return to the mainland. Another important factor which has contributed to the incidence of fighting is the increase in population density and particularly the increase in relational density. For in the supercamp environment more people live together than in the past, and given a system whereby everybody is treated as a relative the net result is that the total number of social relationships has increased remarkably. Thus every person has been laden with a heavier social burden.

ACKNOWLEDGEMENTS

I wish to record my gratitude to the Australian Institute of Aboriginal Studies for financing my main period of fieldwork on Mornington Island, 1966—8. I also wish to thank the Nuffield Foundation, Central Research Fund of the University of London, Geographical and Anthropological Research Division of the London School of Economics, and the Social Science Research Council, for enabling me to continue my research in the years 1970—85. I should like to acknowledge that I have adopted Professor Ken Hale's orthography for Lardil terms (Hale 1981). And finally I would like to thank the Rev. Douglas Belcher, formerly Superintendent of the Mornington Island Mission, for his critical comments on an earlier draft. I should stress that I take full responsibility for the information and interpretations offered in this chapter.

I would regret it if my comments about the mission were to be interpreted as an attack on the missionaries. Many missionaries are well aware that their policies did not always have beneficial results. A proper evaluation of the policies of the missionaries must take historical context into account. Placing children in dormitories seems harsh today, but in the 1920s in Australia I dare say that this was regarded as the best way of educating children. During my main period of fieldwork on Mornington Island it was quite obvious that the Superintendent, the Rev. Douglas Belcher, did his best to move with the times. Indeed in many ways he was well in advance of the policies of the Queensland Government and the Presbyterian Board of Missions. He did all that he could to help preserve the people's traditional culture. He and his wife, Mrs Doreen Belcher, are held in high regard by the Mornington Islanders and I am indebted to them for their warm hospitality.

REFERENCES

Where two dates are given, the first refers to the original edition of a work and the second to the edition used in the text.

Durkheim, Emile 1893/1984: *The Division of Labour in Society.* Introduction by Lewis Coser; translated by W. D. Halls. Contemporary Social Theory. London: Macmillan.

Flinders, M. 1814: *Voyage to Terra Australis*, vol. 2. London.

Fortes, Meyer 1969: *Kinship and the Social Order: The Legacy of Lewis Henry Morgan.* London: Routledge and Kegan Paul.

Hale, K. 1981: *A Preliminary Dictionary of Lardil* (compiled by) Ken Hale, Ann Farmer, David Nash, and Jane Simpson. Cambridge, Mass.: MIT.

Mathew, John 1910: *Two Representative Tribes of Queensland.* London.

McKnight, David 1981: Sorcery in an Australian tribe. *Ethnology*, 20, 31—44.

_____ 1982: Conflict healing and singing in an Australian Aboriginal community. *Anthropos*, 77, 491—508.

Morgan, L. H. 1871: *Systems of Consanguinity and Affinity of the Human Family.* Washington: Smithsonian Contributions to Knowledge 17.

Rose, F. G. G. 1960: *Classification of Kin, Age Structure and Marriage amongst the Groote Eylandt Aborigines: a study in method and a theory of Australian kinship.* Berlin: Akademie-Verlag.

Stanner, W. E. H. 1969: *After the Dreaming* (The Boyer Lectures, 1968). Sydney NSW: The Australian Broadcasting Commission.

Strehlow, T. G. H. 1947: *Aranda Traditions.* Melbourne: Melbourne University Press.

_____ 1970: Geography and the totemic landscape in central Australia: A functional study. In R. M. Berndt (ed.), *Australian Aboriginal Anthropology*, Perth: University of Western Australia Press.

Tindale, N. B. 1962: Some population changes among the Kaiadilt people of Bentinck Island, Queensland. *Records of the South Australian Museum*, 14, 297—336.

Worsley, P. M. 1954: *The Changing Social Structure of the Wanindiljaugwa.* Unpublished PhD thesis. Canberra: Australian National University.

9

'Casuals', 'Terrace Crews' and 'Fighting Firms': Towards a Sociological Explanation of Football Hooligan Behaviour

Eric Dunning, Patrick Murphy and John Williams

INTRODUCTION

This chapter focuses on one of the core aspects of football hooliganism in Britain, namely the fighting between rival fan groups that has come, in the decade up to the mid-1980s, to form a quasi- or unofficially institutionalized part of soccer. Our aim is to contribute to an understanding of football hooliganism by: placing hooligan behaviour in its social context; exploring the sorts of satisfactions that hooligans derive from their disruptive behaviour; investigating the meanings that hooligan fans attribute to their actions; and finally, advancing a 'sociogenetic' hypothesis which explains how the norms and values underlying the fighting of football hooligans may be recurrently produced and reproduced.[1] On this last point, a critical elaboration of Suttles's theory of 'ordered segmentation' is used in an attempt to probe the continuing generation, in specific sections of the lower working class, of a social configuration in which streetcorner gangs, aggressive masculinity and a

This chapter is based on material from the authors' book, *The Roots of Football Hooliganism*, to be published shortly. The research on which it is based was financed by the Economic and Social Research Council and the Football Trust.

[1] We have adopted the term 'sociogenesis' from the work of Norbert Elias. For an example of a sociogenetic explanation of a long-term social process, see Elias (1978a, 1982).

relatively high tolerance of open violence in a whole range of public and private situations are principal components (Suttles 1968: p. 1972). Limitations of space preclude discussion of such important related matters as the explanations of football hooligan behaviour offered by the British authorities (including the football authorities), and by social scientists, and the remedies which the former have proposed to combat the phenomenon. But these are dealt with at some length in our forthcoming book (Dunning, Murphy and Williams, in press).[2]

BACKGROUND: SOME PARAMETERS OF FOOTBALL HOOLIGANISM AS A PROBLEMATIZED FORM OF SOCIAL BEHAVIOUR

Football hooliganism is widely regarded in Britain in the 1980s, as one of the most serious causes for public concern. It ranks beside such issues as the inexorable rise in unemployment, the supposedly ever increasing rates of delinquency, violence and crime, and the recently highly publicized apparent increase in the use of hard drugs, particularly among working-class teenagers. In some circles, indeed, especially because of its implications for Britain's standing in the world, football hooliganism seemingly ranks above such issues as a cause for alarm.

Disquiet over the violent and destructive behaviour of young football supporters has been widespread in Britain since the mid-1960s. However, there appears to be a growing consensus at the time of writing that hooligan behaviour, especially that of English fans both on the continent and at home, has become more entrenched and far more seriously violent. Correlatively, the fear has arisen that the long-term future of association football as a major British professional sport is, itself, seriously threatened.[3] Events in the 1980s have, in fact, conspired to begin at least to translate this fear from threat into

[2] Major sociological contributions to the study of football hooliganism are also offered by Clarke (1978), Hall (1978), Marsh et al. (1978), Robins and Cohen (1978) and Taylor (1971, 1978, 1981a, 1981b). With regard to both theoretical approach and findings there are *some* similarities between all these contributions and our own, but we should especially like to draw attention to the differences.

[3] The precise long-term effects on the game of incidents such as those involving Liverpool fans in Brussels in May 1985 are not, at the time of writing, easy to assess. However, it is not too difficult to make 'informed guesses' about what some of the consequences will probably be. For example, the 'deteriorating' image of the game may well accelerate the long-term tendency for match attendances to decline, and this tendency is likely to be reinforced by the ban imposed later in 1985 on English clubs from European competitions. The latter certainly means that less money will come into the English game at a time when major ground improvements are being legally demanded as a result of the fire in the stadium

166   *Dunning, Murphy and Williams*

reality. Thus, a long sequence of highly publicized, mainly English-inspired hooligan incidents abroad, culminating in those involving Liverpool fans in Brussels, in May 1985, which led to the death of thirty-nine, mostly Italian, football supporters, resulted in the imposition by the European football authorities of an indefinite ban on English clubs from European competitions.

Given the distinctive record of the English in recent years for regularly *exporting* football-related violence to the continent, it was not surprising that football's governing authorities should have felt compelled to take draconian measures against English clubs and their supporters. Over the couple of decades up to the mid-1980s, the phenomenon of football hooliganism has come in continental countries to be referred to as the 'English disease'.[4] However, while the hooligan problem in England may be unique in certain respects — it is, for example, at a relatively advanced stage of development in terms of the complex network of football gang rivalries which exist, and in terms of the degrees of organization and sophistication of the rival 'fighting firms' or 'crews' — there is also considerable evidence that spectator disorderliness at football matches is currently spreading elsewhere. More specifically, football hooliganism seems to be growing to something approaching similar social problem status in a number of European countries, most noticeably West Germany and Holland.[5] Indeed, countries such as Italy[6] and Scotland[7] have longer histories of football crowd disorder. It is, perhaps,

---

at Bradford which also occurred in the spring of 1985. The ban imposed during the same year on alcohol sales at football grounds will further reduce club revenue — some estimates suggest by as much as £4 million per season. Finally, if the poor image of football persists, it is likely that sponsors will begin to re-examine their financial links both with the Football League and particular clubs. Such developments could well have catastrophic if not fatal effects on the finances of many league clubs.

[4] Descriptions of this kind are now common in this country, too, although it was only twenty years ago that football administrators and journalists in England were expressing concern about the prospects of the English game contracting what was considered at the time to be a 'continental disease'. As far as we can tell, football hooliganism was first described as the 'English disease' in 1975 following disturbances in Paris involving Leeds United fans.

[5] The growing problem of football hooliganism in West Germany has given rise to a considerable amount of academic research. For a short bibliography of the relevant literature, see Dunning et al. *Crowd Violence Associated with Football Matches: a State of the Art Review*, prepared for the Sports Council on behalf of the Council of Europe, London, 1985. In Holland, clubs like Utrecht, Ajax and Feyenoord appear to be among those most persistently troubled by spectator violence and vandalism.

[6] For the record of football hooliganism in Italy, see Williams et al. (1984b: pp. 188—9).

[7] The best historical account of football hooliganism in Scotland is provided by Bill Murray (1984). See also Dunning et al. *Working Class Social Bonding and the Sociogenesis of Football Hooliganism*, end-of-grant report to the Social Science Research Council, 1982.

worthy of note that even despite the tragic loss of life in Brussels, young football fans in Italy, West Germany and France are reported to have 'celebrated', and expressed their admiration for the Liverpool fans engaged at the centre of the disturbances which led to the fatal crowd panic.

The hooligan phenomenon undoubtedly differs in identifiable ways in each of the countries named above. The relevant cross-national research remains to be carried out but, in its absence, the following probable dimensions of difference can be identified:

1   the type and scale of the hooligan acts that are committed;
2   the seriousness of the violence and vandalism that tend to be involved;
3   the degree to which hooligan incidents are more or less spontaneous or more or less organized;
4   the numbers and ages of those most typically involved;[8]
5   popular, media and official perceptions of the seriousness of the hooligan problem;
6   the responses of national and local government, the police and the football authorities, to particular hooligan incidents and the hooliganism problem as a whole.

The last dimension is of special interest and importance in this context because of the manner in which, in England, official reactions to hooliganism and the introduction of initiatives designed to curb it have had a tendency to re-shape and spread and even to exacerbate hooligan behaviour (Dunning, Murphy and Williams, in press). Besides such probable differences, however, it is likely that there are also similarities in the football-related disorders of different countries.

VARIETIES OF FOOTBALL HOOLIGAN BEHAVIOUR

As a form of behaviour, the disorderliness of football fans that has come to attract the label, 'football hooliganism', is complex and many-sided. In popular usage, for example, the label includes swearing, and behaviour which, in other social contexts, might well be excused as simple 'high spirits' or

---

[8] The social origins of the fans involved may constitute a further source of potential difference. In our view, however, this is unlikely. Football hooliganism is, in all probability, mainly a working-class phenomenon in all countries. There are exceptions, of course; for example, one of the Juventus fans arrested in Brussels was reported to be the son of a wealthy industrialist. There are comparable exceptions in England, too, but that is what they are: exceptions.

'boisterousness'. In fact, many of the fans who are arrested in a football context have engaged only in behaviour of this kind.

More seriously, the label, 'football hooligan', includes pitch invasions which appear to be deliberately engineered in order to halt a match and which can involve a greater or lesser degree of violence. It also involves fracas between opposing fan groups which vary in their scale, and which are frequently violent and destructive. As we said at the beginning, it is with this latter form of the hooligan phenomenon that we shall be principally concerned in this chapter. More particularly, our argument will be that, although there are many young fans who are drawn into hooligan incidents in specific situations — fans who did not set out for the match with the intention of fighting or engaging in other forms of disorderly and disruptive behaviour — the hard core, who engage most persistently in hooligan behaviour in a football context and elsewhere, view fighting and behaving aggressively as an integral part of 'going to the match'. Fans like these are the central figures in the named and organized football 'gangs' who currently dominate the English hooligan scene. They include: 'the Inter City Firm' at West Ham; 'the Service Crew' at Leeds; 'the Anti-Personnel Firm' at Chelsea; 'the Gooners' at Arsenal; 'the Bushwhackers' at Milwall; 'the Main Line Crews' from Manchester, as well as numerous, less prominent 'casual crews' from other parts of the country. ('Casual' because they share with their larger and better known counterparts an intense interest in, and competition in terms of, expensive 'casual' clothing including Italian leisure wear and 'track-suit' styles).[9] The size of such informal groups varies considerably, ranging from fairly small numbers to hundreds of young fans, depending, for example, upon their position in the national 'terrace status hierarchy' and their ability to attract recruits from more than a local catchment area. Generally speaking, however, the activities of even the largest groups are dominated by a relatively small number of young adult males who are already locally celebrated on account of their toughness, their ability as strategists and their capability of organizing 'the action' and, above all, because of their proven ability as fighters. Rivalries between these groups are intense, especially in large urban areas such as London where a relatively large number of gangs exist side by side in territories which they identify as their own but which are frequently penetrated by rival crews. In such situations, football rivalries are superimposed upon

---

[9] Such styles became national news in Britain, in May 1985, when the arrest and conviction of the core members of the 'Cambridge Casuals' was widely reported. In fact, they had been popular among hooligan gangs — especially in southern England — since the late 1970s.

pre-existing territorial rivalries and acted out, not only in a football context but in non-football contexts, too, such as discos, pubs and clubs.

Usually the gangs come from and identify with a particular local community as well as with a particular football club. However, in some cases, such as at Chelsea, they are recruited from farther afield and form *ad hoc* in the football context, their members being drawn together, for example, because, while their parents have migrated to the suburbs, *they* (the sons) retain strong inner-city identifications. Famous clubs such as Manchester United, whose 'ends' are, or have been, nationally notorious for their hooligan behaviour, also recruit some of their hooligan following from outside the city that they represent; thus, the 'Cockney Reds', from London, are staunch Manchester United supporters.

Confrontations between these rival football gangs vary in terms of scale, form and the contexts in which they take place. They can, for example, take the form of hand-to-hand fighting between a small number of rival fans, or they can involve up to several hundred fans on either side. When they occur in or in the vicinity of pubs, they sometimes involve the throwing of bottles and glasses or the use of these articles in more direct combat. In the most serious incidents, whatever the context, other weapons are sometimes used, such as lightweight and easily concealed workmen's 'Stanley knives', although some crews frown upon the use of 'tools', which they view as cowardly and 'unmanly' in hand-to-hand fighting. Football hooligan confrontations can also take the form of aerial attacks, using as ammunition missiles which range from innocuous plastic cups and apple cores to potentially lethal darts, metal discs, coins (sometimes with their edges sharpened), broken seats, bricks, slabs of concrete, ball bearings, fireworks, distress flares, smoke bombs, golf and billiard balls and, as has been reported on one or two occasions, crude incendiary devices.

Missile throwing can take place inside or outside the ground, although police searches as fans enter grounds have, at the time of writing, restricted the opportunities for missile bombardment inside stadia. As a consequence of the official policy of segregating rival fans — a policy introduced in the 1960s as a means of curbing football hooliganism, but which seems to have had greater success in enhancing the solidarity of football ends and driving hooliganism outside grounds — large-scale fights between rival fan groups on the terraces became relatively rare during the 1970s and early 1980s. Small groups of fans, however, still managed frequently to infiltrate the territories of their rivals in order to start a fight or create what they regard as an 'exciting disturbance'. Participating in a successful invasion — 'taking' somebody else's 'end' — had greater relevance for hooligans in the 1960s but, in specific contexts, it still remains a source of great kudos in football hooligan circles. In the mid-1980s, successful routs of the home end *inside* grounds are much more likely to occur when the English travel abroad to continental grounds which are not yet equipped to deal with manoeuvres of this kind. In the domestic context, when it does occur, fighting tends to take place in the largely unsegregated seated sections of grounds or before the match, for example, in and around town centre pubs. It also takes place after the match when the police are trying to keep rival fans apart and to get the main body of away fans to the railway or bus stations without serious incident. On occasions, rival groups communicate an intention to meet at a particular location before or after the match. Such locations are chosen because the hooligan fans believe that this will enable them to avoid the attentions of the police and give them a chance to establish, without outside interference or fear of arrest, which is the 'superior' crew.[10]

Usually, however, it is *after* matches that the larger scale and more destructive confrontations tend to occur. These often start with a 'run', that is, with a rush of perhaps two or three hundred young male fans, who race along the streets looking for young opposing fans who are identifiably part of the rival 'end',[11] or for a breach in the police defences that will enable them to make contact with their rivals. 'Hard core' hooligans, however, those who are most committed to engaging groups of opposing fans, often operate apart from the main body and use elaborate tactics in an attempt to outflank the police. If they are successful, a series of violent skirmishes, scattered over a relatively large area, usually takes place. Occasionally, vehicles carrying rival supporters are attacked, and confrontations also occur by accident or design, when groups of rival fans *en route* to different matches meet, for example, on trains, the underground or at motorway service stations. In addition, fights sometimes occur *within* particular fan groups, the participants in such cases being drawn, for example, from different city-centre drinking groups or from different local housing estates.

One of the main distinguishing marks of these informally organized 'fighting crews' is the fact that they do not travel to matches on 'football specials' or official coaches but tend, instead, to use regular (Inter-City) rail and coach

[10] Scottish 'casuals', for example, have been known to paste 'newsheets' at railway stations inviting opposing hooligans to fight in a stated street before or after matches. In England, in an attempt to avoid the 'spoiling' attention of the police, younger 'apprentices' of the 'firms' sometimes act as go-betweens in arranging the venue for a fight.

[11] Although innocent fans do sometimes get caught up in hooligan incidents, most of the major 'firms' seek out their counterparts within the rival fan-group. These can usually be identified by their stylistic preferences, their accents, the fact that they move around in large groups, and because they, too, are clearly on the look-out for 'aggro'.

services, or cars and privately hired coaches and vans. Some of their members are known to have connections with extreme Right-wing, racist organizations such as the British National Party and the National Front, although some of the more notorious 'crews', especially those located in the London area, also have increasing numbers of young blacks prominent in their ranks. Less commonly, a small number of 'ends' now appear to be attracting young Asian recruits.[12]

The youths and young men who generally make up 'fighting crews' also reject the forms of dress — the scarves, favours and heavy boots (also the club banners) — that still tend to be widely associated with football hooliganism in popular opinion.[13] Since one of their main objectives in attending matches is to engineer confrontations with opposing fans and, less frequently, with the police, fans of this kind, although they sometimes have agreed marks for recognizing their own members, travel without sporting marks of identification which would advertize them too soon to opposing fans and the police. 'Howie', a 20 year old Leicester 'hard case' whom we interviewed, had this to say about the weekly battle of wits between local fans like himself and the local police:

If you can baffle the coppers, you'll win. You've just gotta think how they're gonna think. And you know, half the time you know what they're gonna do, 'cos they're gonna take the same route every week, week in, week out. If you can figure out a way to beat 'em, you're fuckin' laughin': you'll have a good fuckin' raut. (Leicester slang for 'a fight'). That's why I never wear a scarf, in case I go in (the opposition's) side. I used to wear a scarf but (the police) used to come and fuckin' stop me. Used to grab the scarf and go, 'bang, bang'! I thought, 'I ain't having that. Take it off, they can't grab hold of you . . .

This general description of some of the main parameters of football hooliganism and some of the changes that aspects of it have undergone in the last two decades is consistent with the general point we made earlier, namely that the youths and young men who are regularly involved in the most serious football-related incidents tend to view fighting and confrontations with opposing fans as constituting an important part of attending a football match.

---

[12] Mixed black and white football fighting gangs are prominent at such London clubs as Spurs, Milwall and West Ham United. Impressionistic evidence from Leicester suggests that Asian youths may be becoming increasingly involved in football gangs.

[13] Such tendencies are reinforced, for example by newspaper cartoons which purport to portray hooligan offenders. They do so by representing them as 'skinheads' complete with anachronistic 'bovver' boots and scarves.

The songs and chants which form a conspicuous feature of inter-fan-group rivalry, especially inside stadia, point in the same direction. Although some members of 'fighting crews' regard singing and chanting as lacking in style, and as being the preserve of younger fans or those who are less 'streetwise' than themselves, the main bodies of rival fans direct their attention during the match as much, and sometimes more, to one another as they do to the match itself. They sing, chant and frequently gesticulate *en masse* as expressions of their opposition to and disdain for their rivals. Their songs and slogans are in part related to the match and in part used as a form of entertainment during dull periods of play. But they also have as a recurrent theme provocative taunts ('Munich '58'; 'Aberfan'),[14] challenges to fight, threats of violence to opposing fans and boasts about past victories against rival 'terrace crews'. Each fan group has its own repertoire of songs and chants, but many of these are local variations on a stock of common themes. Central in this connection is the fact that their lyrics are punctuated with words like 'hate', 'fight', 'surrender', 'kick' and 'die', all of which convey images of battle and conquest (Jacobson 1975). Apart from violence and the sorts of provocation already mentioned, symbolic demasculinization of the rival fans is another recurrent terrace theme. It is captured in the frequent reference to them and/or the team they support as 'wankers', and usually accompanied by a mass gestural representation of the male masturbatory act. Yet another recurring theme is the ritual denigration of the community of the opposing fans: but let us turn now to the subject of explanation.

Our concern will be to explore the social generation of the norms and values which are expressed in the most seriously violent forms of football hooligan behaviour. In order to make a start in this direction, we shall first consider the available evidence on the social origin of the fans who are most typically involved in football hooligan fighting. Much of this evidence comes from our own research at Leicester.

[14] 'Munich 1958' is a taunt sometimes aimed at provoking the fans of the Manchester United club. It refers to the aeroplane crash in 1958 in which one half of the then Manchester United team was killed. When the chant was used against United fans at a match in Cardiff in 1974, the visitors responded with chants of 'Aberfan' aimed at the Welsh fans. This chant is a reference to a 1960s tragedy in which Welsh schoolchildren from the village of Aberfan were killed following the collapse of a slag heap onto their school.

FOOTBALL HOOLIGANISM AND THE 'ROUGH' WORKING CLASS:
'ORDERED SEGMENTATION' AND THE FORMATION OF
FAN-GROUP ALLIANCES

Systematic information on the social origins of the fans who fight at football matches is currently rather scarce, but data on those *convicted* for football-related offences are consistent with our own from participant observation. More particularly, both sets of data suggest that the phenomenon is *predominantly* — but by no means solely — the preserve of the lower working class. For example, Trivizas (1980) concluded that over eighty per cent of the persons charged with football-related offences were either manual workers or unemployed. His findings in this respect were similar to those of Harrington (1968), and to the impressionistic conclusion reached by Harrison (1974). And at least some of the subjects in the study at Oxford, by Peter Marsh and his colleagues, confirmed their residence on local housing estates, though the authors of this study did not directly address the issue of class background (Marsh et al.: 1978: 69). Our evidence from Leicester supports this general picture, with one lower working-class council estate accounting for around twenty per cent of the fans arrested at Leicester City home matches between January 1976 and April 1980. (The remainder came predominantly from other council estates.) This sort of evidence raises the question of what it is about the structure of lower working-class communities and the position they occupy in society at large that generates and sustains the pattern of aggressive masculinity that some of their members display at football matches and elsewhere.

A useful lead in explaining the social generation of the 'aggressive masculine style' which seems to be characteristic of lower working-class communities — or at least of specific sections of them — is provided, as we said at the beginning, by the American sociologist, Gerald Suttles (1968: p. 10). His research was carried out in Chicago and focused on materially disadvantaged communities whose overall pattern was one where 'age, sex, ethnic and territorial units are fitted together like building blocks to create a larger structure.' He coined the term, 'ordered segmentation', in order to capture two related features of the pattern of life in such communities: firstly, the fact that, while the segments that make up larger neighbourhoods are relatively independent of each other, the members of these segments nevertheless have a tendency to combine in the event of opposition and conflict, and that they do so entirely without central co-ordination or control; and secondly, the fact that group alignments of this kind tend to build up according to a fixed sequence. The pattern is similar in certain respects to what happens in the 'segmentary lineage systems' discussed by anthropologists such as Evans-Pritchard (1940), and to what Robins and Cohen observed on a North London housing estate (1978: pp. 73ff.). More significantly for present purposes, Harrison refers to what he calls 'the Bedouin syndrome' in the contemporary football context, namely to a tendency for *ad hoc* alliances to be built up according to the following principles: the friend of a friend is a friend; the enemy of an enemy is a friend; the enemy of a friend is an enemy; and the friend of an enemy is an enemy (1974: p. 604).

Our own observations provide some evidence to support the existence of this pattern both on working-class estates and in the football context. In Leicester, intra-estate conflicts involving groups of young male adolescents regularly give way to the requirements of defending the 'good name' of the estate as a whole against rival gangs from neighbouring estates. However, these estates and others from Leicester and the surrounding area regularly align themselves on the terraces and in the seats at the Filbert Street stadium, or outside the ground, in the cause of expressing 'home end' solidarity in opposition to visiting fans. If the challenge is perceived in regional terms then, again, enemies may join forces. For example, Northern fans visiting London often complain about confrontations with combined 'fighting crews' from a number of metropolitan clubs. Euston Station used to be a favourite venue for confrontations of this kind when the North would be 'seen off'. Southerners and Midlanders visiting major Northern cities also voice complaints about attacks from inter-end alliances. Finally, at the international level, club and regional rivalries tend to be subordinated to the interests of national reputation. At each of these levels, of course, especially if opposing groups do not provide a challenge which is perceived to be sufficient to unite otherwise rival fans in common opposition, lower-level rivalries sometimes re-emerge.

Having established some of the ways in which 'ordered segmentation' operates in the football context, let us probe the structure of the sorts of communities which tend to approximate to this pattern in somewhat greater detail. We shall endeavour, in particular, to shed light on how they tend to produce fighting fans more frequently than communities of a different type.

'ORDERED SEGMENTATION' AND THE
FORMATION OF STREETCORNER GANGS

According to Suttles, the dominant feature of a community based on 'ordered segmentation' is the single-sex peer group, or in more common terminology, the 'streetcorner gang'. Such groups, he argues, seem 'to develop quite logically out of a heavy emphasis on age-grading, avoidance between the sexes, territorial unity and ethnic solidarity.' However, Suttles documents the regular occurrence of conflict between 'gangs' of the same ethnic group, and he recognizes elsewhere that ethnic differentiation and solidarity are contingent rather than necessary factors in the development of such 'gangs'. That is, age-grading (perhaps 'age-group segregation' would be a more accurate term), sex segregation and territorial identification appear to be the crucial *internal* social structural determinants. More particularly, the strong degree of age-group segregation in such communities means that many children are sent into the streets to play, unsupervised by adults, at an early age. This tendency is reinforced by a variety of domestic pressures. Segregation of the sexes means that, by adolescence, there is a tendency for girls to be drawn into the home, although some form fairly aggressive 'gangs' of their own or simply 'hang around' with the lads where their status tends to be a subordinate one. As a result of this overall social figuration — and apart from the attentions that they regularly attract from the police and other agencies of the state — adolescent males in communities of this sort are left largely to their own devices and tend to band into groups that are determined, on the one hand, by ties of kinship and close or common residence, and on the other, by the real or perceived threat posed by the development of parallel 'gangs' in adjacent communities. According to Suttles, such communities tend to be internally fragmented but, he argues, they achieve a degree of cohesion in the face of real or perceived threats from outside. An actual or rumoured 'gang fight' engenders the highest degree of cohesion, he maintains, for such fights can mobilize the allegiance of males throughout a community.

We can, perhaps, add to Suttles's formulation by suggesting that adolescent males in lower working-class communities are also bound together by the similarity of their life experiences, perhaps especially by their occupational experiences or, as is becoming increasingly the case (in this, along with many other countries), by their common experience of unemployment. Suttles's argument can also be extended via the suggestion that, to the extent that their structures correspond to the pattern of 'ordered segmentation', sections of lower working-class communities will tend to generate standards which, relative to those of groups higher in the social hierarchy, tolerate a high level of open violence in social relations. Several aspects of the structure of such communities tend to work in this direction. For example, the comparative freedom from direct and continuous adult control experienced by lower working-class children and adolescents, and the fact that so much of their early socialization takes place in the streets in the company of their age and gender peers, means that they tend to interact aggressively and violently among themselves and to develop dominance hierarchies that are based largely on age, strength and physical prowess. These sorts of tendencies are liable to be reinforced by the encouragement given by adults, especially to young males, that they should develop the capacity 'to stand up for themselves' when physically threatened, and by the frequency with which relatively violent means of socialization are employed.

Also crucial to the formation of this pattern is the tendency towards segregation of the sexes and male dominance in communities of this sort. This means, on the one hand, that such communities tend to be characterized by a comparatively high rate of male violence towards women, and, on the other, that their male members are not consistently subjected to 'softening' female pressure. Indeed, to the extent that the women in such communities grow up to be relatively aggressive themselves and to value many of the *macho* characteristics of their men, the aggressive tendencies of the latter are liable to be compounded. Further reinforcement comes from the comparative frequency of publicly visible feuds and vendettas between families, neighbour-hoods and, above all, 'streetcorner gangs'. In short, lower working-class communities of the type we are describing, especially those sections of them to which the adjective 'rough' most literally applies, appear to be characterized by 'feedback' processes which encourage the resort to aggressive behaviour in many areas of social relations, especially on the part of males.

One of the effects of these processes is the conferral of prestige on males with a proven ability to fight. Correlatively, there is a tendency for such males to enjoy fighting and to regard openly aggressive behaviour in certain contexts as both appropriate and desirable. They also view it as a means of gaining status and prestige. As a result, their identities tend to be centred around what are, relative to the standards that are dominant in Britain today, openly aggressive forms of *macho* masculinity. Many males of this kind also have a high emotional investment in the reputation of their families, their communities and, where they are into the 'football action', their 'ends' or 'crews', as aggressive and tough. This pattern is produced and reproduced, not only by the constituent *internal* elements of 'ordered segmentation', but also — and this is equally crucial — by some of the ways in which such communities are locked into the wider society. For example, lower working-class males are typically denied status, meaning and gratification in the educational and occupational spheres, which are the major sources of identity, meaning and status available to males higher up the social scale. This denial comes about as a result of a combination of factors. Thus, the majority of lower-class males do not have — nor does their culture lead them typically to prize — the characteristics and attributes that make for formal educational and occupational success, or for striving in these fields. At the same time, they tend to be discriminated against in the worlds of school and work, in part because they find themselves at the bottom of a hierarchical social structure which seems to require a permanent and relatively impoverished underclass as a constituent feature (Gans 1968).

In addition to these facts, a central difference between the 'rougher' sections of lower working-class communities and their more 'respectable' counterparts, both at the same level of stratification and higher up the social scale, seems to be that, in the latter, openly aggressive or violent behaviour in public situations tends to be normatively condemned whereas, in the former, it receives a higher degree of social toleration and is, in a greater variety of circumstances, normatively sanctioned. A correlative difference lies in the fact that there is a greater tendency in the 'respectable' classes for violence to be 'pushed behind the scenes' and, when it does occur in public, for it to take, on balance, either a defensive or more obviously 'instrumental' form. By contrast, violent or aggressive behaviour in those sections of the lower working class to which the adjective 'rough' most literally applies, tends to be more public, to be more frequently initiated as a means of achieving goals and to take, on balance, a more 'expressive' or 'affectual' form. Furthermore, whilst members of the 'respectable' classes, especially males, are allowed (indeed, encouraged and expected) to behave aggressively in specific contexts which are generally regarded as 'legitimate' (for example, formal sports), such avenues are either unavailable to their 'rough' counterparts, or tend to be regarded by them as too regulated and/or tame (Willis 1978: p. 29).

Because of their close identity with their own communities, and because they have relatively few power resources and are likely, as a result, to experience unfamiliar territories and people as potentially threatening and hostile, the violent propensities of groups in the rougher sections of the lower working class have tended, for the most part, to be expressed within or near their own communities and locales. This is less so today, of course, because of the availability of relatively cheap 'package holidays' and, perhaps above all, because of the increasing tendency for lower working-class males to travel in groups to football matches in different parts of the country and abroad. These violent propensities have also been sporadically expressed in other social contexts, giving rise to moral panics among more established groups. Such contexts have tended to shift under the influence of changes in fashion, for example, from cinemas to dance halls to seaside resorts. However, although the fighting and related activities of lower working-class males have increased and become more prominent at football matches in the two decades up to the mid-1980s, it is also the case that association football provides a relatively *permanent* context for the expression of aggressive masculinity. That is, virtually since its emergence in the late nineteenth century in its modern form, the game has been accompanied by fan disorder, much of it involving physical violence. The incidence of such disorder seems to have varied over time, depending, for example, upon the changing social composition of football crowds and the changing proportions in the wider society of 'rough' and 'respectable' communities. We do not have the space here to sketch in and account for changes in the rates of hooligan behaviour at and in conjunction with football matches over the past century, and, in any case, we have tackled that issue elsewhere (Dunning et al. 1984a). Instead, we shall try in what remains of this chapter to account for the rise of football hooligan behaviour to 'social problem' status in this country around the mid-1960s.

THE EMERGENCE OF FOOTBALL HOOLIGANISM AS A 'SOCIAL PROBLEM'

During the inter-war years and, in fact, right up to the 1960s, English football crowds tended to be praised by the media for their good behaviour. Although crowd disorderliness continued to be reported sporadically as occurring at and in conjunction with Football League matches in that period, this 'subterranean current' tended to be downplayed and, when incidents of misbehaviour by foreign fans or by fans from the non-English parts of the British Isles occurred, reports and, above all, editorial comments tended to emphasize the comparative orderliness of English crowds. In fact, media treatment and crowd behaviour in England around this time seem to have mutually reinforced each other to produce a 'feedback cycle' which had the effect of leading to a more or less continuous enhancement in the 'respectability' of football crowds. In the mid-to-late 1950s, however, in conjunction with the 'Teddy boy'[15] scare and the more general moral crisis of those years over working-class youth, the media picked on and amplified the sort of violent incidents which had always, from time to time, occurred in and around crowded football grounds. Football officials also reacted in an increasingly alarmist manner to such incidents because of their growing concern, during a period of falling match attendances and expanding television coverage of football, with the 'image' of the game. It was, however, the preparations for staging the World Cup Finals in England, in 1966, that appear to have been of decisive significance in this regard. This event meant that English crowds, long held up by the British press as an example to their counterparts in other parts of the world, were about to come under the scrutiny of the *international* media and, in that context, popular newspapers in this country began to focus

---

[15] 'Teddy boy' refers to the young men of generally anti-establishment social demeanour, who affected Edwardian styles of dress in 1950s' Britain.

increasingly on football hooliganism as a potential threat to the country's international prestige. By November, 1965, a number of stories warning of the consequences of *televised* misbehaviour had already been prominently featured in the popular press and when, in that month, a dead hand grenade was thrown onto the pitch by a Milwall fan during the encounter of his team with London rivals, Brentford, the *Sun* printed the following story under the headline, 'Soccer Marches to War':

The Football Association have acted to stamp out this increasing mob violence within 48 hours of the blackest day in British soccer — the grenade day that showed that British supporters can rival anything the South Americans can do. The World Cup is now less than nine months away. That is all the time we have left to try and restore the once good sporting name of this country. Soccer is sick at the moment. Or better, its crowds seem to have contracted some disease that causes them to break out in fury.[16]

Around the time of the 1966 World Cup, too, the popular press started sending reporters to matches to report on crowd behaviour and not simply on the game itself. Not surprisingly, these reporters saw incidents which, although by this time they were undoubtedly on the increase, had always tended to occur. In this way, the rate at which football hooliganism was *reported* began to be amplified disproportionately to the *factual* rate of increase that was occurring. What is more, because it had the advantage of selling papers in an increasingly competitive industry, and because of the increase in the moral and political panic about youth violence which occurred around that time, they tended to report such incidents in a sensationalistic manner, often using a military rhetoric. Thus, football grounds came increasingly to be portrayed as places where fighting and disruptive incidents, and not just football, regularly took place. This drew in young males who found incidents of this kind satisfying and exciting, adding to the already existing momentum for more orderly spectators to withdraw their support, especially from the goal-end terraces, and contributing to the situation in which we find ourselves in 1985, that is, one where disruptive incidents at football are larger in scale and a much more regular accompaniment of ínatches than used to be the case, and where the English hooliganism problem has been exported abroad to an extent sufficient to lead to a ban on English clubs playing matches on the continent. The mass media did not cause this process on their own, of course, but they can be said, as a kind of self-fulfilling

16 *The Sun*, 8 November 1965.

prophecy, to have played an important part in bringing about football hooliganism in its distinctive mid-1980s' form.

Football is, in a number of ways, a highly appropriate context for the sorts of activities that members of the 'fighting crews' and their younger apprentices find meaningful, exciting and enjoyable. As a result, once they have been attracted there, they tended to stay. At a football match, for example, they are able, in a context that provides relative immunity from arrest and from direct, person-to-person censure, to act in ways that are generally frowned upon and reacted to with alarm by officialdom and 'respectable' society. Both travel to matches, and the game itself can generate high levels of excitement, the focus of which is a contest - a 'mock battle' with a ball — between the male representatives of two communities. Though formally controlled and in a sense more abstract, and usually less openly violent), the game is in many ways analogous to the sorts of confrontations in which the hooligan fans engage — it is also a form of ritualized masculinity struggle. Also, to the extent that the away team brings with it large numbers of supporters, a ready-made group of opponents is provided and, in that context, the rivalries that exist between groups of local 'hard cases' can be at least temporarily submerged in the interests of 'home end' solidarity.

CONCLUSION

By way of conclusion, it is important to stress that our argument is not that youths and young men from the lower working class are the *only* football hooligans. Nor is it that all adolescent and young adult males from lower working-class communities use football as a context for fighting. Some fight elsewhere and others hardly fight at all. Our point is rather that youths and young men from the 'rougher' sections of the lower working class (we do not regard the concepts, 'rough working class', and 'lower working class', as synonymous in any simple sense) seem to be the most central and persistent offenders in the more serious forms of football hooliganism.

It should also be clear from this paper that we are not proposing any of the 'single factor' explanations — drink; 'permissiveness'; the National Front; unemployment — which are prominent in public debate about the hooliganism issue. Of these, unemployment probably has the greatest claim to central causal statuis but only in a complex and indirect sense. Thus, it is certainly the case that the communities which tend to produce the majority of hooligan fans are those which persistently have the highest levels of unemployment. They also tend to be the hardest hit in times of economic recession. But, whilst unemployment — along with poverty — clearly plays a crucial part in producing and reproducing many aspects of the structure and social character of lower working-class communities, it cannot be said that there is a simple correlation between it and the probability of involvement in football hooligan fighting. For one thing, football hooliganism began to reach its current peak in the mid-1960s at a time when unemployment was relatively low. For another, the currently high level of joblessness has probably impeded at least some 'hard cases' from continuing their activities at football. In other words, hooligan fans who remain in work are better able to maintain their football links, though, of course, account has to be taken in this connection of the dependency of some of them on 'the black economy' and simple crime. Finally, some of the most violent 'fighting' crews come from relatively prosperous London.

Nor is it our contention that, because hooliganism at football matches can be shown to be deeply rooted in the British past, it has, therefore, been entirely unchanging in its form, content and consequences. Among the factors at work shaping the specific character of the 'football hooligan phenomenon' since the late 1950s have been:

1 the structural changes that have been occurring within the 'rough' and 'respectable' sections of the working class, and in the relationships between them;
2 the rise of a specifically teenage leisure market;
3 the increased ability and desire of young fans to go to away matches on a regular basis both in this country and abroad;
4 changes in the structure of the game itself and in the relations between clubs and supporters;
5 specific attempts by the football authorities to curb hooliganism and the involvement of central government in this process;
6 changes in the structure and operations of the mass media, particularly the advent of television and the emergence of the 'tabloid' press with its competition-generated and populist concept of 'newsworthiness';
7 the recent virtual collapse of the youth labour market.

In our view, each of these factors — which are, in some ways at least, historically specific — has made a contribution of some significance to the forms, contents and extent of football hooliganism since the 1950s. However, our research leads us to believe that many of the values which underlie and are expressed in football hooligan fighting are relatively persistent, deeply rooted and long-standing features of specific sections of the working class. It follows, if our arguments are sound, that an adequate understanding of the phenomenon requires: (1) not only an analysis of social (including economic) developments since the Second World War but also an *historical sociological*

182   *Dunning, Murphy and Williams*

(developmental) account of the manner in which such communities and the values their members espouse have been produced and reproduced over a much longer span of time; and (2) a diachronic account of variations in the extent to which football has formed a context for the expression of these values. Until such an understanding has been achieved, official and media discussions of football hooliganism will remain at their presently high level of superficiality, and attempts to eradicate or curb the phenomenon will, at best, fail to hit the mark, or at worst, displace and perhaps even exacerbate it.

REFERENCES

Clarke, John 1978: Football and working class fans: tradition and change. In Roger Ingham (ed.), *Football Hooliganism: the wider context*, London: Inter-Action Imprint.
Dunning, E., Murphy P. and Williams, J. 1984a: Football hooliganism in Britain before the First World War. *International Review for the Sociology of Sport*, 19, 215–40.
_____ 1984b: *Hooligans Abroad: the behaviour and control of English fans in continental Europe*. London: Routledge and Kegan Paul.
_____ in press: *The Roots of Football Hooliganism*. London: Routledge and Kegan Paul.
Elias, Norbert 1978a: *The Civilizing Process*. Oxford: Basil Blackwell.
_____ 1978b: *What is Sociology?* London: Hutchinson.
_____ 1982: *State Formation and Civilization*. Oxford: Basil Blackwell.
Evans-Pritchard, E. E. 1940: *The Nuer*. Oxford: Oxford University Press.
Gans, Herbert J. 1968: Urbanism and suburbanism as ways of life. In R. E. Pahl (ed.), *Readings in Urban Sociology*, London: Pergamon Press.
Hall, Stuart 1978: The treatment of 'football hooliganism' in the press. In Roger Ingham (ed.), *Football Hooliganism: the wider context*, London: Inter-Action Imprint.
Harrington, J. A. 1968: *Soccer Hooliganism*. Bristol: John Wright.
Harrison, Paul 1974: Soccer's tribal wars. *New Society*, 29, 604.
Jacobson, Simon 1975: Chelsea rule — okay. *New Society*, 31, 780–83.
Marsh, P., Rosser, E. and Harré, R. 1978: *The Rules of Disorder*. London: Routledge and Kegan Paul.
Murray, Bill 1984: *The Old Firm: sectarianism, sport and society in Scotland*. Edinburgh: J. Donald.
Robins, D. and Cohen, P. 1978: *Knuckle Sandwich: growing up in the working class city*. Harmondsworth: Penguin.
Suttles, Gerald 1968: *The Social Order of the Slum: ethnicity and territory in the inner city*. Chicago: Chicago University Press.
_____ 1972: *The Social Construction of Communities*. Chicago: Chicago University Press.

Taylor, Ian 1971: Football mad: a speculative sociology of football hooliganism. In Eric Dunning (ed.), *The Sociology of Sport: a selection of readings*, London: Frank Cass.

_____ 1978: Soccer consciousness and soccer hooliganism. In Stan Cohen (ed.), *Images of Deviance*, Harmondsworth: Penguin.

_____ 1982a: On the sports violence question: soccer hooliganism revisited. In Jennifer Hargreaves (ed.), *Sport, Culture and Ideology*, London: Routledge and Kegan Paul.

_____ 1982b: Class, violence and sport: the case of soccer hooliganism in Britain. In Hart Cantelon and Richard S. Gruneau (eds), *Sport, Culture and the Modern State.* Toronto: Toronto University Press.

Trivizas, Eugene 1980: Offences and offenders in football crowd disorders. *British Journal of Criminology* 20, 276—88.

Willis, Paul 1978: *Profane Culture*. London: Routledge and Kegan Paul.

10

Violence in Rural Northern Ireland: Social Scientific Models, Folk Explanations and Local Variation (?)

Graham McFarlane

INTRODUCTION

This chapter is a study of the way in which social scientists and lay observers have attempted to understand the violence in rural Northern Ireland: the focus is on an audience trying to make sense of the relationship between the Catholic/Protestant (or Nationalist/Unionist) division, and of the acts of killing and serious injury perpetrated by members of one side on the other. A total account of the situation in Northern Ireland obviously requires a detailed objective enquiry into the evolving goals and ideologies of the performers of violence (cf. Guelke 1982), yet there is a danger that the viewpoints of those who witness, and seek to interpret this violence will be neglected. The peril of such neglect is that the situation will not be grasped fully, for social scientists and lay observers constitute different sectors of the 'public opinion' to which the performers, wittingly or otherwise, appeal.

The spectators of the violence in Northern Ireland fall into many categories, and my study will have to be somewhat selective. In this regard, some preliminary comments are in order. Firstly, while attitudes of the Northern Irish elite to the violence have been given a fair hearing (for example, Galliher and de Gregory 1985), and while professional social science theorizing about the 'Troubles' has been piling up at a prodigious rate, the views of the broader public have not been a focus of much academic discussion. What will be revealed in this chapter is the way in which these particular views compare with the models (theories) of the social scientists. Secondly, violence as it occurs between ordinary Catholics and Protestants is not given a great deal of attention in the literature, where considerations of the events of the fifteen

years up to 1985 concentrate on the confrontation between the British Army
and paramilitary organizations:[1] violence among ordinary people gets analyzed
only when levels of 'sectarian' killing are so high that they cannot be ignored
(Dillon and Lehane 1973). Rectifying this general neglect, the focus here will
be precisely on the way in which violence between ordinary people is perceived
and understood.

This chapter moreover deals with the population of *rural* Northern Ireland,
not just because rural areas of the province have traditionally been the
anthropologists' stamping ground, but also because anthropological research
in these parts has been cited by some writers as evidence that Northern
Ireland as a whole has built-in cultural brakes against genocide (Kuper 1981).
I do not want to get embroiled in a general discussion of the 'meaning' of
violence for rural people in Northern Ireland, although this too might merit
attention in any overall view of the situation. Certainly, for most of those who
are the subject of study here, as for most of the rest of the English-speaking
world, the commonsense understanding of violence has as its core the idea of
physical harm to the person — specifically, physical harm which is in some
way unacceptable. As a category of action, violence can be graded by degrees
of intensity, and even stretched to include words, and also physical harm done
to inanimate objects (buildings, etc.). However, the kind of violence which is
culturally associated with the Northern Ireland 'Troubles' is classifiable as
extreme violence, that is, killings and deliberate serious injury. Where
'violence' is used in an unqualified way in the text, it may be assumed that it is
of this particular type. I accept that the complete understanding of such
extreme violence requires its contextualization in a broader framework
comprising all the acts to which the label 'violence' might be attached. I
intend to fulfil this 'anthropological duty' at least to some extent in the pages
which follow, by providing the necessary ethnographic comment.

Let me start by looking at the viewpoints of the 'Troubles' offered by
professional social scientists.

---

[1] The most prominent paramilitary organizations during this period have been the mainly
Catholic 'Provisional IRA' (Irish Republican Army), and the mainly Protestant 'UDA'
(Ulster Defence Association). The former has always been a proscribed organization, the
latter not. The latter should not be confused with the 'UDR' (Ulster Defence Regiment), a
part-time — and effectively Protestant — regiment of the British Army, upon which a
considerable part of the burden of maintaining state security has fallen, especially in rural
areas. For present purposes, Ulster is a synonym for Northern Ireland.

SOCIAL SCIENTIFIC MODELS OF THE CONFLICT IN NORTHERN IRELAND

I speak of social scientific models here with some hesitation. The label 'professional commentators' model' would perhaps be more appropriate, since the 'Northern Ireland-study' industry involves journalists, as well as geographers, political scientists, psychologists, sociologists, and last, but not least, social anthropologists. Even so, the models constructed by all these commentators are replete with social scientific logic and language, so it is worthwhile to group them. And yet, distinctions have to be made. The most noticeable division is between models constructed by social anthropologists and those constructed by other social scientists — the differences will be apparent as I proceed.

In the analysis of the Northern Ireland problem, the concern of the *non*-anthropologists has generally been to identify the various factors which account for the existence and tenacious persistence of the structural opposition between Catholics and Protestants. And until recently, most theorizing has begun with the assumption that 'Catholic' and 'Protestant' are religious labels serving to obscure what are more fundamental issues. Let me give a brief resumé of the varieties of this kind of theorizing. First of all, there are analyses which see the polarization and conflict between Catholic and Protestant as at least partly a product of relative deprivation felt by the minority (Catholic) population, relating to housing, jobs and legal rights (Birrell 1972; Hadden et al. 1980; Moxon-Browne 1981; Cormack and Osborne 1983).[2] Then there are theories which tie these issues into a more general process of 'internal colonialism' (Hechter 1975), 'imperialism' (e.g. Collins 1984) or the workings of British capitalism (O'Dowd et al. 1980). In elaborations of this second type of theory, some writers see polarization and conflict as a result of the manipulations of the Unionist bourgeoisie, which duped the Protestant working class into believing that its sectarian (or ethnic) loyalty was more important than class interests, and which backed this process of mystification with a measure of real discrimination in favour of Protestants (Farrell 1976; Bew et al. 1979; Patterson 1980).[3] Meanwhile, other writers attribute such mystification equally to the Catholic bourgeoisie

---

[2] See Hewitt (1981) and Kelley and McAllister (1984) for reconsiderations of this viewpoint.
[3] These are just three of the more sensitive examples. See also Bell (1976, 1984) and de Paor (1971).

in the Republic of Ireland, who encouraged northern Catholics to pursue 'Green' (Nationalist) rather than 'Red' (socialist) politics. Among all the commentators mentioned so far, there is disagreement about the geographical units that should be taken into account, and about the spatial spread of the economic processes which are held to be the base for political action. Many of the commentators are both nationalists *and* socialists, so there is a tendency to concentrate on Ireland as a unit in its relation to Great Britain.

This brings me to a final group of writers, who see variations in the patterns of economic growth within the British Isles as a whole as having created the different kinds of society in Ireland. According to them, the predominantly Protestant north-east of Ireland emerged as part of an industrial zone which included Clydeside and Merseyside; while the rest of Ireland, predominantly Catholic, remained agrarian. The conflict emerged as much from the 'bottom up' as from the 'top down', when the expanding industrial economy in the nineteenth century drew Catholic rural immigrants into the north-east industrial area, challenging the Protestant working class (Miller 1978). A conclusion that could be drawn from the entirety of this immense variety of theorizing is that, now, many aspects of the 'Green Marxist' theories of the development of the conflict are out of fashion. Marxist and non-Marxist writers are today much more likely to emphasize, as the catalyst for the conflict, a complex interplay of groupings *within* each bloc, especially within the Protestant bloc (e.g. Boserup 1972; Wright 1973; Bew et al. 1979; Nelson 1984).[4] However, common to all this work is a general political economy orientation — an emphasis on political interests based on economic foundations.

Still more factors are added by other writers, though less as alternatives as to round out the picture. Thus, geographers stress territoriality, and the defence of territory, as factors in the conflict which give it its particular spatial form (e.g. Boal 1969; 1972; 1982), whilst psychologists examine both the psychological effects of conflict and the psychological forces which maintain it.[5] More recently, religious ideology, and competition over the superiority of one set of symbols, have been taken up as important areas of research. Religion and its emotional charge has at last been lifted out of the realm of epiphenomena of political and economic processes and given centre stage by such writers as Hickey (1983) and Bruce and Wallis (1985).

An overall attempt to understand the conflict in Northern Ireland will

[4] Burton (1978) considers groupings within the Catholic population.
[5] For a controversial statement, see Fields (1977); see also Fraser (1973), Harbison and Harbison (1980) and Heskin (1980).

plainly have to incorporate many of the factors isolated in these various models. But to assess the literature fully would be an awesome task, not least because different factors will have had different degrees of importance in different historical periods. Meanwhile, a good deal of what the writers have to say theoretically, reads like the mental gymnastics of politically-motivated 'bricoleurs'. Thankfully, evaluation and assessment is not the task to be attempted here. I intend instead to take out the shared elements in all the theories — the central themes which seem to give them a coherence.

First, the theories are all holistic in perspective; they tend to treat Northern Irish society as an undifferentiated entity — local variations and peculiarities are played down. Second, the authors seem to assume that the most useful data comes from surveys of historical documents, government publications and other secondary sources, together with a limited number of formal and informal interviews. Little need is seen for the researcher to be involved intimately (and for a long term) with those who are the subjects of research.[6] Third, the picture of Northern Ireland is drawn mainly from materials derived from urban areas like Belfast and Derry. Rural Northern Ireland (where a substantial proportion of the Province's population resides) is largely set aside, and treated as insignificant in the march of political history,[7] or else as analytically unproblematic: absorbed within an overall view of Northern Ireland and its problems, it gets to a large extent lost. The fourth point is the most important: the theories all treat political violence between Catholic and Protestant (and, indeed, between Irish and British) as an expectable and logical consequence of conflict. In a sense, the explanation of violence and the explanation of conflict are the same. Outbreaks of violence between Catholics and Protestants, at different times and places, are seen both as indicators of the collision of interests within Northern Ireland society and as the result of them. Thus treated, political violence is allowed to support a general assumption that relations between Catholic and Protestant have a fundamentally negative charge — a charge which lurks behind a thin veneer of day-to-day normality, underpinning a 'problem' which, given the right conditions, can erupt at any moment. At times, the unsurprising nature of extreme violence seems to be stretched into a kind of justification for it.

The social anthropologists' model of Northern Irish society and its conflict is very different. It has been created almost exclusively from materials relating to rural and village studies (still the focus of most social anthropology

[6] To an extent, Burton (1978) and Nelson (1984) are exceptions here.
[7] At least, that part of political history which begins in the nineteenth century, following the shift in the balance of Unionist power away from the landed gentry.

in the British Isles), which are characterized by the researcher's lengthy involvement in the day-to-day life of the people whose activities and ideas are under purview. As they look at sectarian or ethnic relations, social anthropologists generally concentrate on two theoretical matters: how people deal with the perceived division between Catholics and Protestants, and, following this, how various aspects of daily social interaction serve not only to maintain the division, but also to counteract its centrifugal force. The important contribution of social anthropology is its clear statement of the complexity of the situation from the standpoint of the Northern Irish — a complexity which stems from the fact that the identities, 'Catholic' and 'Protestant', are just one set among a number available to people. Thus, these religious identities interact, overlap and at times conflict with identities emerging from the domains of class, neighbourhood, friendship and kinship. 'Catholic' and 'Protestant' identities can be overplayed and underplayed, as one moves from situation to situation (Donnan and McFarlane 1983). Social anthropology has also reaffirmed the sociological common-place that it is vital to distinguish clearly between expressed attitudes towards the 'other sort' in general, and day-to-day interactions with individual members of the category. Actions towards particular Catholics and Protestants can apparently be at variance with 'general' attitudes, and the discrepancy is usually dealt with by means of the notion that the Catholic or Protestant concerned is somehow 'different' from the rest.

Whilst others, in pursuit of the large-scale picture, play down possible local variation, social anthropologists tend to stress the unique character of 'their' communities. In return, their critics maintain that they often cannot see the wood from the trees, which is a charge having at least two thrusts. One is a version of the standard 'political economy' criticism of community studies, namely that processes empirically investigated at the local level are better seen as refractions of broader scale processes. The other is the accusation that few comparisons are made as between the various local studies, especially comparisons concerning levels of violence and conflict. In short, whilst social anthropologists may describe — indeed celebrate — local peculiarities, they make no attempt either to substantiate the differences or to explain them.

Although there is some justice in this representation of their endeavours, a model of rural Northern Ireland can be taken from the social anthropologists' writings. In this model, a *modus vivendi* is seen to prevail, which has found expression in a value that stresses that division in the community be played down and harmony played up. It has been noted already that social anthropology has been concerned to understand both opposition *and* integration. One can go further and argue that without exception its practitioners have concentrated rather more on integration than on conflict.

Leyton puts the position most clearly when he remarks that 'the true enigma is not why so many have died: rather, it is why so few have been killed' (Leyton 1974: p. 194). At heart, Leyton's community is a peaceful one, where social relations between the two sides 'have been marred by violence only twice in the past fifty years' (1974: p. 193), and where Catholic and Protestant have lived together 'in relative peace throughout the current conflict' (1974: p. 186). In 'Kildarragh', we are told, there are 'two, yet one' (1974: p. 194). Working in much the same part of Northern Ireland, Larsen similarly highlights forces which, she says, counterbalance 'attempts to bring conflict into the open'.[8] Harris puzzles over the same sort of problem in her study of 'Ballybeg'. Like Leyton, she notes the 'apparent paradox of intermingled yet separate populations' — the phenomenon of people in different groups who had 'close relationships whilst remaining essentially separate' (1972: p. ix). Her energies are accordingly devoted to showing what the inhabitants of Ballybeg have in common (1972: chapters 4, 5 and 6), and though all social relationships in the area are 'pervaded by a consciousness of the religious dichotomy' (1972: p. xi) she is able to reveal it as a community 'in which there was a vast amount of tolerance and goodwill' (1972: p. xiv).

Other writers are concerned to an even greater extent about levels of harmony in their respective communities. Buckley's research was in an area where binding forces are of such strength that conventions prohibiting mixed marriages appear to be weakening (1982: p. 127) — conventions which elsewhere are as strong as ever (McFarlane 1979). Overt harmony would reach its peak at the annual village festival, when Catholic and Protestant combine to produce an occasion when 'religion and politics are absent' (1982: p. 153). Bufwack similarly puts immense stress on factors which counterbalance conflict (1982). Peace in 'Naghera' is generated by a variety of factors: by ties, such as those of class, which cross-cut the religious divide; by the existence of 'civic morality' (i.e. a sense of shared humanitarianism); and by simple rational expediencies which emerge as people have to live side by side.

The variation between these social anthropological accounts may be summarized in terms of a relative weighting of opposition (conflict) and integration. For Harris, Larsen and, to some extent, Leyton, integration and opposition are roughly in balance, but it is a fragile balance, not least because of the broader context of paramilitary violence. Meanwhile Buckley and Bufwack point to the relatively greater strength of 'positive' forces. 'Gentle People' inhabit Buckley's rural community, and Bufwack's Naghera is

---

[8] Quoted in Leyton (1974: p. 197), from a personal communication.

presented as a haven in a 'sea of strife' (this may be the publisher's metaphor, but the overall vision comes through strikingly in the book). Even Leyton's Kildarragh gives evidence of 'relative stability in the midst of violent rhetoric and violent act' (Leyton 1974: p. 194).

These differences aside, practically every community is presented as if it is *reacting* to sectarian violence, rather than actively re-creating it. In a number of places, this is explicit. Thus, Leyton wonders for how long the forces of integration will withstand 'external pressure' (1974: p. 198), and worries that their fragility may be crushed by 'forces outside Northern Ireland' (1974: p. 186), whilst Bufwack describes the inhabitants of Naghera as confronting a sectarianism 'which they did not originate' (1982: p. 10). Glassie presents the same imagery for the community of Ballymenone — where the 'Troubles have hurt, but not killed the neighbourly ethic' (1982: p. 150).

In an obvious sense, these last observations can be taken to mean that local level events cannot be completely understood without reference to what is going on outside the community, nor without reference to the historical tradition of violence and sectarianism at all levels of Northern Irish society. One could say that they effectively amount to token acknowledgement of the analytical deficiencies of 'local studies' (see above). But this is not the crux of them. What they essentially reflect is the social anthropologists' central image of the rural community, and specifically the role of *violence* within it: in all the anthropologists' works, the existence of local level violence is played down. Whereas in the models of other researchers, political violence is regarded as self-explanatory, in the models of the social anthropologists it is largely set aside. One of the major reasons for this can be revealed if we turn our attention now to the interpretations of the situation in Northern Ireland which are offered by the rural folk themselves.

FOLK INTERPRETATIONS

The viewpoints expressed by their informants are obviously of crucial significance to anthropologists. And where Northern Irish viewpoints are concerned, the salient fact is that, whilst the Protestant—Catholic division is clearly expressed (most often in terms of negative stereotypes), so too are other differences and distinctions based on class and locality. Indeed, it is clear that rural folk see these distinctions as partially overlapping. Moreover, although people will definitely speak of a 'community' of Catholics and a 'community' of Protestants when they refer to Northern Ireland as a whole, separate Catholic and Protestant communities are not invariably perceived in the local arena, except in certain areas where one side is overwhelmingly in the majority. Thus, the model which the anthropologist is most usually offered is one of a single community which is divided — 'the house with two sides', as Leyton's and Larsen's informants put it. Division and unity are both features of the folk model.

The folk models normally embrace an historical explanation of the Northern Ireland conflict as well, typically in terms of events which have become part of the province's commemorative culture. And they are often laced with versions of the arguments presented by social scientists; as one would expect, there is slippage between all the models of the conflict. Thus, the 'bosses', the 'fur coat brigade', the 'Brits', and world-wide communism are all blamed for the divisions in the community, not to mention other bogeymen such as the priests, the politicians, the godfathers, and the Papacy.

There is rather little discussion of violence *per se* in social anthropology, and it is not surprising that there is little in the literature on Northern Ireland about how the rural 'folk' explain it (or indeed the lack of it). However, a clue is given in certain less-than-idealistic Northern Irish opinions about the state of play within rural communities — opinions which contrast nicely with the image, such as some writers offer, of a people dominated by the pursuit of a value of harmony (cf. Glassie 1982). Among Protestants in Ballycuan, where I conducted fieldwork in 1975—6, it was stated that the Catholics would be fools to cause real trouble in an area where they were a small minority and where only four roads led into and out of the village.[9] My evidence more importantly suggests that most rural Northern Irish will explain quite differently the state of political *division* and *conflict* in Northern Ireland, and particular cases of *violence* (what little I can glean from reports of other areas in Northern Ireland indicates the same). Accordingly, whilst people may concoct models of conflict which are reminiscent of those of the professional social scientist, this is only when they wish to explain the existence of the problem in general; actual instances of violence are quite another matter. In the folk model, violence is *not* self-explanatory, even in terms of an overall perception of opposed interests.

The essence of a folk explanation of violence is revealed in the fact that killings and bombings within the home community tend to be blamed on outsiders. People may distrust the intentions of their neighbours of the opposite religion, and they may see the 'other sort' fundamentally as political opponents, but it is difficult for them to believe that such deeds could be carried out by fellow townsmen or villagers. They admit, of course, that each area has its own hot heads — the 'hard cases' who may be expected to get

---

[9] Elsewhere, Catholics are capable of being equally tactical (Larsen 1982).

involved in violence, especially in the 'hot' season of marching and commemoration. Yet they insist that such individuals do not normally get involved in *extreme* violence: fist fighting, with the aim of giving someone a 'good digging', is usually their limit. What is evident is that, in the popular scheme of things, explanations of extreme violence have to be coupled with some special factor. Drunkenness is sometimes invoked, but this is associated with all levels of violence, so something more is still required. In order to account for the numerous sectarian killings in Belfast and elsewhere in the 1970s, a very popular theory in Ballycuan at the time linked murder with drugs. Several people assumed that since Belfast had the majority of such killings, the drug trade must be very heavy in the city. If drugs are not cited, the general idea that a person is psychologically 'sick' is offered instead. Psychological illness is even more likely to be blamed when people are confronted with the reality that one of their own community has been responsible for a killing. Except as a very last resort, the plain fact of sectarian extremism is seldom mentioned; something else must have pushed the person to carry out the killing.

The folk image, then, is one in which Northern Ireland in general, and local communities in particular, are at the mercy of a minority of uncontrollable individuals — who are outsiders to the local community, although they may be Northern Irish. Now, one could be forgiven for being astonished at this, considering the force with which people in Northern Irish rural areas express political and religious antagonism against the 'other sort'; the immediate response ought to be a degree of scepticism, to say the least. Is not this view a self-conscious public facade, a kind of rhetoric masking a more 'genuine' understanding of violence in which political and religious differences feature strongly?

The Northern Irish certainly have many discussions in which violence as a principle is either condoned or threatened. Even over particular acts of violence there is often a good deal of prevarication. Alongside condemnations, previous actions carried out by the victim's 'side' are quoted — this is the 'but' response which follows expressions of horror. Thus: 'It's terrible, but that crowd do worse . . .', or 'People who do that sort of thing must have something missing, but there's bad on both sides', or 'Sure it would sicken you . . . but d'ye remember what some of that crowd did to that fellah in . . . ?' The assumption is that violent deeds are explicable, perhaps even justified, given what occurred before. In Scott and Lyman's terms (1968), such comments constitute 'accounts' — statements which in a culturally-standardized way bridge the gap between acts that occur, and ideas about what acts are acceptable. However, two points might be stressed about the apparent ambiguousness in the people's statements. First, even if outrage about violent acts is a facade which masks true feelings, it is a facade which makes sense only against a background of a shared cultural understanding that violence needs further explanation than can be obtained by simple reference to Catholic and Protestant differences of interest. It is the essence of such 'accounts' that prevarication over condemning particular deeds does tend to include conversational elements which make the perpetrator somehow different from the rest of society, and/or sets the action beyond the pale of normality. Second, to look at the issue from another perspective, violent acts between Catholic and Protestant are rarely celebrated by rural people in Northern Ireland. If the paramilitary activist is praised, it is more likely in terms of how much he or she has sacrificed in the defence of Ireland or 'Ulster'. The risks taken, the self-injury sustained, the freedom given up; these are the elements which will be stressed.

There can of course be no doubt that a view of extreme violence, as something perpetrated by individuals who are in some way outside the bounds of normal society, is to a considerable extent a construction of the mass media, which stems from its involvement in the politics of outrage.[10] Elliot has argued that the picture of violence presented by the media is one of randomness and senselessness, just like a natural disaster (1976). However, such a picture comes close to being sustained in day-to-day social encounters as well; when killings occur, each community reacts as communities typically react to crises whatever their source. In discussion, at least one shared version of events is produced; details are mulled over, especially details which seem too gruesome to be presented by the media: 'It'd make you ill, to think what they did to him. His brother was sick'. Conversations regularly contrast the violence of the so-called doorstep murders with a notion of quiet domesticity: 'He was just sitting there watching T.V. with the wains when they came to the door'.[11] Of course, there is much conjecture about the perpetrators: 'Did you see anyone strange around, Mary? The "News of the World" over at . . . said she saw a car a bit like our Willie's going past her house.' The negative effects on the community are not forgotten. 'You find it hard to even look at any of "them" when this happens to one of your own. They look so *sleekit* (treacherous) and you wonder about them. You just have to remember they're not all the same, sure they're not?'

People's reaction to violence is also tailored in respect of to whom they are talking. In Ballycuan, if it is suggested that one's own side carried out the

---

[10] See Curtis (1984) for a rather controversial view of this process.

[11] That political conflict should be excluded from the private domain of the home is reminiscent of the Spanish culture described by John Corbin, this volume.

event, and one is speaking to one of 'them', then one is outraged and volubly so. But supposing it was one of their side who stood accused, one would not only be outraged, but would go in search of outrage. One could go further, and argue that the social norm in Northern Ireland communities, that one should generally avoid talking about the divisions between Catholics and Protestants, is slowly being replaced by a norm that one should say something about acts associated with this division. Such norms and practices can help maintain a view that one's political opponents are not automatically one's physical enemy. Among a few on the Catholic side, another procedure is now discernible. The shooting of local Protestants who are members of the part-time security forces is sometimes accompanied by the relabelling of the victims as 'Brits', or even as 'Black bastards' — as people who are totally beyond the bounds of the normal community. This procedure leaves unchallenged the overall positive image of the community, and the unacceptability of the practice of extreme violence among its members. Needless to say, Protestants look at such shootings rather differently.

One final point plainly asserts itself. Since most of their informants join in the politics of outrage, it may not be very surprising if these viewpoints on the community, and explanations of violence, have captured the imagination of anthropologists. And this returns us to the problematic mentioned earlier. This is that the folk to whom anthropologists have spoken, and the anthropologists themselves, may have constructed and presented an image of rural Northern Ireland as a whole which cannot easily be reconciled with the killings and bombings that have occurred in various areas. The reality of rural Northern Ireland is that there has been a considerable amount of violence — violence not emphasized by the anthropologists. Possibly, a resolution of this problematic can be found. Maybe the folk perceptions of violence in fact vary from place to place, perhaps in response to the respective levels of violence in these places.

LOCAL VARIATION IN INTERPRETATIONS OF VIOLENCE?

The question of variation between communities begs other questions, and these have to be tackled first. In the first place, are folk interpretations of violence as generally held *within* individual communities as the existing reports seem to suggest? It is not implausible that anthropologists have over-generalized about their communities. Critics from other disciplines certainly maintain that social anthropologists have not taken their ideological blinkers seriously enough, and that they are therefore as 'slanted' as the other researchers on the Northern Ireland problem. Because anthropologists tend to occupy the middle ground in the politics of the province (though many of them are outsiders), it is not impossible that they have *chosen* to emphasize the more positive viewpoints of their informants. One can indeed see hints of this in the literature: Bufwack transparently celebrates the anti-sectarianism of the socialist Republican Clubs (renamed Workers' Clubs), whilst Harris's research would be a remarkable intellectual bulwark for the New Ireland group or even the Alliance Party. However, this kind of charge is always difficult to handle, and I would not know how to assess it without doing more research on the researchers.

One might approach the issue from a different angle. The possibility should be entertained that social anthropologists have obtained most of their data from limited sections of the communities. Perhaps they have gleaned information on local perceptions from people with whom they have most in common, namely the educated elite. This sector of the community tends to occupy the political middle ground, and is usually unequivocal in its condemnation of violence. However, this does not seem to have happened. In fact, it is the non-elite who are predominant as informants in Northern Irish studies, as they are in the bulk of anthropological studies conducted in Europe. Could there, then, be a bias in favour of the perceptions of one gender? Rosemary Harris suggests that, in farming areas, women are likely to express more bitterness towards members of the opposing camp, and are likely to invoke more strongly negative stereotypes of the 'other sort'; she explains this in terms of the domestic centredness of the typical farm wife, and her lack of opportunity to mix with members of the opposition (Harris 1972: p. 178). Possibly, women such as these have had a muted voice in the social anthropologists' construction of each community's image of itself? Yet, there is no evidence that rural women feature less than men in anthropological samples, especially in village studies, and, even if women do exhibit stronger attitudes, these certainly do not include an unequivocal support of extreme violence.

More meaningful variation might be yielded in the viewpoints as between the generations. Even casual visitors to Northern Ireland can notice that the ideas and expressions of youth may be decidedly different from those of their parents: for some youth, various kinds of violence between Catholic and Protestant has a relatively great legitimacy, and moreover seems to be self-explanatory.[12] Anthropologists have possibly avoided the youth sector, and so have given a skewed version of what the rural community 'thinks'. In this regard, it is significant that local people *incorporate* youth in their ideas about

---

[12] See Jenkins (1983) and Nelson (1984) on Protestant youth.

'hot heads'. In the small towns and villages, it is youth which is regularly blamed for fighting between the two camps. The 'lads' or 'young fellahs' certainly seem as positive in their attitudes towards fights and other violence between 'Fenians' and 'Prods' as any youth in the city estates.[13] These attitudes tend to be construed via notions of licenced extremism — as a kind of playful stage through which young men, especially, have to pass (cf. Buckley 1983). On the other hand, in the remoter countryside, the majority of young men and women appear to hold viewpoints which are remarkably akin to their parents, stressing opposition to the 'other sort', but also opposition to the violence (though perhaps not to an abstract notion of violence). I think it is fair to say that rural youth does have a relatively muted voice in social anthropological research. However, because of this such variations, as between village youth and the youth of the remoter countryside, have to be entered tentatively; sufficient confirmatory data are just not available. More importantly, it is difficult to guage the extent to which the positive attitudes of village youths towards violence is stretched to include the extreme violence of killing and maiming.

Even if anthropologists have *not* overgeneralized the way in which a community presents itself, it remains possible that the image they have obtained is consistently skewed, because of elements in their relationships with their informants. Informants may simply have told the anthropologists what they assumed the latter would wish to hear. There is a general feeling among the Northern Irish (certainly among the Protestant population) that outsiders regard sectarianism as irrational, especially if they are educated and elite outsiders. It follows that countryfolk would likely present the researcher with a relatively positive and optimistic view of the conflict. An alternative is that people might be unwilling to express their true opinion, not so much because they felt the listener would not appreciate it, but because to do so might be dangerous. Either way, 'moderate' opinion would be more emphasized.[14] Yet my feeling is that these contentions have to be put aside. There is no real evidence from the anthropological literature of informants being reluctant to voice strong opinions once the researcher has been incorporated into the local networks.

On balance, I would say that researchers *have* allowed an adequate picture

[13] 'Fenians' is the historically-derived term for supporters of the Republican cause, and 'Prods' is the vernacularized abbreviation for Protestants.

[14] Political scientists have pointed out that opinion polls in Northern Ireland prior to elections tend consistently to overestimate moderate opinions, probably for a mixture of these reasons.

of the views on violence held in those communities in which they have worked. Accordingly, a distinction can be made between folk models of the general structure of Northern Irish society and folk explanations for particular instances of violence — with folk ideas making no intrinsic link between the two. Accordingly, we may turn with some confidence to the question of variation in the perceptions of violence *as between local communities*. A first suggestion here follows the commonsense idea that violence tends to feed upon itself and create still wider divisions in communities; communities might be compared over time and space in order to discover whether there is variation in folk theorizing in response to the realities of violent acts (cf. Harris 1979). After exposure to violence, people might be expected to shift their perceptions towards something like the social science models put by the non-anthropologists — towards a view that violence is an intrinsic consequence of the division between Catholic and Protestant.

However, a review of the ethnographies strongly invites the conclusion that there is a remarkable permanence in the viewpoints over time and space. Firstly, there seem to be no real differences among studies relating to the various recent historical periods, namely (i) the 1950s; (ii) the late 1960s (prior to the generally accepted start of the current troubles in 1968—9); and (iii) the 1970s, following some of the really crucial events in the commemorative calendar (Bloody Sunday, Bloody Friday, etc.) and during the period when tit-for-tat killing was rife. (Table 1 lists the studies carried out 1950—84.) Secondly, there is a general consistency in viewpoints even among communities varying in terms of demographic balance (i.e. whether predominantly Catholic, predominantly Protestant or equally proportioned). Thirdly, such consistency is discernible even in the face of variation in the number of violent actions perpetrated by the paramilitary. Viewpoints in my research area of rural North Down, where acts of extreme violence have been comparatively rare, are similar to those in Bufwack's 'haven of peace amid a sea of strife' in South Down, in spite of the fact that the latter's research was conducted at a time when a number of particularly vicious killings had been committed on Protestant members of the part-time security forces.

It might be as well to account for this constancy over time and space, rather than to identify sources of variation in folk imagery. How can folk interpretations of the conflict and violence remain so consistent, in spite of varying levels of violence? How do people square their views of violence with the reality of it? To some degree, the answers have been given already. The point to stress is that the level of violence has simply never been so high that the predominant folk model is compromised. The notion that violence is to be blamed on outsiders or on the psychopathic shortcomings of insiders may indeed remain even as violence increases still more, not least because it is

Table 1 Social anthropological research on Catholics/Protestants
in rural Northern Ireland, 1950—84

Researchers	Period of research	Location(s)
Blacking et al. (personal communication)	mid-1970s	Ballycuan, North Down Drumness, South Down Glenleven, South Fermanagh Glentarf, North Antrim
Buckley	late 1970s/ early 1980s	Kilbeg, North Down Listymore, North Antrim
Bufwack	early 1970s	Naghera, South Down
Glassie	mid-1970s	Ballymenone, South Fermanagh
Harris	1950s, 1970s	Ballybeg, South Tyrone
Larsen	early 1970s	Kilbroney, South Down
Leyton	mid/late 1960s	Blackrock, South Down Aughnaboy, South Down
McFarlane	mid/late 1970s	Ballycuan, North Down
McFarlane and Donnan	ongoing	Ards, North Down

constructed and reconstructed in both the media and everyday conversation. Moreover, as migration brings about the decline of the mixed Protestant—Catholic community, so the sheer existence of such a model may help people deal with this decline — it can help maintain a sense of stability in the midst of perceived chaos.

However, one surmises that there must come a time when a model such as this can no longer be sustained in the face of repeated acts of violence. Especially among minorities in mixed areas, one would expect there to be a shift in perception about responsibility for killings and attempted killings — towards blaming 'them' for violence, and towards seeing killing as an automatic, intellectually unproblematic outcome of the basic division in Northern Irish society.

There has not been much in the way of in-depth research on this topic, so it would be audacious to point precisely to the parts of Northern Ireland where this kind of reasoning has become prevalent. Even so, population movement (always an indication of community strain in urban areas in Northern Ireland)

and attitude surveys sponsored by the media would appear to point to its emergence among the minority Protestant population in the rural border areas. Within Northern Ireland as a whole, this area has the second highest level of violent activity (Murray 1982), and it is an area which has witnessed some 62 per cent of the fatal incidents which have occurred in rural parts (Poole 1983). Most of the killings have been the work of Republican activists, and many of the victims were part-time members of the security forces who were also associated in some way with farming or the service industry which supports it. The Protestant population is in a minority in this area, mostly living in isolated farmhouses, and many of the farms have changed hands in recent years, some of them passing into the hands of Catholics. In the context of the symbolic value of land in the rural border area (Harris 1972: p. 168), the recent successes of the Nationalist (Republican) groupings in local government elections, and the history of the 'door-step' murders in the area, it is not surprising that border Protestants have re-emphasized their centuries-old 'siege mentality' (or 'bawn' mentality, referring to the fortified farmhouses built in the area in the seventeenth century). This local Protestant vision can indeed only get more established as the responsibility for state control is handed over to the Northern Irish (as opposed to British) security forces, and as the number of individual killings at place of work, home and leisure increases as a proportion of total killings (Roche 1985). What this means is that members of the security forces shot by activists will increasingly be Protestant (for only some three per cent of the Northern Ireland security forces are Catholics), and will be increasingly attacked within the community. There is no evidence that Protestants recognize that someone was shot because he or she was a 'Brit', rather than a Protestant; the act is read as sectarian, despite the assurances of many Catholics that Protestants as such have nothing to fear. Under these circumstances, Protestants may increasingly see violence, and the approval of violence, as an intrinsic feature of the basic opposition in Northern Ireland society.

CONCLUSION

In this chapter, I have contrasted the interpretations of violence in rural Northern Ireland which are offered by social scientists with those offered by the rural folk themselves. Being closely attuned to (perhaps entranced by) the interpretations of rural people, social anthropologists have to some considerable extent assimilated the people's model of the community in their analytical models. In this way, attention comes to be put firmly on the forces of integration, as well as on the forces of division. While social anthropologists have said very little about violence *per se*, people in the countryside generally insist that violent acts are aberrations, which can only be interpreted in terms of some kind of diminished responsibility.

These viewpoints obviously do constitute a 'cultural brake' against the emergence of a total disintegration of rural Northern Ireland (and probably large areas of urban Northern Ireland as well), and they can also be taken as a guage of the nature of the 'gap' between Catholic and Protestant. There can be no doubt that rural Northern Ireland, like the rest of the province, has created by word and deed an environment in which extreme violence, and/or ethnic segregation, can thrive as options. Yet the existence of the 'cultural brake' means that the country as a whole is not at the moment on a downhill course to open warfare. I hope I am not being too pessimistic in accepting that there is some evidence in certain rural areas that the folk interpretations of violence which I have set out here are slipping into disuse. When the models of (non-anthropologist) social scientists and those of lay observers begin to converge, the brake starts fatally to be loosened.

REFERENCES

Bell, G. 1976: *The Protestants of Ulster*. London: Pluto Press.
_____1984: *The British in Ireland: a Suitable Case for Withdrawal*. London: Pluto Press.
Bew, P., Gibbon, P. and Patterson, H. 1979: *The State in Northern Ireland, 1921—1971* Manchester: Manchester University Press.
Birrell, D. 1972: Relative deprivation as a factor in the conflict in Northern Ireland. *Sociological Review*, 20, 317—47.
Boal, F. W. 1969: Territoriality on the Shankill/Falls divide in Belfast. *Irish Geography*, 6, 30—50.
_____1972: The urban residential sub-community: a conflict interpretation. *Area*, 4, 164—8.
_____1982: Segregation and mixing: space and residence in Belfast. In F. W. Boal and J. N. H. Douglas (eds), *Integration and Division: geographical perspectives on the Northern Ireland problem*, London: Academic Press.
Boserup, A. 1972: Contradictions and struggles in Northern Ireland. *Socialist Register*, 9, 157—92.
Bruce, S. and Wallis, R. 1985: Defender of the faith. *Times Higher Education Supplement*, 661, 15.
Buckley, A. D. 1982: *A Gentle People: a study of a peaceful community in Ulster*, Cultra: Ulster Folk and Transport Museum
_____1983: Playful rebellion: social control and the framing of experience in an Ulster community. *Man*, 18, 383—93.
Bufwack, M. S. 1982: *Village without Violence: an examination of a Northern Irish community*. Cambridge, Mass: Schenkman.

Burton, F. 1978: *The Politics of Legitimacy: struggles in a Belfast community*. London: Routledge and Kegan Paul.

Collins, T. 1984: *The Centre Cannot Hold*. Dublin: Bookworks, Ireland.

Cormack, R. J. and Osborne, R. D. 1983 (eds): *Religion, Education and Employment*. Belfast: Appletree Press.

Curtis, L. 1984: *Ireland: the propaganda war. The British media and the 'battle for hearts and minds'*. London: Pluto Press.

De Paor, L. 1971: *Divided Ulster*. Harmondsworth: Penguin.

Dillon, M. and Lehane, D. 1973: *Political Murder in Northern Ireland*. Harmondsworth: Penguin.

Elliot, P. 1976: Misreporting Ulster: news as field dressing. *New Society*, 38, 398—400.

Farrell, M. 1976: *Northern Ireland: the Orange State*. London: Pluto Press.

Fields, R. M. 1977: *Northern Ireland: society under siege*. New Brunswick: Transaction Books.

Fraser, M. 1973: *Children in Conflict*. Harmondsworth: Penguin.

Galliher, J. F. and de Gregory, J. L. 1985: *Violence in Northern Ireland: understanding Protestant perspectives*. Dublin: Gill and Macmillan.

Gibbon, P. 1975: *The Origins of Ulster Unionism*. Manchester: Manchester University Press.

Glassie, H. 1982: *Passing the Time: folklore and history of an Ulster community*. Dublin: O'Brien Press.

Guelke, A. 1982: The changing politics of Ulster's violent men. *New Society*, 61, 171—3.

Hadden, T., Hillyard, P. and Boyle, K. 1980: Northern Ireland: the communal roots of violence. *New Society*, 54, 268—71.

Harbison, J. and Harbison, J. (eds) 1980: *A Society under Stress*. Somerset: Open Books.

Harris, R. 1972: *Prejudice and Tolerance in Ulster: a study of neighbours and 'strangers' in a border community*. Manchester: Manchester University Press.

Harris, R. 1979: Community relationships in Northern and Southern Ireland: a comparison and a paradox. *Sociological Review*, 27, 41—53.

Hechter, M. 1975: *Internal Colonialism: the Celtic fringe in British national development*. London: Routledge and Kegan Paul.

Heskin, K. 1980: *Northern Ireland: a psychological analysis*. New York: Columbia University Press.

Hewitt, C. 1981: Catholic grievances, Catholic nationalism and violence in Northern Ireland during the civil rights period: a reconsideration. *British Journal of Sociology*, 32, 362—80.

Hickey, J. 1983: *Religion and the Northern Irish Problem*. Dublin: Gill and Macmillan.

Jenkins, R. 1983: *Lads, Citizens and Ordinary Kids: working-class youth lifestyles in Belfast*. London: Routledge and Kegan Paul.

Kelley, J. and McAllister, I. 1984: The genesis of conflict: religion and politics in Ulster, 1968. *Sociology*, 18, 171—80.

Kuper, L. 1981: *Genocide: its political use in the twentieth century*. Harmondsworth: Penguin.

Larsen, S. S. 1982: 'The two sides of the house': identity and social organization in Kilbroney, Northern Ireland. In A. P. Cohen (ed.), *Belonging: identity and social organization in British rural cultures*, Manchester: Manchester University Press.

Leyton, E. 1974: Opposition and integration in Ulster. *Man*, 9, 185—98.

_____1975: *The One Blood: kinship and class in an Irish village*. St Johns: Memorial University.

McFarlane, G. 1979: 'Mixed' marriages in Ballycuan, Northern Ireland. *Journal of Comparative Family Studies*, 10, 191—205.

McFarlane, G. and Donnan, H. 1983: Informal social organization. In J. Darby (ed.), *Northern Ireland: the background to the conflict*, Belfast: Appletree Press.

Miller, D. W. 1978: *Queen's Rebels: Ulster loyalism in historical perspective*. Dublin: Gill and Macmillan.

Moxon-Browne, E. 1981: The water and the fish: public opinion and the Provisional IRA in Northern Ireland. In P. Wilkinson (ed.), *British Perspectives on Terrorism*, London: George Allen and Unwin.

Murray, R. 1982: Political violence in Northern Ireland, 1969—1977. In F. W. Boal and J. N. H. Douglas (eds), *Integration and Division: geographical perspectives on the Northern Ireland problem*, London: Academic Press.

Nelson, S. 1984: *Ulster's Uncertain Defenders: Loyalists and the Northern Ireland conflict*. Belfast: Appletree Press.

O'Dowd, L., Rollston, B. and Tomlinson, M. 1980: *Northern Ireland: between civil rights and civil war*. London: CSE Books.

Patterson, H. 1980: *Class Conflict and Sectarianism: the Protestant working class and the Belfast labour movement 1868—1920*. Belfast: Appletree Press.

Poole, M. 1983: The demography of violence. In J. Darby (ed.), *Northern Ireland: the background to the conflict*, Belfast: Appletree Press.

Roche, D. 1985: Patterns of violence in Northern Ireland in 1984. *Fortnight*, 218, 9—10.

Scott, M. B. and Lyman, S. M. 1968: Accounts. *American Sociological Review*, 33, 46—62.

Wright, F. 1973: Protestant ideology and politics in Ulster. *European Journal of Sociology*, 14, 213—80.

11

Violence and Will

David Parkin

While violence can reasonably be classed together with other such odd-job words as evil, fear or sexuality in the multiplicity of its referents, there are nevertheless some recurring senses in the use of the term in English, as is evident from the chapters making up this volume. Whichever one of the several distinctive connotations is preferred, English-speaking anthropologists are bound to fit their ethnographic experience to it, however much they also take into account native renderings. My own approach is to acknowledge this distorting effect, but then, through a series of shifts and counter-shifts in translation, to allow the ethnography itself to distort the English term and so both deconstruct it and probe its more hidden implications. In this chapter, insights into English notions are produced through examining the ethnography of an African society.

The substantive 'violence' in English, as Riches notes in his comments on Anglo-Saxon usage in the first chapter, strongly connotes the use of physical force, usually unlawfully. Through metaphorical extension it also refers to less immediately physical acts — 'doing violence to someone's reputation', etc. Anglo-Saxon usage is, of course, not sacrosanct. Thus, Foucault, taking what is perhaps as much a primary sense of the French 'violence' as any other, is able to regard discourse as a 'violence inflicted upon events through the distortions it imposes' (cf. Sheridan 1980). Copet-Rougier, in this volume, indeed makes explicit the French connotations of the word. She is led to contrast observable physical harm (which in the society she discusses is exacted on communities from the outside) and such invisible noxious practices as witchcraft (operating inside the community) whose physical effects are evident only by being inferred from subsequent sickness and death, yet are central to the people's metaphysical understandings of power, rivalry and individuality.

In English, the contrast which Copet-Rougier introduces is perhaps most crudely obvious in terms of a distinction between violence and 'violation'. In this regard, the substantive 'violence' has a primary sense of a) determination or destruction through physical force, which is regarded as b) beyond the law. Sometimes the use of violence is justified by those in authority as a necessary response to opposition, but it is rarely referred to as such, and is more normally couched in acceptable idioms (e.g. 'state of emergency', 'measures taken in the interests of national security', 'detention centres', etc.). This sense of violence clearly presupposes questions of institutionalized legitimacy, so that the rule-governed physical force exerted by, say, prison wardens in the performance of their duty is not in the eyes of the law called violence, but becomes so if in some way the wardens are found to have gone beyond certain standards of conduct. The chapters in this volume, in particular by Dunning and colleagues and by McFarlane, explore some of the varying interpretations that different sections of a population will have of acts which only some of them will characterize as violent.

The verb, 'violate', in English, gives an interesting semantic complementarity to 'violence'. The best synonym is probably 'desecrate', and, while the desecration of, say, church relics or an old master in an art gallery is clearly a destructive act beyond the law, it is the notion of extreme defilement of aesthetic values and beliefs rather than of actual physical harm done that is primary. I once recorded a case from Kenya of a man who deliberately urinated on a copy of the Koran. The Holy Book survived its ordeal and was left unmarked, but that in no way reduced the severity of its 'violation'. Many other examples could be given of this primacy of the aesthetic and religious over the physical, and those in this book include Moeran's study of properly executed violence as beauty in Japan, the contributions by Corbin and Marvin on Spanish style (even elegance) in the conduct of both political challenge and the bullfight, and the chapter by Heald on the craft of ritual performances involving bodily mutilation and on the images these are expected to evoke.

Here I am interested in the analytic potential in the relationship between the two notions of violence implied in the discussion so far: between violence as physical destruction and 'violence' as metaphysical desecration. The former may seem to overlay the latter in many Western societies, possibly because in these societies the value given to the inviolability of private property for its own sake supersedes in importance notions of metaphysical and, so to speak, spiritual perfection or wholeness — breaking into a man's car is a more criminal offence than rudely disturbing him at prayer or while contemplating a work of art. Such an overlay is, in contrast, by no means so clear in the African society I worked in and shall discuss, and in which the destruction of metaphysical order (whether or not physical persons or things happen also to be broken) is of greater concern than the actual physical harm perpetrated, insofar as the two can be distinguished. Consonant with this is the common emphasis in this, and many other African societies, on a violent deed being followed by purification as much as by direct retribution. But the relative significance between physical destruction and metaphysical desecration cannot be static. In 'African society' there must be circumstances when the component of sheer physical destruction becomes the most heinous fault, the act effectively being no longer a sin occasioning metaphysical disorder, but a crime against authority. In the particular society studied here, such a transformation remains largely implicit, but its potential is evident in certain (metaphysical) notions about harmful forces which are autonomous of, and external to, the individual actor — which emergent authorities could theoretically harness as instruments of physical control. Importantly, such notions seem to correspond with certain ideas in British society referring to the accountability for violence. As a result, non-Western ethnography generates insights into the English-speakers' concept.

In order to examine these matters I will first of all introduce some material drawn from British society in the 1980s, and then move on to my African data. In discussing violence in British society I start with the intentionally ethnocentric assumption that I shall be looking at acts which are regarded by at least some people as unlawful uses of physical force; the politician may refer to terrorism as violence, whilst his own policy is that which his opponents in turn call violence.

I should like to lead the discussion by considering some acts which do not by themselves inflict violence in the above sense but which indirectly encourage violence and whose encouragement comes from the law. Let me refer here to a poster recently issued by the London Metropolitan Police. It is less than one metre square and depicts a young man, possibly a teenager, his hands pressed hard against the outside of a car window; directed out of the poster at the onlooker, his eyes burn with what could be anger, frustration, hatred, desperation or hopelessness. The car remains 'inviolate', the boy's 'violent' intentions are thwarted, and you, the onlooker, are enjoined to take up this frustrated 'violence', so to speak, and to 'Block his knock-off' (written in large letters across the top of the poster). Some smaller versions ask 'Have you blocked his knock-off?', or advertise 'Blocking his knock-off!' (see plates 1 and 2). Non-native speakers of English might well miss the collusive act of violence in which the onlooker is invited by the police to engage. The surface rendering of the phrase simply means 'Stop his theft'. But the reversed idiom, 'knock his block off' ('Knock his head off'), is strongly provocative and combative and is certainly associated with physically violent encounters. It cleverly draws on an intense indignation that may easily turn the ordinary, mild, person-in-the-street householder into violent defender of his/her

Plate 1   *(reproduced by kind permission of the Commissioner
of the Metropolitan Police)*

Have you Blocked his Knock-off?

How to protect yourself in the autocrime crisis

1 REMOVE the ignition key and activate the steering lock.

2 TAKE all your belongings with you or put them out of sight.

3 PARK in a sensible place, avoiding unlit areas at night.

4 MARK your car and its contents and fit an anti-theft device.

For more advice contact your local Police Station.

METROPOLITAN POLICE
Lock it - Mark it, watch where you park it!
AUTOCRIME WATCH

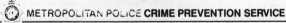

METROPOLITAN POLICE **CRIME PREVENTION SERVICE**

Plate 2   (reproduced by kind permission of the Commissioner of the Metropolitan Police)

property. There is an explicit appeal in some versions to the sanctity of the family and private property.

Pocock's work on the British Mass Observation archives enabled him to conduct a thumbnail survey of attitudes in Britain to evil-doers (1985). This suggested a distinction between a minority with relativistic and circumstantial views of evil, who can excuse gross perpetrators, and a majority whose more absolute image of evil precludes such forgiveness, and who suggest or allude to the most heinous punishments. Since most people probably alternate at some time between such attitudes, it may be best to see this as separating out viewpoints rather than whole, fixed categories of persons, though there is no doubt some polar clustering, and it is conceivable that in other social formations, or in different eras, the absolutist views are in a minority. The police poster is in any event clearly aimed at the majority factor, and indeed can be said to be directed at the mob element of many violent situations.

Of course, it is true that countervailing sanctions normally restrain, and it would be rare in Britain to have a mob stoning a car thief. But the Victorian responses in the hue-and-cry after thieves, the lynchings in parts of the United States not so long ago and the existence of both these phenomena in the 1980s in, say, parts of urban Africa, suggest that the creators of the police poster are right in assuming an urban potential for collective violence of this kind.

The poster is additionally clever in that it can in fact be explained by its apologists as no more than an appeal to drivers to ensure that they lock their cars in the most secure manner possible, which is eminently sensible advice. Information in leaflets fronted by the photo does indeed give sober and undramatic instructions on car protection. The question then is, if the advice is so reasonable, why should appeal to it be made in such a violent idiom? Why not a 'rational' appeal: 'Locking cars prevents theft'. The reversed phrase, 'Knock his block off', directed at a confused-looking teenage boy by a police authority itself soliciting public support and involvement, strikes me as extremely violent, and other onlookers (the minority view?) have reacted similarly. An obvious answer to the question of why this particular presentation should have been used is that its shock-effect engages the attention of passers-by who would otherwise not give it a second glance. Part of the shock-effect is indeed achieved precisely through the paradox of unlawful violence being implicitly encouraged by the lawful defenders of the peace.

Whereas the Dickensian hue-and-cry and the lynchings of the American South drew openly on mob rule in relatively unpoliced eras or situations, the poster invites public collusion in potential violence within and as part of a systematically policed society (which is not, however, a police state in the sense that more explicit directives may be used; e.g. 'Report to the authorities anyone speaking ill of the state', etc.). What the poster tries to do is to make lawful that which is, in other presentations, unlawful. Thus, for citizens to lynch car thieves is for them to take the law into their hands and, therefore, out of the control of the state — which cannot be tolerated, for that same power can be turned against state authority. But to have citizens commit such acts (or some more subtle equivalent) with and through the indirect leadership of one of the arms of the state (e.g. the police), is at once to secure the loyalty of the (presumed) majority and also to convert an unlawful use of physical force into a lawful use.

We are in this situation dealing with the question of the relationship between violence and consent (see Turton 1984: pp. 22—4). As well as ambivalence in the definition of violence in Britain in the mid-1980s, there is ambivalence concerning the place and role of the police both with regard to a purportedly democratic convention by which all people vote for their political representatives, and to a public which is held to determine the means by which such representatives rule. In short, do the police serve the public or master it?

Stated thus, the question is naive, for no holder of power can exclusively do one or the other. The question can be re-phrased as being whether the one, servant or master, masks the greater effects of the other. Phrased now differently, how do people regard those who act as the executive agents of authority? Do they view them as ontological extensions of themselves, that is, as resembling ordinary citizens but having a special (and sometimes unpleasant) public job to do? Or do they regard them as ontologically quite different from themselves, treating them as another dimension of humanity — indeed even as being non-human? The point about executive authorities — those who actually are seen to exercise control over subjects — is that their 'true' intentions and volition are always open to speculation and re-interpretation as their relationships to their subjects or wards change.

The police are not alone, and similar questions may be asked of, say, judges who pass death sentences and of hangmen who execute the deaths. Thus, does the hangman see himself as providing the necessary public service and even as sacrificing himself for it, or does he actually enjoy the job or see it as a means of avenging himself on humanity, etc.? The subjects will ponder such questions even if they find it difficult themselves to give moral judgements on actions carried out by such agents of authority.

These questions of office vis-à-vis intentionality go beyond the normal anthropological concern with the duality of office and incumbent. The secular king may be judged a morally bad person but regarded as a politically good (i.e. efficient) king, and so will not be usurped. The divine king, however, is both a moral as well as political figure (as is the Piaroa shaman described by Overing in this volume), and so immoral acts on his part affect the qualities of his kingship and his kingdom, and may lead to his elimination. I suspect that the serious questions which the minority in Britain in the mid-1980s ask about the police, as regards either general matters or such specific issues as the confrontation with striking miners and their pickets, are similar to those asked of the divine king. It is not a matter merely of whether the police are suitable persons for the jobs they are doing in terms of, say, education or aptitude. It is more whether the police, as persons, are beginning to depart from the minority definition of human morality, and thereby tainting irredeemably the fabric of society, in the same way that the 'contaminating' agents of the Left are held to account (or so it seems) in the majority view.

The alleged minority view, then, is that the police should be moral agents, ideally responsible to themselves and their 'community' for their own actions, and autonomous of the state in a role defined as that of civic duty; as with the divine king, should the police fail morally, they fail civically. The alleged majority view is that the police are morally neutral and perform tasks, sometimes necessarily ruthless, which are ordained by the central state. Here, like a secular head of state, they are judged more by their efficiency — which may itself justify their morality. Translating into general terms, while the majority regard perpetrators and their crimes of violence as answerable to the judgements of the state alone, the minority re-define such responsibility as a moral one to be borne by the perpetrators themselves, sometimes even independently of the judgements of the state.

Such contrasting views can be glossed as outer- and inner-directed accountability for violence. Where accountability is outer-directed, violence is explained and resolved centrifugally from individual to state; where it is inner-directed, it is interpreted centripetally within as small a set of relationships as possible and ultimately in terms of the personal morality of the perpetrator himself. Outer-directedness leads to the state exercising punishment, claiming to act on behalf of all society; meanwhile, inner-directedness tends towards attempts at small-group rehabilitation. Interestingly, however, both views may end in the violent death of the individual when each is taken to its extreme. The state's ultimate sanction is of course capital punishment. Yet it is also the case that a highly developed personal sense of moral accountability may induce suicide in the wrong-doer, who sees himself as having violated the high moral standards expected of him.

Rolling the points of the argument backwards, I think that we can see this last distinction between self-inflicted and other-inflicted violence as reflecting in part the distinctions between a) self-accountability versus blaming others; b) divine versus secular kingship; c) the 'bobby' as member of a moral community versus the 'bill' or 'pig' as humanly dissociated oppressor; and, finally, d) violence as a kind of personal sacrifice thought by the agent as morally necessary, but also open to the judgement of others, versus violence as a recognized and less questioned means to a specific end, for example, the maintenance of the state. In this way, a number of otherwise disconnected social and ontological phenomena can be viewed as partially represented in each other.

To return to the police poster, I believe that its paradoxical nature — obliquely encouraging unlawful violence with the complicity of the law — expresses the dilemma in 1980s' Britain over the definition of the nature, and the extent of the use of violence. The debates that surround these issues are too well-known to require elaboration here. Moreover, they are pithily expressed in the different languages of the many interests involved, from accusations directed at the 'emerging police state' to utterances of despair at the 'dissolution of communal morality/religion, etc.'. Putting one of the points very simply, a question arising out of the poster, and which occurs in the debates, is to ask whether violence is definable in terms of personal morality or social law; and whether violence is therefore *a part of* the person, and ultimately to be dealt with by him alone, or *perpetrated by* him (i.e. projected out of him), and only amenable to treatment by external agents. Let me now turn to some of my African material for some comparisons. I want to see how much this debate concerning a contrast between the 'moral individual' and the 'morally neutral state' can be said to exist in one society I have studied.

Among the Giriama, one of the Mijikenda peoples of Kenya, self-inflicted violence, ín the form of suicide, co-exists with violence directed at other persons. Following the above analysis of modern Britain, one would expect these two modes of violence (suicide and murder) to be accompanied by two separate explanatory schemes of causation: that which identifies and blames the 'other' (murder), and that which attributes responsibility to the self (suicide). But this simple dichotomy does not seem to apply among the Giriama, for, while people do of course distinguish suicide (by hanging) from murder (by knife or by arrow), they nevertheless regard both as instances of 'bad death', a category including, in addition, such other 'untimely' deaths as accidents (falling from a palm tree, drowning, burning, snake-bite, car crash, etc.). Thus the distinctiveness of murder and suicide at one level is, at another, subsumed within a single metaphysical concept — of 'bad death'. Are murder and suicide then the same or different for the Giriama? And if they are aspects of a single metaphysical idea, does this ambivalence (to an outsider) tell us something of the issues surrounding the questions relating to violence in Britain?

Some translation of the concept of 'bad death' is first necessary. The Giriama term is *kufwa kwa viha* (or *vihani*), to die in war. *Viha*, war, is a key concept. In fact it is best translated as violence, for it refers not only to death in battles but also to that arising from domestic disputes, as well as from random 'accidents'. *Viha*, then, is a term which applies to the types of actions and occasions which are captured by the English senses of 'violence through intentional use of physical force' and 'violation of the fullness of life': for accidents, murder, and being slain in battle are events which cut life short and detract from the wholeness of the person. The concept does not appear to refer specifically to the unlawfulness of violence. But it does refer to something which may be said to presuppose the elaboration of an idea of law, namely a notion of defilement, with which Giriama legal concepts co-exist.

The metaphysical ideas relating to 'bad death' centre on the notion that men and women who kill — in battle as warriors, in village quarrels or by accident — have the blood of their victims in them, and are now subject to the negative state of what is known as *kilatso* (derived from *mulatso*, blood).[1] 'Bad death' (or *viha* death) refers to the subsequent murders, suicide, acts of violence or accidents, which these individuals carry out and which are attributed to this condition. Actual motivations for these acts may certainly be identified, as we see later in examples. But *kilatso* is held to subsume them, translating them, so to speak, into action.

Kilatso's negative state must be removed by purification: as a force, it is effectively autonomous, and it may therefore turn back on the killers' own families and cause many deaths. In a similar vein, the victims, including those who have died from accidents, must be ritually dissociated from their own homesteads. There are a number of elements in this. The victims are buried outside their homestead (and in some Mijikenda groups simply thrown into the bush); they are not dressed in the calico *sanzu* cloth which is customary for corpses, but are buried in the clothes in which they died; their bodies are not placed on wooden planks in the grave; the funeral is one day less than normal and the burial position is different (and accords with the nature of the death); and death itself must be purified through the slaughter of a ram, although many cattle and goats are slaughtered as well. In addition, the mother and father of a victim must sleep, and have sexual intercourse, outside the homestead on the night after the day of the burial. The exception here is when the deceased is a man and there are no surviving parents: at the end of the second mourning ceremony, the bereaved widow must have sexual

---

[1] *Mulatso*, from which *kilatso* is derived, has more positive connotations, including that of natural skill.

intercourse outside the homestead 'in the forest or bush' with a man who is paid for the job, but who is not of the Mijikenda peoples (i.e. who is a complete outsider), and who will unsuspectingly carry the *kilatso* away with him. The unsuspecting man is often characterized as being an up-country Luo. The homeland of the Luo people is very distant, but they migrate to work all over Kenya. Their characterization as carriers-away of *kilatso* is as to an enemy (though cordial relations are otherwise the norm): from the far outside, they came too close or were foolishly lured, and must pay the consequences. In a parallel manner, widowers must seek a distant prostitute for the same purpose, paying her in the usual way, so that she too is unsuspecting. These latter obligations are designed, it is said, to divert the *kilatso* from the home and to send it away. *Kilatso* is sometimes also spoken of synonymously as *kifo*, death.

All the above ritual obligations are binding, for failure to carry them out will bring sickness and death to the deceased's own homestead. To ignore such duties is to flout Giriama concepts of cosmological or 'natural' law, just as the deaths themselves are a breach of this same cosmological order.

The contaminating and contagious effects associated with bad deaths are illustrated by the following abbreviated case:

1 Kazungu, the owner of a teashop, was attacked with a knife by one of his young employees, following accusations over the misuse of money. The latter was restrained by others present and did no harm.
2 It was claimed generally that the young attacker had a 'spirit in him' because, together with six older men, he had killed another older man who they had alleged was a witch.
3 The young man had been arrested at the time of the murder but released because he was classed as a 'juvenile'.
4 It was claimed now that 'the blood of the (murdered) old man is in him' and that 'he will continue to kill others until he is purified by a traditional doctor' (here referring to the persisting effects of *kilatso*).
5 Even after the young man's attack on Kazungu, neither Kazungu nor anyone else wished to call in the police, nor accuse him in Court: Kazungu said he pitied the 'boy', and others felt that no useful purpose would be served in taking the action.

Though the offender's youth might seem to prompt this apparent leniency, much the same attitude characterizes older attackers, even when death results. The police are kept at bay and modern courts treated cautiously and used only some time after the event, for example to secure compensation. What is striking is the tendency to attribute blame, where possible, to factors beyond the instigator's control.

As a somewhat broad general proposition, then, the occurrence or commission of 'bad death' is the responsibility of individuals only insofar as they or their kin (agnates) have failed to carry out purification rituals. Although motivations are mentioned, a cold malice lying behind such deaths is not stressed, and there is no focus on a killer's intentionality; and this explains why 'accidents' can be classed together with *crimes passionelles* and suicides as being of the same kind of metaphysical disturbance.

In Giriama thought, notions of 'bad death' are importantly contrasted with notions of witchcraft, to which other deaths (such as 'natural cause' deaths) are attributed. Witches are held as directly responsible for their malicious destructiveness and for the deaths they cause, even if their reasons, such as revenge, are understandable. They must confess, or in some way be called to account through their own subsequent misfortunes and even death.

These two sets of ideas do, however, clearly overlap in one special case of *viha* death, namely that resulting from a falling coconut which, in its outer casing, is very heavy. In those areas of Giriama country in which coconut palms grow, paths linking homesteads constantly pass under palms. Yet it is extremely rare to hear of persons being hit. In fact, coconuts are so valuable that they are felled before they become over-ripe. Nevertheless, the odd one does fall while it is still maturing. In the rare event of a falling coconut killing someone, the victim is buried outside the homestead in the standard manner for a *viha* death, but in addition it will be concluded that the victim must have been a malevolent person — a witch (*mutsai*) whose witchcraft turned back on to him or her. There is, however, no reference to the person's intentions at the time of the accident. The witchcraft here acts as an external, autonomous agent, like *kilatso* (which is itself very occasionally spoken of as a spirit).

This overlap in ideas is reflected in an ambivalence concerning the role of witchcraft in *viha* deaths generally. In most discussions of cases, or when talking in the abstract, people do not consider witchcraft as having played a part in *viha* deaths. But for one or two people closest to the victims, the death may be claimed as the result of the work of a witch who 'sent' the conditions of the death.

Any death, then, including a 'bad death', is for someone or other, likely to be regarded as due to one or more forms of witchcraft (of which there are many kinds among the Giriama). And explaining a 'bad death' as motivated by (to give an example) a rival lover's jealousy and *also* from some quite different person's witchcraft, need not in fact be inconsistent or contradictory. After all, although a rival lover might be expected to express jealousy, and even to become violent, this by itself is not enough to push someone to the point of killing his adversary (knife fights between young men competing for the same girl are not uncommon). Only a few knife fights end in death and, as among the Azande, there will be some Giriama wishing to know whose witchcraft creates these exceptions. With suicide, there is similar reasoning. The factor that motivates it is believed to rest in the sorrow or shame of the person concerned (indeed, much of a diviner's work consists of diagnosing and tracing the causes of personal dependence), but an ultimate cause can always be ascribed, if so desired, to some form of witchcraft.

Utsai is the most general term for witchcraft; it is also a generic term, subsuming various other kinds of witchcraft. The internal classifications are extensive and, at certain points, varying — with new ones always being brought in. But they are all premised on the human witch's intention to cause harm, whether as a calculated act of revenge or as malice arising uncontrollably from a jealous or grief-stricken heart. Even the use of so-called protective magic may be construed as witchcraft: desperate victims lay the *fingo* medicine in the paths of their suspected attackers or use other methods to catch witches, themselves running the risk of being accused of witchcraft should their magic appear to be successful. As I was often told, 'nearly everyone is a witch, for does not a man feel bitterness when his son (or whoever) dies?'

Witchcraft construed as such is of course common to much of Africa. It is a view which places mankind's destructiveness in the hands of mankind itself, however much spirits and occult forces may be used in the process. In contrast, a 'bad death', although possibly willed by an enemy's witchcraft, is, in its suddenness and abruptness, placed beyond the normal sphere of humanity. Witches are bad but, as the quotation given above indicates, they are like other humans. However, when witchcraft results in a 'bad death', it ushers in contamination that will be endless unless purified: 'bad deaths' point in the direction of harmful forces which threaten to become autonomous of individual humans, witches or non-witches.

As is suggested by the symbolism surrounding the disposal of the corpses of victims of 'bad deaths', these forces arise from outside the homestead and must be returned there. The witch at least belongs as a human being within the homestead moral community. Witchcraft (*utsai*) is therefore the sinister but inevitable dimension of relations between people of a single homestead, or of nearby homesteads, while *viha* (the violence of 'bad deaths') refers to relationships external to these domains. (But when responsible for a 'bad death', the witch causes an overlap of outside and inside which must be separated.)

That *viha* refers to externally directed relationships comes out in statements about the origin of the concept itself. Giriama society is divided into six named sections, which are remembered even today by elders. These sections were, it is claimed, ideally endogamous. But young men would sometimes raid another section for a woman and one of them would marry her. This was called 'the war (*viha*) of young men'. After discussion, the elders of the men's section would agree to a fine being paid to the girl's section, 'for otherwise the *mbari* (meaning anything from tribe, section, clan, to patrilineal descent group) would be destroyed as many would be killed'. The elders of both sections would meet together and eat the fine in the form of livestock.

However idealized this account may be, it suggests that the meaning of *viha* is more than simply the kind of war that might occur between the Giriama and such quite unrelated peoples as the Maasai. The concept of *viha* is also tied up with the question of where the appropriate line is between exogamy and endogamy, and of how to maintain it. It presupposes both attack and reparation, or disruption and re-order. It is interesting, therefore, that in contemporary times, *viha* deaths reproduce the theme of integrated inside versus disruptive outside *within* a wider cosmos in which disorder must be repaired. As it was once put to me by an elder, 'Bad deaths are *viha* (war) because they must not enter the homestead. They are of the outside'.

We may speculate that other themes are also reproduced in modern times. Thus, though section endogamy no longer exists, there is a pronounced preference for local endogamy, that is, for marriage between different patriclans but *within* a neighbourhood community. Marriages of this sort make up the majority. By contrast, prospective marriages with spouses at some geographical distance are often spoken of with distrust, and have to be checked out carefully beforehand to ascertain whether 'bad' *viha* deaths involving *kilatso* and its effects have occurred in the spouse's immediate local descent group. Other contaminating afflictions, such as those caused by breaches of seniority rules, incest, or adultery taboos (called *mavingane* and *kirwa*), have also to be checked out, as have such diseases as leprosy and tuberculosis.

In other words, geographical closeness represents the easily ascertainable purity of prospective in-marrying groups, while marriages between partners dwelling far from each other precludes such certainty. By itself this is unsurprising. However, it is also the case that from within the neighbourhood community people are likely to encounter those who will bewitch them. It is not normal for witches to afflict their victims at a distance. We thus have the formula:

$$\text{local endogamy} = \text{low } \textit{viha} \text{ risk}$$
$$= \text{high } \textit{utsai} \text{ (witchcraft) risk}$$

or,

$$\text{local exogamy} = \text{high } \textit{viha} \text{ risk}$$
$$= \text{low } \textit{utsai} \text{ risk}$$

That local exogamy *is* seen as an alternative, albeit a less preferred one, is evident in the occasional choice, on the part of a particular family which feels besieged by local witches, to arrange to have a son or daughter married at some distance. The distant marriage is often a prelude to a physical movement by part or the whole of the family to the area of their new affines. The move enables the family to become part of a new neighbourhood and reproduce the preference for local endogamy. At the same time it thrusts them into a new set of local relationships whose intensity will in time be expressed in witchcraft.

In this possible cycle of movements, we see that the fears associated with *viha* (as 'outside' violence) and those of *utsai* (as 'inside' witchcraft) do push against each other, when either is extreme. Thus while all deaths, including *viha* deaths, *are* caused by witchcraft in the eyes of at least some, it is the *viha* in 'bad deaths' which is the focus of concern. In such *viha* deaths, the urgent need is to purify, not to find the witch. In non-*viha* or 'ordinary' deaths, no purification is necessary, but the witch must be identified and made to pay, the more so if his victim is relatively young. Remembering the claim that, at some time or other, 'everyone is a witch', non-*viha* deaths point to the moral sensibilities and responsibilities of people living near each other. *Viha* deaths go beyond such problems of direct personal accountability.

Here, I want to suggest that there is a link between, a) this idea of *viha* violence as emanating from outside the individual and his moral community, and b) the putative *majority* view in Britain of individual violence as a problem mainly to be dealt with by the state, including the police. *Viha*, after all, refers to forces which are not just from outside, but from over and above the local community. It is in some respects similar to the idea of the state sitting on local communities, and surveying and punishing them (if I may use an image which borrows from Foucault's panoptic perspective). The difference is that the state seeks and sometimes obtains legitimacy in the eyes of its subjects. *Viha* violence is neither a legitimate nor illegitimate use of force. It is, so to speak, potentially destructive power that is unharnessed by human political figures. Yet it touches on ideas of the state, or at least of conquest, in its reference to war by one cultural group against another. More normally, in referring to 'abrupt' and violent deaths, it gives form to people's fears of unexpected and amoral forces in human destruction. It is a relatively short step from here to situations in which powerful people use *viha*-like fears to sanction their rule, at some point by actually demonstrating this capacity — as in mass public executions.

In a parallel manner, I see a link between the Giriama understanding of witchcraft and the *minority* British view of violence. The Giriama blame and take action against witches. But they also see witches as reflections of themselves as ordinary human beings, and as a regrettable but inevitable part of the moral community, occasional witch purges notwithstanding. The British minority seeks to place even the most heinous acts within a moral framework shared by everyone, and tries to understand their motivation. Violence may even be regarded by the minority as a means of explanation: terror on the terraces indicates the despair of the unemployed and disillusioned, who are nevertheless fellow members of society, among whom, but for the grace of good luck, heritage or innate skills, go the rest. How similar in many respects this is to witchcraft, among the Giriama and many other African peoples, as a system of explanation.

Viha is, then, violent potential. Under the conditions of political conquest, institutionalized hierarchy, and centralized authority, it may be realized, and even brought within the moral community as the legitimate use of force, though not always uncontestably. I believe that it is this potential, this *viha*, which the London police poster, with which I began, is trying to capture. *Viha* violence among the Giriama is autonomous: it comes from outside. Whoever captures *viha* has transferred to him that autonomous potential for violence. The parallel with the police is, I think, clear. To have that autonomy would convert the police into the state. Hence the seriousness of the debate in Britain about the accountability of the police.

But where in all this is the distinction I drew earlier, before introducing the Giriama material, between murder and suicide as examples of outer- and inner-directed violence? Among the Giriama both murder and suicide are grouped together in the same category, as being 'bad deaths' of *viha*. I think that the logic for this is that in this society, *both* are seen as outer-directed — as emanating from outside the individual. Murder is clearly so. But suicide is also, in the sense, as the Giriama put it, that the individual does *not* kill himself voluntarily but only because the amoral actions of his fellow men oblige him to. As in Britain, Giriama suicides are, we would say, the result of an intense shame, or personal rebuttal, felt by the victim, who may sometimes view his act as moral revenge. It is as if society ruthlessly imposed itself on the victim, who has nothing to answer with but his life. Given the somewhat cosmological casting of the idea of society among the Giriama, the view from the victim is of irrepressible forces outside, over and above him. This is not unlike the idea of the tyrannical state, but it also includes something of the idea of violence which is politically unharnessed. With murder at one end clearly located outside the moral community, and with witchcraft at the other end as central to the definition of the moral person with all his understandable frailties, suicide occupies a middle position: the individual cries for tolerance, but yields to, and thereby acknowledges, forces which defy his definition of the proper, moral community. This predicament could well be applied to the desperate teenager in the London police poster. There is a thin line between suicide that he or another like him might commit and the violence done against him by those who would, consciously or unconsciously, collude with the poster's exhortation: 'Bl(kn)ock his Kn(Bl)ock off!'

The question of the individual in relation to such corporate violence brings us, in the way of a conclusion, to the question of to what extent violence emanating from 'corporate' sources is regarded as intended; who, if anyone, are seen as the conscious perpetrators? In their contemporary view of themselves, the Giriama preserve certain aspects of their traditional lack of political centralization. But their characterization of *viha* as 'outside' violence (beyond human individual control) is in fact like the view of the tyrannical state held by some subjects in politically centralized societies. However, just as some Giriama will occasionally attribute even *viha* deaths to the malevolence of witches, so some individuals in state political systems will identify those within the state whom they hold responsible for the violence intentionally inflicted on them.

The views of such individuals may never do more than typify a minority pitted against the majority, but they sometimes become part of a wider political consciousness, which itself may or may not thereafter fragment. The equivalent among the Giriama would be to blame without question all *viha* deaths on witches, eventually dissolving the notion of *viha* itself, and so more firmly attributing the causes of violence to various human beings rather than to external, impersonal, and autonomous sources of violence. Going further, it is evident from studies of African witch-hunting movements that heightened witch-consciousness may be a kind of political consciousness; they amount to the levelling of blame against human ritual experts, or simply against human scapegoats who are believed to operate against the community. Such movements are, however, often only temporary or cyclical in nature.

Such a multi-perspectival view of the organized use of force is akin to the view of power held by Weber, which presupposes resistance to its use and conflicts over the right to exercise it (1947: p. 132). To this I would add that we may also look at the conflicting interpretations of what constitutes corporate violence. By contrast, Radcliffe-Brown is normally credited with a consensual view: for him political authority depends on physical coercion (or the threat of it) recognized as legitimate by most members of a polity (1940: p. xiv). But in fact Radcliffe-Brown is here characterizing what I have called the majority view: that physical force may justifiably be used by acknowledged political leaders. A corrective from Weber is to stress the dynamic and potentially changing nature of the relationship of minority to majority.

A useful concept which accommodates both the idea of the engulfment of the individual, and changing representations of violence, is that of totalization.

The term has a number of related scholarly connotations, especially from Hegel and Marx. Laing's and Cooper's discussion of Sartre's usage is particularly relevant to the problem of violence (1964: pp. 14—15), and I adapt it for my own purposes. Totalization starts as a cumulative objectification of different individuals, who are lumped together, given a common label and concrete existence, and even a sub-culture. This group is thereafter absorbed within a larger, more totalizing group, which eventually undergoes the same fate, and so on.

Totalization neither releases nor dissolves, so to speak, any of the absorbed groupings, even though they are no more than 'creations of being' (i.e. they are given objective existence through the judgements of others rather than through their own intentions and activities). An absorbed group can neither disappear, be replaced, nor be destroyed 'without also destroying the individuals who make it up' (1964). It is fixed within the totalizing process and its individual members can only re-define themselves consciously through the activities of the larger group of which they are now part.

Purely from impression, I think we have seen something of this process in Britain, as regards the identification, largely by the mass media, of increasingly inclusive groups of individuals engaged in the perpetration of violence. We may start with the street gangs which were the subject of common complaint during the mid-1950s and the early 1960s, mainly in national and local newspapers. Youths would roam town centres in drunken states, attacking each other and causing a general disturbance to residents and passers-by. In this context, the original 'Teddy-boys' were taken as the sartorial expression of youthful deviance, and of street violence and criminality. Soccer crowds, meanwhile, were benign. But in the mid-to-late-1960s and early 1970s, as a result of isolated instances, these were taken up by the media as contemporaneously the most representative perpetrators of youthful violence — which again extended to criminal acts against property and persons. Importantly, the violence of the street gangs was absorbed within this new category. The so-called terrorists of the soccer terraces were later cast as war-like marauders who roamed Europe's cities, the focus on their violence culminating in the most recent attempts by police to place them 'panoptically' under closed-circuit television surveillance.

In the early 1980s, in the context of bitter strikes, particularly in the coal fields, in protest at closures and redundancies against a background of rising unemployment, attention on the perpetrators of violence widened still further to include both young and not-so-young men. The category of criminal violence was often invoked to include picketing, especially when instances of injury and even death could be used to substantiate the charge.

Then, at about the same time, but continuing when the strikes ended, community riots against the police occurred in a number of inner city areas in Britain. Interestingly, many newspaper and television reports strained to characterize these as 'racial riots', in the face of scattered evidence that some whites as well as blacks opposed the police. Yet a wider and more rhetorically manageable category was thus constructed, which clearly made sense for the media, whose primary aim is to present simplified accounts for as large a readership or audience as possible — in their presentations, news is typically regarded as entertainment in the guise of information, with news broadcasts among the most popular television programmes. At the time of writing, one may anticipate that the result of this entire process will be the emergence of more unambiguously racial violence than previously existed, in the manner of a self-fulfilling prophecy. Ultimately, the 'problem' of violence may be widened to include ethnic as well as (and perhaps eventually superseding) socio-economic or class factors.

If, then, we follow the political rhetoric reported and provided by much television and many newspapers in Britain during the three decades up to the mid-1980s, the compass has evidently extended successively over violence in the streets, in the soccer grounds, at the picketing gates and in racially mixed inner-city areas — with the long-standing violence in Northern Ireland being given curiously routinized coverage and set apart from these other kinds of violence. Except for Northern Ireland, it is as if the scale of violence associated with a previous group (e.g. street gangs) is somehow absorbed within that of the next (soccer crowds, and then pickets/strikers and community protesters). None of the groups has disappeared, for they are each used historically, through parallels and comparisons, to plot the alleged trend in modern society towards greater civil violence. With so many collective activities, especially among the young, charted in this totalizing manner, it becomes difficult for individuals to redefine either themselves or the groupings of which they are judged to be members. Mud not only sticks; it also gives recognizable shape to those against whom it is repeatedly hurled, creating layer upon layer. Earlier 'creations of being' are reinforced by later ones.

Further wider reinforcement is provided, again through the media, by the global drama of international conflict, which is often phrased in science-fiction language (star-wars, etc.), and sustains interest through its promises and threats of ever-increasing scales of violence. As regards ordinary citizens, it is not perhaps that physical violence has become more prevalent in any objectively measurable sense, as that more people look to the world as a whole, and articulate what they see as the only *permissible* response to an alleged current dilemma: destroy or be destroyed.

REFERENCES

Laing, R. D. and Cooper, G. D. 1964: *Reason and Violence*. London: Tavistock.
Pocock, D. 1985: Unruly evil. In D. Parkin (ed.), *The Anthropology of Evil*, Oxford: Basil Blackwell.
Radcliffe-Brown, A. R. 1940: Preface to M. Fortes and E. Evans-Pritchard (eds), *African Political Systems*, London: Oxford University Press.
Sheridan, A. 1980: *Michel Foucault*. London: Tavistock.
Turton, A. and Shingeharu Tanabe 1984: Introduction. *History and Peasant Consciousness in South East Asia* (Senri ethnological studies 13) Osaka: National Museum of Ethnology.
Weber, M. 1947: *The Theory of Social and Economic Organization*. New York: Free Press.

Glossary

acephalous society	society whose constituent units lack coordination through some permanent institutionalized authority.
affine	a relation established through marriage.
agnate	co-member of a patrilineal descent group (q.v.).
anthropophagy	cannibalism.
Azande	a people of southern Sudan, famous in anthropology for their beliefs relating to witchcraft.
bilateral kinship	relationships (of kinship) traced through one's father or through one's mother.
clan, lineage, descent group	division of a population in terms of descent from some distant ancestor. *Clan* implies that the precise links between living members and the distant ancestor are not known. *Lineage* implies that such links are known. *Matriclan, matrilineage, matrilineal descent* membership in these groups is transmitted to the next generation by females only (group structure is based on mother—daughter ties). *Patriclan, patrilineage, patrilineal descent* membership is transmitted by males only (group structure is based on father—son ties).
classificatory kinship	the association of a genealogically distant kinship relation with a genealogically close one by grouping them under the same term. In this way, for example, one's mother's mother's brother might be called 'mother's brother'. (See footnote 12, chapter 8 in this book.)
cognate	relative by kinship (q.v.).

consanguines	relatives who, actually or putatively, share a common 'biological' heritage.
corporate group	group which retains its identity independently of the recruitment or demise of its members, and which presents itself to outsiders (and is so seen) as an undifferentiated entity.
cross-cousin	the relationship between the children of a brother and sister.
descent group	(see *clan*).
Durkheimian	Emile Durkheim, 1858—1917, French sociologist, one of whose main propositions was that the actions of the human individual should be seen as being constrained by a social or moral order which functions independently of that individual.
endogamy	rule that one's partner in marriage should be selected from within a specific group or category of relatives.
epiphenomenon	something that appears by consequence and unintendedly.
ethnography	the observations constituting the raw material of anthropology.
ethology	the study of social behaviour from a biological perspective.
exogamy	rule that one's partner in marriage should be selected from outside a specific group or category of relatives.
generic	term applied to a class of objects or phenomena.
genetrix	natural ('biological') mother.
incest	sexual relations between kin (normally close kin) among whom sexual relations are disallowed.
kinship (kin)	relation between people built up from links between parents and children, and siblings.
lineage	(see *clan*).
matriclan, matrilineage, matrilineal descent	(see *clan*).
matrilateral	relationship of kinship traced through one's mother only.
negative reciprocity	economic transaction governed by the rule that one should maximize one's material advantage, regardless of the 'other's' interests.

nuclear family	social group consisting of a married couple and their children.
Nuer	a people of southern Sudan, famous in anthropology for their acephalous, segmentary lineage organization.
objectification	the expression of something as an object for perception.
ontology	the study of the essence of things.
panopticon	the name coined by Jeremy Bentham for a circular prison in which convicts may be viewed from a central well.
parricide	homicide of a father by his child.
patriclan, patrilineage, patrilineal descent	(see *clan*).
patrilateral	relationship of kinship traced through one's father only.
patrilocal	residence upon marriage where the married couple live with the husband's people (specifically, with the husband's father).
polygamy	state of marriage in which an individual has two or more spouses.
polygyny	variety of polygamy in which a man has two or more wives (opposed to *polyandry*, where a woman has two or more husbands).
Rousseau	Jean-Jacques Rousseau, 1712–78, French philosopher, one of whose essential concerns was to distinguish the state of society (represented by men) from the state of nature (represented by animals).
segmentary (*social structure*)	a social structure whose groupings have an inherent capacity to split, and then later recombine. For instance, a patrilineal descent group (q.v.) typically splits in terms of the differentiation between the senior and junior wives of the founding polygynous (q.v.) ancestor.
Weberian	Max Weber, 1864–1920, German sociologist, one of whose main propositions was that insights into human action must derive essentially from the subjective understandings of the actor.

List of Contributors

Elisabeth Copet-Rougier is Chargée de Recherche at the Centre National de la Recherche Scientifique (CNRS) (Laboratoire d'Anthropologie Sociale), Paris.

John Corbin is Lecturer in Sociology in the School of Economic and Social Studies, University of East Anglia, Norwich.

Eric Dunning is Senior Lecturer in Sociology at the University of Leicester.

Suzette Heald is Lecturer in Social Anthropology in the Department of Sociology, University of Lancaster.

Graham McFarlane is Lecturer in Social Anthropology at the Queen's University of Belfast.

David McKnight is Senior Lecturer in Social Anthropology at the London School of Economics, University of London.

Garry Marvin is Lecturer in Social Anthropology in the School of Economic and Social Sciences, University of East Anglia, Norwich.

Brian Moeran is Lecturer in Anthropology in the School of Oriental and African Studies, University of London.

Patrick Murphy is Lecturer in Sociology at the University of Leicester.

Joanna Overing is Senior Lecturer in the Anthropology of Latin America, London School of Economics, University of London.

David Parkin is Professor of Anthropology in the School of Oriental and African Studies, University of London.

David Riches is Lecturer in Social Anthropology at the University of St Andrews, Scotland.

John Williams is Fieldwork Director in the Department of Sociology, University of Leicester.

Index